THE UNIVERSITY OF MICHIGAN
CENTER FOR SOUTH AND SOUTHEAST ASIAN STUDIES

THE MICHIGAN SERIES IN SOUTH AND SOUTHEAST ASIAN LANGUAGES AND LINGUISTICS

Ann Arbor, Michigan

CRITICAL STUDIES IN INDIAN GRAMMARIANS I:

THE THEORY OF HOMOGENEITY [SĀVARṆYA]

Madhav Deshpande

Ann Arbor
Center for South and Southeast Asian Studies
The University of Michigan
1975

The Michigan Series in South and Southeast Asian Languages and Linguistics, 2

*Open access edition funded by the National Endowment for the Humanities/
Andrew W. Mellon Foundation Humanities Open Book Program.*

Library of Congress Catalog Card Number: 75-36896

International Standard Book No. 0-89148-052-8

Printed and bound by CPI Group (UK) Ltd, Croydon, CR0 4YY

ISBN 978-0-89148-052-5 (paper)
ISBN 978-0-472-12774-0 (ebook)
ISBN 978-0-472-90170-8 (open access)

To my Gurus,

eastern and western

CONTENTS

CONTENTS

There are few problems indeed
connected with Pāṇini that have
been solved as yet in such a way
as to make fresh investigations
or additional support superfluous.

PAUL THIEME

PREFACE

For the last few years, I have been interested in the concept of homogeneity (*sāvarṇya*) in the Pāṇinian and non-Pāṇinian traditions of Sanskrit grammar. In 1972, I published "Pāṇinian Procedure of *Taparakaraṇa*: A Historical Investigation," in *Zeitschrift für vergleichende Sprachforschung*, Band 86. In this article, I had touched upon some aspects of the notion of homogeneity, but that was not the focus of the article. Afterwards, I continued my researches in the evolution of this notion in *Pāṇinian* and non-*Pāṇinian* traditions of Indian grammar. This has given me an opportunity to go through each text carefully, and see how the notion of homogeneity is defined and implemented in different ways. I have tried to be historical, not in the sense of arriving at a definite chronology of various texts, but in the sense of attempting to find the most natural interpretation of the texts as far as possible. After having studied different systems individually, I have tried to present the possible evolution of this concept.

To some of the readers it may appear that I could have presented this material in a more condensed form. However, after having taught Pāṇini in the West for some years, I have realized the need for being more explanatory. The traditional Indian pundits remember the whole rule, if only the first word is mentioned. That is, however, not the case in the West. Except for a few really good scholars, reading a work on grammar is still very difficult for most Westerners. The arguments are involved. The traditional writers take many things for granted. In order to make such texts intelligible to non-traditional readers, it is very necessary to provide the background material with as much clarity as possible. I have tried my writing on my advanced graduate students, and have attempted to find out exactly what kind of "explanation" they really need, in order to understand the arguments clearly. Coming from India, and having studied grammar traditionally, I used to take too much for granted. But thanks to my Western students, I have had the opportunity to come down to the earth, and discuss many points in detail. Therefore, I have striven to make my exposition as "readable" as possible, and have purposefully refrained from "unreadable condensation." I hope it serves its purpose.

I thank Mr. Jame Bare with whom I have discussed most of the material presented here. Having a student like him was certainly more than pleasure to me. He often raised more questions than I could find answers for. It may be mentioned that his Ph. D. dissertation "Phonetics and Phonology in Pāṇini," just submitted to the Department of Linguistics, the University of Michigan, is, in many respects, a continuation of the same line of research, and contains a good deal of discussion of homogeneous-representation. I have continued my own research in this field, after the completion of this book, and the results of that research are gradually being published in the form of independent articles. [Ref. "The Scope of Homogeneous-Representation in Pāṇini," appearing in the *Annals of Oriental Research*, University of Madras; "Phonetics of /V/ in Pāṇini," appearing in the *Annals of the Bhandarkar Oriental Research Institute*, Poona; "Phonetics of short /a/ in Sanskrit," appearing in the *Indo-Iranian Journal*; and "New Material on the *Kautsa-Vyākaraṇa*," appearing in the *Journal of the Oriental Institute*, Baroda.]

I am also thankful to my friend and colleague Dr. Peter Hook for having gone through some portions of this work, and for insisting that I should explain more, rather than condense the arguments. I thank Prof. S. D. Joshi, Poona, and Prof. George Cardona, Philadelphia, whom I occasionally consulted. Prof. Cardona also helped me with some of the most rare books from his personal collection. I am grateful to Prof. Alton Becker, Director, Center for South and Southeast Asian Studies, University of Michigan, for providing me a research grant to visit India during the summer of 1974. I am also indebted to Prof. R. N. Dandekar, Secretary, Bhandarkar Oriental Research Institute, Poona, and to Dr. Trivikram Dharmadhikari, Secretary, Vaidika Saṁśodhana Maṇḍala, Poona, for allowing me to use their rich manuscript collections, and obtaining microfilms of the necessary materials. I must express my gratitude to Prof. K. V. Abhyankar, Poona, for letting me use copies of some of the unpublished manuscripts in his possession. Finally, I thank the Publications Committee, CSSEAS, University of Michigan, for accepting this work for publication.

Madhav Deshpande
Ann Arbor
29 September 1975

Note: Due to the technical problems in underlining dotted Sanskrit letters, they have been left without the underline, while other letters in a word have been underlined. Since single dotted letters could not be underlined, no single letters have been underlined, but they have been put in between vertical slashes, e.g. /a/. *This does not, in this book, have the normal linguistic significance of "a phoneme," but just refers to that particular Sanskrit sound.* The same convention has been followed for the short-forms in Pāṇini's grammar, e.g. /a-Ṇ/.

PART ONE

THE PĀṆINIAN TRADITION

CHAPTER 1

PRINCIPLES OF HISTORICAL INVESTIGATION

1.1. Grammatical procedures in Pāṇini's grammar have undergone a variety of interpretations at the hands of Kātyāyana, Patañjali and their followers. At each step in the tradition we encounter conflicts between the older grammarians (prācīna) and the neo-grammarians (navya). These are relative terms and their referents keep on changing with time. The chief criterion of validity in the Pāṇinian tradition is that every explanation must be ultimately in consonance with Patañjali's Mahābhāṣya. Franz Kielhorn explains this principle:

> Where there is a difference of opinion between Pāṇini and Kātyāyana, or between Kātyāyana and Patañjali, or between all the three, the native grammarians attach a higher value to the views of Kātyāyana to those of Pāṇini, and a higher value again to those of Patañjali to those either of Kātyāyana or Pāṇini. That such should be the case is not unnatural.[1]

The well known traditional maxim of the Pāṇinians says: yathottaram munīnām prāmāṇyam "The later the sage, the greater his authority." The grammarians belonging to a later period in history are bound to have more information. They possess knowledge of the earlier grammars and also knowledge of the linguistic changes which took place later on.

1.2. However, this principle is unhistorical from a different point of view. The original meaning of the rules of an ancient grammar is gradually lost under the weight and supposed authority of later interpretations. S.K Belvalkar succinctly points out this element of unhistoricity:

> They (the more orthodox grammarians) accordingly tried to invent new maxims of interpretation, tending to show, after a very diligent analysis of the works of the three great sages, that such defects as Chandragomin and others tried to find in the Pāṇinian grammar were in it already implicitly provided for. This procedure was no doubt unhistorical, but so was that of Kātyāyana or of Patañjali.[2]

While studying the works of the ancient Indian grammarians, a modern scholar has to take care that he is not himself trying to impose any unhistorical interpretation on these works.

1.3. In the course of the historical investigation into the tradition of Indian grammarians, we shall follow a principle which is laid down by Patañjali in his oft-quoted statement: siddhaty evam, apāṇinīyaṁ tu bhavati "The correct result is established thus, but the method becomes un-Pāṇinian." In this statement, Patañjali draws a line of demarkation between notions of theoretical or applicational effectiveness of an interpretation and its historical validity or its conformity with Pāṇini's intentions. With this distinction, it is possible to make a fourfold system of classifying various interpretations in the Pāṇinian tradition.

[A] siddhyaty evam, pāṇinīyaṁ ca bhavati: "The correct result is established thus, and the procedure is also Pāṇinian."

[B] Siddhyaty evam, apāṇinīyaṁ tu bhavati: "The correct result is established thus, and yet the procedure becomes un-Pāṇinian."

[C] naivaṁ siddhyati, pāṇinīyaṁ tu bhavati: "The correct result is not established thus, and yet the procedure is Pāṇinian."

[D] naivaṁ siddhyati, apāṇinīyaṁ ca bhavati: "This way the correct result is not established, nor is the procedure Pāṇinian."

The types [A], [B] and [D] are quite clear, but [C] needs

some clarification. This is usually the reason why Kātyāyana feels like proposing changes, additions etc. in Pāṇini's rules. In many cases, Kātyāyana believes, with ample justification, that a certain formulation of Pāṇini is bound to lead to some incorrect results.[3]

1.4. The two aspects of each of these classifications are not contradictory to each other, but they are significantly different. The aim of a historian of the Pāṇinian system is not to prove Pāṇini's grammar to be absolutely perfect, complete and free of errors. His function is to see how Pāṇini stands in his own right. If an ancient king lost a battle, no historian can make him win that lost battle. Similarly a historian should not refrain from recording inconsistencies and inadequacies in Pāṇini's grammar. It is the hard duty of a historian to detach later interpretations from Pāṇini. At the same time, he must look at different successive interpretations from the point of the historical development of the grammatical system. An un-Pāṇinian interpretation could very well be a significant step in the development of grammatical theory and it must be given the credit that it deserves. Paul Thieme, whose work on Pāṇini is perhaps the best example of this historical approach, clarifies the methodology of historical research:

> In the end, we have to return to Pāṇini's formulations themselves, to compare his work, so to speak, with its own method, and to wring evidence from its weaknesses, which will betray something of its historical limitation: the merciless eye of the historian will not heed the beauty of the edifice in its entirety, but will be intent on looking for unassimilated elements which disturb its harmony, for flaws that might be due to the author being influenced by older sources, or not yet having reached certain stages of development.

1.5. In studying the theory of homogeneity (savarṇa) and its historical development, we shall not limit ourselves to the Pāṇinian tradition alone, but will undertake a thorough investigation of the entire range of the grammatical and phonetic science in India. We will first study this conception in the Pāṇinian tradition, and then pass on to the Prātiśākhyas, Śikṣās and post-Pāṇinian grammatical systems. We shall study not only the definitions of homogeneity in these systems, but in each case, we must also study its implementation in those respective systems. With identical definitions, we do find quite different implementation of this conception, and this involves different kinds of historical relationships among various systems.

CHAPTER II

PĀṆINIAN THEORY OF HOMOGENEITY

2.1. Pāṇini's grammar is headed by the well known fourteen Śiva-sūtras, the rules which are traditionally believed to have been given to Pāṇini by the Lord Śiva. Most of the modern scholars now believe in Pāṇini's authorship of these rules and their genetic relationship with the formation of his grammar.[5] There rules are as follows:

1) /a/ /i/ /u/ /Ṇ/
2) /ṛ/ /ḷ/ /K/
3) /e/ /o/ /Ṅ/
4) /ai/ /au/ /C/
5) /h(a)/ /y(a)/ /v(a)/ /r(a)/ /Ṭ/
6) /l(a)/ /Ṇ/
7) /ñ(a)/ /m(a)/ /ṅ(a)/ /ṇ(a)/ /n(a)/ /M/
8) /jh(a)/ /bh(a)/ /Ñ/
9) /gh(a)/ /ḍh(a)/ /dh(a)/ /Ṣ/
10) /j(a)/ /b(a)/ /g(a)/ /ḍ(a)/ /d(a)/ /Ś/
11) /kh(a)/ /ph(a)/ /ch(a)/ /ṭh(a)/ /th(a)/ /c(a)/-/ṭ(a)/ /t(a)/ /V/
12) /k(a)/ /p(a)/ /Y/
13) /ś(a)/ /ṣ(a)/ /s(a)/ /R/
14) /h(a)/ /L/.

These serve as a fundamental reference catalogue of certain sounds, arranged in a particular order conducive to the proper and concise formulation of the grammatical rules. Its purpose is not to give an inventory of all Sanskrit sounds, nor to teach correct pronounciation, but purely to facilitate concise formulation of rules.[6]

2.2. The rule P.1.3.3 (hal-antyam), in its final interpretation, says: "[In the instruction], a final consonant [is termed it]," and the rule P.1.3.9 (tasya lopaḥ) says: "There is deletion of that [which is termed it]." Thus, all consonants occurring at the end of the Śiva-sūtras are termed it. The other term for it is anubandha. An it sound is a metalinguistic marker attached to a grammatical element. These markers will be given in capital letters and are unconditionally deleted. Though they are deleted and never appear in the object language, their functional significance still continues to operate. The rule P.1.1.71 (ādir antyena sahetā) says: "The initial [sound of a group] together with a final it [denotes the intervening members and itself]." Applying this rule to the Śiva-sutras, we can formulate shortforms (pratyāhāra) such as /a-K/, /i-K/ etc. The shortform /a-K/, for instance, stands for all sounds from /a/ to /K/, excluding the markers. Thus /a-K/ stands for /a/, /i/, /u/, /ṛ/ and /ḷ/.[7]

2.3. Then comes the notion of savarṇa "homogeneous sound." This term is sometimes rendered as "homorganic sounds," but that should be a more appropriate translation of the term sasthāna. The notion of savarṇa involves things in addition to the organs. Paul Thieme believes that the term savarṇa was borrowed by Pāṇini from some ancient Śikṣā text,[8] while Burnell holds that Pāṇini took over this term from the ancient Aindra grammar and redefined it.[9] Whatever be its source, Pāṇini offers us a definition. The rule P.1.1.9 (tulyāsya-prayatnaṁ savarṇam), in its traditional interpretation, means: "[A sound having in common with another sound a] similar internal effort [at a point] in the mouth [is termed] homogeneous [with respect to the other sound]." As we shall see, this is what the rule must mean.

2.4. Kātyāyana found the wording of this rule to be unsatisfactory. Following the usage of his times, Kātyāyana interpreted the term āsya-prayatna to stand just for internal effort.

Then he objected that such a definition would make two sounds homogeneous, if only they had the same internal effort, despite the difference in their points of articulation.[10] This is undesirable, since this would make the sounds /j/, /b/, /g/, /ḍ/ and /d/ homogeneous with each other. He answered this objection by reformulating the rule:[11] "The correct result is, however, established by [defining] a homogeneous sound [as the one which shares with another sound] the same point of articulation (deśa) and [the same] internal effort (prayatna) in the mouth (āsya)." This is what Pāṇini ought to teach and probably intended to teach.

Instead of accepting Kātyāyana's formulation, Patañjali reinterprets Pāṇini's rule to get at the same meaning. The word āsya normally means "mouth," but Patañjali explains it to be a taddhita-formation: asye bhavam [āsya+yaT] "that which lies in the mouth," i.e. the point of articulation and internal effort. But the latter has been already mentioned by Pāṇini by the word prayatna. Thus finally the word āsya stands for "point of articulation" and prayatna stands for "internal effort."[12] These are the two conditions for homogeneity.

2.5. Though we know what the rule ought to teach, the historical situation still remains unclear. In the Śikṣās and the Prātiśākhyas, the term āsya-prayatna stands only for internal effort.[13] Breloer handled this term in the same way.[14] In his early work, Paul Thieme believed that "Pāṇini's terminology is yet less developed. His expressions āsya-prayatna and mukha-nāsikā-vacana seem to betray that he did know the doctrine of sthāna and karaṇa, which is familiar to the Prātiśākhyas."[15] However, Pāṇini, who uses terms like mūrdhanya "cacuminal, retroflex" (P. 8. 3. 55) and oṣṭhya "labial" (P. 7. 1. 101), could not have been unfamiliar with points of articulation. Yet we may agree with Thieme's following statement: "Auch sthāna wird von Pāṇini nicht in dem technischen Sinn 'Artikulationsstelle' vervendet, sondern heisst ein fach 'Platz, Stelle.' "[16] Later on Thieme gave an explanation of āsya-prayatna, which seems more probable:

> Paninis Fassung der Definition lässt vermuten, dass er den Ausdruck *prayatna* noch nicht in dem späteren Sinne von 'Artikulationsweise' (*spṛṣṭa*, *īṣat-spṛṣṭa*, *vivṛta* usw.) gebrauchte, sondern in einem weiteren, so dass er auch die Artikulationsstelle ein begriff (der *āsya-prayatna* von *k* würde demnach *kaṇṭha-spṛṣṭa*, der von *p* *oṣṭha-spṛṣṭa* gewesen sein unsw.). Diese Annahme liegt um so näher, als Pāṇinis Sprachgebrauch auch sonst mit der phonetischen Terminologie der Prātiśākhya nicht in Einklang zu stehen scheint.[17]

However, this involves some assumptions about the meaning of the term *prayatna* being different in Pāṇini. This is doubtful, since he uses the term again in P.8.3.18 (*vyor laghu-prayatnataraḥ śākaṭāyanasya*), which has its parallels in the *Prātiśākhyas*. [Whitney, APr, p. 83.] Actually, there is perhaps even an easier explanation of Pāṇini's *āsya-prayatna*. We could interpret the word *āsya* "mouth" as a general term covering all points on the vocal tract. This is evident from his parallel usage of *mukha* in P.1.1.8 (*mukha-nasikā-vacano'-nunāsikaḥ*). No *anunāsika* "nasal" sound is produced in the whole of the mouth, but it uses some point of articulation along with *nāsikā* "nose." For such a general conception of points on the vocal tract, Pāṇini used the general terms *mukha* and *āsya*.

In Sec. 11.7, we shall see that the term *āsya-prayatna* had a different meaning in the pre-Kātyāyana times. It included not only the internal effort, but also points on the vocal tract. Pāṇini was not alone in this usage and there were ancient *Śikṣā*-texts with the same usage. This will help us revise Thieme's oft-repeated notion that P.1.1.9 (*tulyāsya-prayatnaṁ savarṇam*) is concise but not precise, and that the *vārttika* on this rule, i.e. *siddhaṁ tv āsye tulya-deśa-prayatnaṁ savarṇam*, alone is both concise and precise. [Thieme (1935), p. 93.]

By the time of Kātyāyana, the term *āsya-prayatna* became restricted to internal effort alone. This restricted notion is seen in the *Vājasaneyi Prātiśākhya* 1.43 (*samāna-sthāna-karaṇāsyaprayatnaḥ savarṇaḥ*). This created a problem for Kātyāyana and, therefore, he reformulated P.1.1.9 to fit the terminology of his days. Patañjali's interpretation of āsya as āsye bhavam is only partially correct, because he says that āsya in this extended meaning stands for both sthāna "point of articulation" and karaṇa "internal effort" [MB, Vol. I. Sec. I. p. 155]. [The term karaṇa here does not stand for "articulator" or "active organ," see: Sec. 10.5.5.] If that were the case, then P.1.1.9 would be mentioning the internal effort twice. Actually Kaiyaṭa and Nāgeśa do realize this problem, but somehow try to explain it away. [MB-P, and MB-P-U, Vol. I Sec. I. p. 155.] From a historical perspective, thus, Pāṇini was concise and precise in his definition, and does not stand in need of any reformulation or reinterpretation.

2.6. Thus, two sounds are homogeneous with each other, if they share the same points of articulation and internal effort. Thieme points out the relation of the term savarṇa with the term varṇa in its abstract sense.[18] Patañjali clarifies that the notion of savarṇa is based on difference (bheda) between sounds. He says that if the term "homogeneous" were to apply to those sounds alone, which have all identical features, then the designation would be useless.[19] Thus, the homogeneous sounds must agree with respect to two features, but may differ in other respects, i.e. the external efforts, quantity, nasality and pitch. Patañjali says that the term āsya also qualifies the term prayatna, thus excluding those efforts which lie, in some sense, outside the mouth (āsyād bāhyāḥ).[20]

2.7. In Pāṇini's grammar, nasality does not affect homogeneity of sounds. But this exclusion of nāsikā "nose" from the conditions of homogeneity poses some problems. Nāgeśa has a long argument on the status of nāsikā "nose." Does it fall within āsya "mouth?" Is it a point of articulation or an internal effort or an articulator? According to the Pāṇinīya-Śikṣā, nāsikā "nose" is a point of articulation. Nāgeśa says that in P.1.1.8 (mukha-nāsikā-vacano'nunāsikaḥ), Pāṇini mentions nāsikā along with mukha "mouth." Therefore, for the purpose of grammatical considerations, nāsikā is excluded from mukha. Since the words mukha and āsya are synonyms, the same applies to āsya.[21] Whether this reasoning is true or false, the conclusion is certainly right. A conclusive proof that nasality does not affect homogeneity in Pāṇini is offered by the fact that he includes semi-vowels in his procedure of savarṇa-grahaṇa "representation of homogeneous sounds" [P. 1.1.69]. This is only to enable them to cover their nasal counterparts.

2.8. There is also another important doctrine concerning homogeneity which must be mentioned here. This is the doctrine of sarva-sthāna-sāmya "identity with respect to all points of articulation." If a sound has two points of articulation, say x and y, then it can be homogeneous only with that sound which has x and y as its points of articulation. It cannot be homogeneous with a sound that has only x, or only y, or x and z as its points of articulation. Though, nāsikā "nose" is considered to be a point of articulation by the Pāṇinians, it is not taken into account. According to the later Pāṇinian tradition, /v/ and /l/ are both dental (dantya), but /v/ is also labial (oṣṭhya). Thus they cannot be homogeneous. Actually, there is a greater chance of /v/ being only oṣṭhya "labial" for Pāṇini, Kātyāyana and Patañjali, rather than being dantyoṣṭhya "labio-dental" as believed by the Kāśikā-vṛtti and the later tradition. [For details, see my article "Phonetics of v in Pāṇini," appearing in the Annals of the Bhandarkar Oriental Research Institute.] Similarly, the sound /ai/ is both kaṇṭhya "produced in throat" and tālavya "palatal." The sound /au/ is both produced in throat and labial (kaṇṭhauṣṭhya). Though they share one common point of articulation, they differ in the other and hence they are not homogeneous. Though this principle is not explicitly stated by Pāṇini, it can be deduced from his rules.

2.9. With this background, let us take a brief survey of the phonetic categories adopted by the Pāṇinian tradition. Since Pāṇini's rules do not contain elaborate phonetic details, we have to depend on the traditional account, and then examine it critically. According to the points of articulation, sounds are classified as spṛṣṭa "with contact of the articulator and the point of articulation," īṣat-spṛṣṭa "with slight contact," vivṛta "open, without contact" and saṁvṛta "closed." The category of vivṛta "open" was later subdivided by Patañjali into īṣad-vivṛta "slightly open," vivṛta "open," vivṛta-tara "more open" and vivṛta-tama "most open." This is an important subclassification and it played a great role in later dialectic. Here we need not go into the details of the external efforts and other minor points, since our discussion does not concern them.

2.10. For Pāṇini, the sounds termed ūṣman, i.e. /ś/, /ṣ/, /s/ and /h/, and vowels have the same internal effort. They are all vivṛta "open." Thus, there is a possibility of some vowels being homogeneous with certain ūṣmans. To counter such a possibility, Pāṇini formulated P.1.1.10 (nājjhalau) which says that the sounds denoted by the shortforms /a-C/ and /ha-L/ are not mutually homogeneous. This rule actually intends to deny homogeneity of all vowels and consonants with each other. However, its interpretation poses certain grave problems, which will be considered later in detail. Since Pāṇini's definition was clearly couched in featural terms, it created another problem for him. The short /a/ was a saṁvṛta "closed" sound, but long and extra-long varieties were vivṛta "open." In order to get their homogeneity, Pāṇini ruled that the short /a/, within the grammatical system, is an open sound. The final rule of his grammar, P.8.4.68 (a a), reinstates the closed /a/ sound in the object language. K. C. Chattopadhyaya (1974) holds a different opinion on this point. He thinks that Pāṇini had an open (vivṛta) short /a/, which was natually homogeneous with /ā/ and /ā3/. In post Pāṇinian times, under the influence of Dravidian languages, the short /a/ became a closed sound. To account for this short /a/, later Pāṇinians inserted P.8.4.68 (a a). He tries to show that most of the Prātiśākhyas and Śikṣās support his argument. I disagree with Chattopadhyaya, and have dealt with his argument in my article "Phonetics of Short A in Sanskrit," appearing in the Indo-Iranian Journal.

After thus defining the term savarṇa, Pāṇini introduces a procedure, which is well known as savarṇa-grahaṇa "representation of homogeneous sounds." The rule P.1.1.69

(aṇ-udit savarṇasya cāpratyayaḥ) says: "A sound [which is denoted by the short-form] /a-Ṇ/ [with /Ṇ/ in the Śiva-sūtra /l(a) Ṇ/], or a sound with the marker /U/ stands for its homogeneous sounds and for itself, unless it is an affix." This is widely used in the rules of Pāṇini. Its details will be discussed later on.

2.11. Apart from P.1.1.9 (tulyāsya-prayatnaṁ savarṇam) and P.1.1.69 (aṇ-udit savarṇasya cāpratyayaḥ), Pāṇini uses the term savarṇa in eight rules. They are as follows:

1) P.1.1.58 (na padānta-dvirvacana-vare-yalopa-svara-savarṇānusvāra-dīrgha-jaś-car-vidhiṣu)
2) P.6.1.101 (akaḥ savarṇe dīrghaḥ)
3) P.6.1.102 (prathamayoḥ pūrva-savarṇaḥ)
4) P.6.1.127 (iko'savarṇe śākalyasya hrasvaś ca)
5) P.6.4.74 (abhyāsasyāsavarṇe)
6) P.7.1.39 (supāṁ suluk pūrva-savarṇāccheyāḍāḍyāyā-jālaḥ)
7) P.8.4.58 (anusvārasya yayi para-savarṇaḥ)
8) P.8.4.65 (jharo jhari savarṇe)

In some of these cases, the term savarṇa or the compound with that term continues into the following rules. The term is mostly used in the context of vowels, semi-vowels and stops, except in a few cases. For instance, in the rule P.8.4.65 (jharo jhari savarṇe), it is also used with respect to /ś/, /ṣ/ and /s/. These sounds have no homogeneous sounds other than themselves.

Another point that needs to be noted is that P.1.1.69 does not mean that all the sounds incorporated in the shortform /a-Ṇ/ must have homogeneous sounds other than themselves. The sounds /h/ and /r/ have no homogeneous sounds other than themselves. The rule says that the /a-Ṇ/ sounds stand for their homogeneous sounds, if they have any.[22]

Kunhan Raja (1967) has raised the question of the limit of /a-Ṇ/ in P.1.1.69. He argues that /a-Ṇ/ even in this rule is limited only to the first Śiva-sūtra. In my article "The Scope of Homogeneous-Representation in Pāṇini" [appearing in the Silver Jubilee Volume of the Annals of Oriental Research, University of Madras], I have extensively dealt with this question. The conclusion of this article is that /a-Ṇ/ in P.1.1.69 certainly extends to /Ṇ/ in the Śiva-sūtra /l(a)-Ṇ/; however, no practical purpose is served by the inclusion of semi-vowels in P.1.1.69. The theoretical purpose is quite obvious. [Also see Appendix A.]

2.12. To sum up, we might say that the procedure of savarṇa-grahaṇa "homogeneous-representation" is a procedure built of five steps discussed earlier. There are many differences of opinion concerning the exact interpretation of these five stages. At times we have proposals for additional postulates which make some of these stages unnecessary. Some of the differences are rooted in the differences between alternative priciples of interpretation.

2.13. Here it is necessary to see how a difference in theoretical axioms affects the final output of a grammar. Let us consider two hypothetical situations.

> Situation [A]: Suppose that we have a rule R_1 which contains the term a. Is it possible to apply the rule R_1 to the term a in the same rule? Let us say that the rule R_1 is as follows: "a stands for a, b and c." If the rule R_1 applies to itself, then the term a in the rule itself could stand for a, b and c. Thus, the rule could be rewritten as: "a, b and c stand for a, b and c." This could mean that each one of them could stand for all of them. If the rule does not apply to itself, then a stands for a, b and c; b stands for b, and c stands for c.
>
> Situation [B]: If there are two rules, R_1 and R_2, such that R_2 presupposes R_1, is it possible that R_2 could apply to R_1 or a part of it? This gives us two alternatives. Either R_2 may apply to R_1, or it may not apply.

By combining the alternatives in [A] with those in [B], we could get several possible ways. Most of these alternatives are reflected some way or the other in the discussions in the Pāṇinian tradition, along with certain other postulates.

CHAPTER III

KĀTYĀYANA'S THEORY OF ĀKṚTI-GRAHAṆA

3.1. As an alternative to Pāṇini's procedure of savarṇa-grahaṇa "representation of homogeneous sounds," Kātyāyana proposes the philosophical procedure of ākṛti-grahaṇa "mention of a sound-universal." He says: "[The desired morphophonemic procedure] is established by understanding the sound-universal [as being mentioned in the Śiva-sūtras and elsewhere]," and Patañjali explains this as: "[In the Śiva-sūtras and elsewhere], the universal of the sound /a/ is taught and it will cover the whole class of /a/ sounds [including long and extra-long varieties]. Similarly are [taught] the universals of the sounds /i/ and /u/."[23] In this view, the particular sounds uttered in the Śiva-sūtras could be understood as tokens standing for the types or sound universals which cover all the particular sounds belonging to that type or sharing that universal. This is like the sentence: "A brahmin should not be killed." The statement does not mean that, leaving aside one brahmin, the rest of them could be killed, but rather that anybody who belongs to the class of brahmins or shares the universal brahmin-ness should not be killed. Thus what is intended is not a single brahmin, but the universal brahmin-ness.[24] Kātyāyana adds that this notion of a universal extends to consonants also.[25] Just as the universal of /a/ covers /ā/, similarly the universal of /y/ covers /ỹ/. However, the universal of /k/ does not cover /kh/ and other members of that varga. Kātyāyana clearly points out that this universal-mention is not an explanation of Pāṇini's homogeneous-representation, but an alternative to it. If one is adopted, the other is almost unnecessary. Kātyāyana says: "In P.1.1.69, the /a-Ṇ/ sounds need not be mentioned, since the sound universals are mentioned [in the Śiva-sūtras]."[26] Thus, in the theory of universal-mention, no homogeneous-representation is necessary for vowels and semi-vowels, but it is still necessary for the homorganic groups of stops (varga). Thus, Kātyāyana is proposing a partial modification of Pāṇini's system.

3.2. The distinction between these two procedures needs to be clearly understood. According to the theory of universal mention, the sounds listed in the Śiva-sūtras are a type listing, without P.1.1.69. On the other hand, Pāṇini lists individual sounds and then states P.1.1.69 whereby they could stand for their homogeneous sounds.[27] Recently, Scharfe[28] and Ghatage[29] seem to have fused one into the other. Biardeau[30] discusses savarṇa in the context of ākṛti, but leaves an impression that she does not consider them to be different alternatives. On the background of this, a clear differentiation of these two seems to be of vital importance. Kātyāyana is bringing a non-Pāṇinian notion into Pāṇini's grammar. This new notion of varṇākṛti "sound-universal" is a philosophical interpretation of the old class-conception of varṇa, the real sound, where features of quantity, nasality and accent were non-distinctive for inclusion in a varṇa. Thus a-varṇa could cover /ā/ and /ā3/, the varṇa of /y/ could cover /ỹ/. However, the varṇa of /k/ could not cover /kh/ and other homorganic stops. For this purpose, the notion of varga was used along with -varṇa. Pāṇini's expanded definition of savarṇa was a sophisticated attempt to cover both of these older notions under a single generalization. Kātyāyana brought back the older notions in a new philosophical form. Thus his notion of ākṛti worked for the older notion of varṇa, while he still retained Pāṇini's savarṇa-grahaṇa to account for the older notion of varga. A detailed discussion of this older notion of varṇa is taken up later in the context of the Prātiśākhyas.

3.3. As it has been already explained, Kātyāyana's theory partially replaces Pāṇini's homogeneous-representation. The fact that this new theory does not belong to Pāṇini is realized by the traditional commentators. Bhaṭṭoji Dīkṣita says: "This view [of universal-mention] is not intended by the author of the sūtras, since he incorporates [the term] /a-Ṇ/ [in P.1.1.69]."[31] He further states: "The author of the sūtras does not formulate [his rules] after having seen the vārttikas [of Kātyāyana]."[32] Nāgeśa and some of the later commentators on his works clearly bring out this historical development.[33] The commentary Cidasthimālā on Nāgeśa's Laghu-śabdendu-śekhara says that if we accept the rules related to the procedure of savarṇa-grahaṇa, then there is no ākṛti-grahaṇa.[34]

3.4. The theory of universal-mention needs to be subjected to a critical examination, both for its merits and drawbacks. Pāṇini clearly defined savarṇa in featural terms, but there is no clear definition of a sound-universal found anywhere in Kātyāyana's vārttikas. Patañjali explains that the universal of /a/ is mentioned [in the Śiva-sūtras] and it will cover the whole family of /a/ sounds.[35] Bhartṛhari, in his Mahābhāṣya-dīpikā, sheds some light on this notion:

> The desired [coverage of many varieties] is established by universal-mention. In shortforms and in other rules, a universal is prescribed, and not an individual. Resorting to an individual [in order to mention a universal] is like this: It is thus advised to an inhabitant of the Nārikela island: "This is a bull. You should not touch him with your feet." Though he is advised actually with respect to a young, black and skinny bull, still he does not touch even an old, tawny and fat bull.[36]

Thus when one hears /a/, he develops a notion of some generic features. When he hears /ā/, he recognizes the same generic features in /ā/. This is how a person identifies the same universal in different instances. This seems to be the import of Bhartṛhari's explanation.

3.5. Since there is no clear definition of a universal, nor of any standard way of recognizing its presence, this notion certainly seems to be very impressionistic. We are not sure if the origin of this notion lies in phonetic considerations, or somewhere in the realm of realistic metaphysics. Perhaps this is an outcome of a combination of different influences. Kātyāyana himself uses frequently the grammatical terminology of the Prātiśākhyas, which was replaced by Pāṇini with new terms.

In this old terminology, we have a conception of varṇa which stands for "the real sound" or class of sounds which differ only in features like quantity, nasality and pitch. There also existed a conception of varga "group of homorganic stops" alongside with the class-conception of varṇa. Kātyāyana was obviously familiar with this conception. At the same time, early schools of Mīmāṁsā were coming up in pre-Kātyāyana days. He was deeply interested in their philosophical speculations, and quoted their controversies in great detail. The two important names are those of Vyāḍi, who held Vyakti-vāda "doctrine of individuals," and Vājapyāyana, who held the opposite doctrine of Ākṛti-vāda "doctrine of universals." Most probably, under the influence of Vājapyāyana's thoery of universals, Kātyāyana reinterpreted the old conception of varṇa and came up with the doctrine of varṇākṛti "sound-universal." Even in this new philosophical form, the notion still remained very much impressionistic or conventional.

The system of Mīmāṁsā considers sounds (varṇa) to be eternal, and these eternal sounds are manifested by physical sounds which are not eternal. However, the relation between non-eternal physical sounds and eternal linguistic sounds is not that between a universal and individuals which share that universal. The eternal sound is like an eternal individual.[37] The notion of sound-universals is found used in the system of Nyāya. This system believes that the sounds of a language are not eternal, their existence being limited by their production and disappearance. Yet we have a perception of identity each time we hear certain sounds: "It is the same /g/ sound, which I heard before." This perception of identity is due to the common universal shared by many instances.[38] Kaiyata's explanation of the sound-universal /k/-ness is very similar to the Nyāya view. He says: "The universal /k/-ness etc. pertains to individual sounds or is manifested by specific instances of sounds.... The [sound] individuals are infinite and they are produced [in contrast to the eternal universals]."[39] It must be remembered, however, that Kātyāyana's notion belongs to a very ancient period of philosophy, and most of the systematic works in different philosophical schools are certainly post-Kātyāyana.

3.6. The ambiguity concerning how many varieties a certain sound-universal can cover is reflected in several discussions in Kātyāyana's own vārttikas and in Patañjali's Mahābhāṣya. In his introductory remarks on Pāṇini's grammar, Kātyāyana has raised questions as to the purposes of the Śiva-sūtra listings. One of the alleged purposes is the proper teaching of all the sounds in Sanskrit.[40] To this Kātyāyana presents an objection by saying that if this is the purpose, Pāṇini should list all the varieties of sounds differing in pitch, quantity and nasality.[41] A reply to this objection is given by saying that the Śiva-sūtras are a list of sound-universals, which would naturally cover all these varieties.[42] Then comes an objection to this reply: "If [one says that] the desired [coverage of necessary varieties] is established by the mention of sound-universals, then a prohibition of [vowels that are possessed of] constriction of mouth or other similar faults has to be laid down."[43] This objection amounts to saying that just as a sound-universal covers all the correct or unfaulty (śuddha) instances, similarly it would also cover those instances which involve faults. A sound-universal is shared by correct as well as by incorrect instances, and there is no philosophical reason why a sound-universal could represent only the correct instances. Patañjali observes that if one accepts this doctrine of universal-mention, one may have to make an all out effort to reinstate the correct varieties of sounds.[44] The upholder of universal-mention suggests that these faulty varieties of sounds could be given metalinguistic functions, and could then replace the whole system of marker-sounds in Pāṇinian rules.[45] Patañjali says that this could be done, but then the procedure becomes un-Pāninian.[46] Even though it is easy to talk of constructing rules for reinstating the correct varieties, in actuality, it would be a very difficult task. Compared to the correct varieties, faults are too many to count. This is surely not an advisable procedure.

3.7. Patañjali then continues the argument of the upholder of universal-mention. He asks as to where could these faulty varieties occur. They could not occur in augments (āgama), substitutes (vikāra), affixes (pratyaya), verb roots (dhātu) or nominal stems which are either derivable from the enlisted smaller items or which are directly listed by Pāṇini. Pāṇini taught all these items with correct pronounciation. The only items which are left are the nominal stems which are underivable and are not listed by Pāṇini. It is suggested that even these should be listed in order to teach their proper pronounciation.[47] K. V. Abhyankar explains the purport of this suggestion:

> This is the final conclusive solution to the difficulty raised above, viz. that if in the formation of words faulty utterances are made for signifying grammatical operations, those faults would remain in the words after their formation also. The author says here that the original crude bases of words are uttered faultless and thereafter in the process of formation, augments, substitutes, affixes and the like are also uttered faultless; as a consquence no occasion arises for formed words being attended with faulty utterances.[48]

It is doubtful if it is a conclusive solution. It is quite clear that it is a suggestion for a complete listing of underived nominal stems, which does not exist in Pāṇini. Patañjali, in other contexts, makes it clear that such a listing of underived nominals involves prolixity (tad guru bhavati, see n. 47). Bhartṛhari suggests that finally we have to rely on the usage of the natural speakers of Sanskrit (śiṣṭa) to determine correctness of words, and the same reference is to be the authority in excluding these faulty varieties.[49] Thus the procedure of universal-mention finally involves too many assumptions.

3.8. There are many other problems which confront the upholder of universal-mention. According to Pāṇini, the original root in the forms kalpate and kḷpta is √kṛp. From this root, we first derive the forms karpate* and kṛpta*, and then /r/ and /ṛ/ are replaced by /l/ and /ḷ/. For both the changes, there is only one rule, P.8.2.18 (kṛpo ro laḥ), which literally means: "/r/ of [the root] √kṛp is replaced by /l/." The constitution of /r/ and /l/ is such that they contain vocalic and consonantal elements fused together. Thus:

$/ṛ/$ is $\frac{1}{4}/ə/ + \frac{1}{2}/r/ + \frac{1}{4}/ə/$ and

$/ḷ/$ is $\frac{1}{4}/ə/ + \frac{1}{2}/l/ + \frac{1}{4}/ə/$.

If parts of a composite sound are looked upon as independent sounds and could be represented by independent sounds, then there is no problem in the present case. The sound /r/ in the rule would stand for independent /r/, as well as for /r/ that forms a part of /ṛ/. The same would apply to /l/.[50] But if the so-called parts of a composite sound have no independent reality and cannot be represented by independent sounds, then we may have to have a separate rule for substituting /ṛ/ by /ḷ/.[51]

At this stage, Patañjali offers two solutions which would avoid formulation of an additional rule. The second solution runs as: "Or, rather, it should be understood that in both [the cases, i.e. rah and lah], only the class-sound (sphoṭa) is mentioned. Thus the sound heard as /r/ (ra-śruti) is replaced by a sound heard as /l/ (la-śruti)."[52] This passage has given rise to many interpretations in the context of the celebrated theory of sphoṭa. However, we shall restrict ourselves only to those considerations which are pertinent in the context of the notion of sound-universals.

3.9. Bhartṛhari explains the above argument as follows: "Or, the word sphoṭa-mātra indicates that this is a universal-mention. . . . The purpose of universal-mention is that it covers both /r/ sounds, one which is independent and the one which forms part of /ṛ/."[53] Thus, the universal of sound /r/ covers, according to Bhartṛhari, the sound /r/ which forms part of /ṛ/. Kaiyaṭa expresses the same view.[54] Thus the rule says: "In the case of the root √kṛp, the universal of /r/ is replaced by the universal of /l/."[55] Nāgeśa, on the other hand, is not ready to accept a sound-universal which covers independent and dependent varieties.[56]

3.10. Just as there is a consonantal element in /ṛ/, similarly there is also a vocalic element which is called ac-bhakti "a split vowel."[57] Just as /a/ covers long and extra-long varieties by homogeneous-representation (p.1.1.69), similarly one may extend this coverage to the vocalic particles in /ṛ/ and /ḷ/. This objection could also be raised in the theory of universal-mention. The universal of /a/ might be said to cover these vocalic particles.[58] But Bhartṛhari says that /a/ in no way can stand for these vocalic particles. He remarks: "This vocalic particle of quarter-mora quantity is not found anywhere else. There is no homogeneity. A part [of a composite sound] does not have a phonetic effort and points of articulation, independent from those of the whole. This vocalic particle is also incapable of manifesting the sound-universal of /a/ etc."[59] Kaiyaṭa points out that the perception of this vocalic particle is very indistinct and is not capable of manifesting any sound-universal.[60] Nāgeśa agrees with Kayaṭa's judgement.[61]

3.11. In Pāṇini's Śiva-sūtra: ṛ-ḷ-K, the sounds /ṛ/ and /ḷ/ are listed separately. No two sounds directly listed in the Śiva-sūtras are mutually homogeneous with the only exception of stops. A similar argument is offered by Bhaṭṭoji Dīkṣita for /e/ and /o/ not being homogeneous with /ai/ and /au/.[62] Kaiyaṭa clearly says that /ṛ/ and /ḷ/ are not homogeneous with each other for Pāṇini, though they are so for Kātyāyana.[63] In the real usage, the sound /ḷ/ occurs only in the forms of √kḷp. This is noted by Patañjali, all of whose other examples are pure fabrications.[64] Thus, Pāṇini did not need separate rules for guṇa and vṛddhi changes of /ḷ/, since he took care of the only occurrence of /ḷ/, the root √kḷp, by the above explained way.

Literally, P.1.1.51 (ur aṇ ra-paraḥ) says: "The /a-N/ replacements of /ṛ/ are immediately followed by /r/." Based on this rule is the notion of some modern authors that the guṇa for /ṛ/ is /ar/, and its vṛddhi is /ār/. Actually for Pāṇini, the term guṇa applies only to /a/, /e/ and /o/, while the term vṛddhi applies only to /ā/, /ai/ and /au/. But /a/ and /ā/ which replace /ṛ/ are immediately followed by /r/.[65] To derive kalpate, we start from karpate* and replace /r/ by /l/. Thus there is no occasion for /ḷ/ being directly changed to /al/. Thieme is certainly right when he points out that there is no guṇa to /ḷ/ in Pāṇini's system.[66]

3.12. Kātyāyana proposes that /ṛ/ and /ḷ/ be considered mutually homogeneous.[67] These sounds actually have different points of articulation and they would not normally become homogeneous in Pāṇini's system. Kātyāyana imposes this homogeneity, for specific purposes.[68] If /ṛ/ is homogeneous with /ḷ/, /ṛ/ can stand for /ḷ/ also. Thus the rule P.1.1.51 (ur aṇ ra-paraḥ) would mean: "The /a-Ṇ/ sounds which replace /ṛ/ and /ḷ/ are immediately followed by /r/." Patañjali sees this situation arising.[69] He counters such a possibility by saying: "I shall rule that [the /a-Ṇ/ substitutes of] /ḷ/ will be followed by /l/. This provision has to be given. [This provision] would be prescriptive, if the term 'homogeneous' is not [applied to /ḷ/ with respect to /ṛ/]. The same [provision] would help avoiding [the possibility of the /a-Ṇ/ replacements of /ḷ/ being followed by] /r/, if [the term 'homogeneous'] is applied [to /ḷ/ with respect to /ṛ/]."[70] This is a very significant statement. Patañjali suggests here that if /ṛ/ and /ḷ/ are not homogeneous, as in the view of Pāṇini, there is no fear of the /a-Ṇ/ substitutes of /ḷ/ being followed by /r/. But then Pāṇini does not provide that they will be followed by /l/ either. Such a proviso has to be made to account for the fictitious examples, or grammatical expressions involving /ḷ/.

3.13. Now a question arises as to how to understand Kātyāyana's statement on homogeneity of /ṛ/ and /ḷ/, in the light of his doctrine of universal-mention. Kātyāyana does not give us any direction in this case. Patañjali is also silent. Coming down to Bhartṛhari, we find the following explanation:

> When we accept the statement that /ṛ/ and /ḷ/ are homogeneous, and also when P.1.1.69 is rejected due to universal-mention, then, despite the difference of the sound [/r/ and /l/ in /ṛ/ and /ḷ/], they [i.e. /ṛ/ and /ḷ/] have the same universal, just as short and long [corresponding vowels have the same universal].[71]

Bhaṭṭoji Dīkṣita refuses to accept that /ṛ/ and /ḷ/ have the same sound-universal. According to his view, /ṛ/ cannot cover /ḷ/ unless we make a special provision.[72] He suggests that we should take out the term /a-Ṇ/ from P.1.1.69, following Kātyāyana, and put in /ṛ/ in its place. Thus P.1.1.69 should be rewritten as /ṛ/-udit savarṇasya etc.[73] This way /ṛ/ will cover /ḷ/. He also suggests that homogeneity between /ṛ/ and /ḷ/ has to be optional, or otherwise it would create several other problems.[74]

Nāgeśa accepts a different doctrine. He thinks that Kātyāyana's statement imposes the same universal on /ṛ/ and /ḷ/.[75] Some of the commentaries on Nāgeśa's Laghu-śabdendu-śekhara try to show that the word savarṇa itself could be interpreted to mean "having the same universal" (sajātīya), since the word varṇa is sometimes synonymous with jāti in the sense of "caste."[76] In fact, Liebich does interpret the word savarṇa as: "von gleicher Kaste" [see n. 344]. Hari Dīksita refers to poetic interchangeability of /r/ and /l/ and says that for these reasons the sounds/ṛ/ and /ḷ/ could have the same universal.[77] Of course, Kātyāyana had a very specific purpose in prescribing their homogeneity, i.e. obtaining a general rule for guṇa and vṛddhi of /ḷ/ being followed by /ḷ/. This seems to have been his only limited purpose. He needed this to explain usages with /ḷ/, which came about through incapability of proper pronounciation (aśaktija) and imitation of such usages (anukaraṇa) etc. No traditional grammarian ever clarified this limited purpose of this imposed homogeneity, except for the fact that Bhaṭṭoji Dīkṣita thought it to be optional and not obligatory throughout the grammar.

3.14. There is another kind of ambiguity involved in the notion of universal-mention, which has been discussed at some length by some of the later commentators. They classify universals into pervading universals (vyāpaka-jāti) and pervaded universals (vyāpya-jāti). The universal of the sound /a/ of which Kātyāyana and Patañjali speak covers the whole class of /a/ sounds (sarvam a-varṇa-kulam), and this is the pervading universal. However, there are also pervaded universals, such as the restricted /a/-ness, which covers only the short varieties. Similarly, we can have /ā/-ness pervading only the long varieties, and /ā3/-ness pervading only the extra-long varieties.[78] Thus, we have the following scheme of coverage:

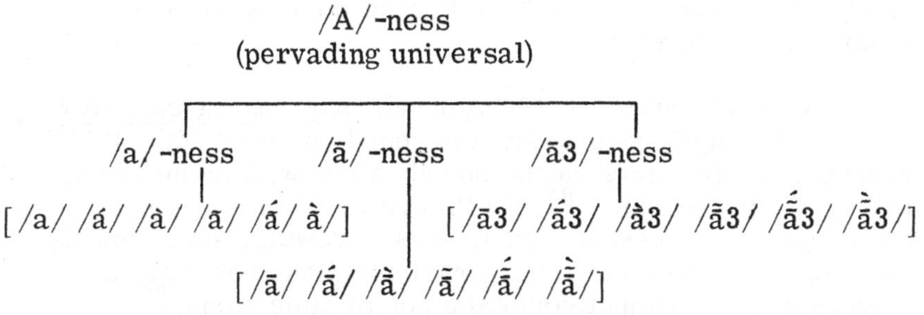

It has also been discussed whether the Śiva-sūtras contain the pervading universals or the pervaded universals. Each of these alternatives has a different implication. If the Śiva-sūtras contain the pervading universals, then there is no need of the procedure of homogeneous-representation in those cases. But if they contain the pervaded universals, then we still need that procedure. Suffice it to say that Kātyāyana intended the first alternative.

3.15. As a merit of this theory of universal-mention, it should be pointed out that its acceptance helps us to get rid of the rule P.1.1.10 (nājjhalau). This rule intends to deny any possible homogeneity between vowels and consonants. In the theory of universal-mention, vowels and consonants have different universals and hence there is no scope of homogeneity or co-universality of any vowels with consonants. Thus, despite the fact that /ā/ and /h/ have the same internal effort and point of articulation,[79] they do have different universals, and hence there is no problem. This has been noticed by some of the commentaries on Nāgeśa's Laghu-śabdendu-śekhara.[80] Another benefit could also be derived from this theory. Despite the difference of internal effort between /a/ and /ā/, they share the same universal, and hence we do not need anything like Pāṇini's pronounciation of /a/ as vivṛta "open," within the system, and its reinstatement to saṃvṛta "closed" by P.8.4.68 (a a). As far as I know, no grammarian has noticed this point. As we shall see later, those grammatical traditions, which accepted the impressionalistic notion of varṇa and savarṇa, were never faced with this problem. Kātyāyana's notion of universal is equally based on such conventional impressionism, and he, therefore, did not have to face the problem that Pāṇini was faced with.

3.16. Pāṇini's rule P.1.1.69 (aṇ-udit savarṇasya cāpratyayaḥ) says: "The /a-Ṇ/ sounds and the sounds marked with /U/ represent their homogeneous sounds along with themselves, if they are not affixes."[81] By this rule, the process of homogeneous-representation applies to vowels, semi-vowels and stops. In the view of universal-mention, however, a universal of /k/ cannot cover the homorganic stops.[82] Kātyāyana is aware of this short-coming and he only suggests removal of /a-Ṇ/ sounds from homogeneous-representation. Thus he still retains homogeneous-representation for stops. This means, we would still need the rule: udit savarṇasya. Since this rule contains the term savarṇa "homogeneous," we still need the definition of homogeneity (P.1.1.9), which still remains a general definition and covers even those sounds, which are already covered by universal-mention. Thus the procedure of universal-mention cannot function by itself, and needs assistance of homogeneous-representation. On the other hand, the latter can very well function by itself. The difficulty in accepting both the procedures simultaneously is that both of them presuppose opposite philosophical doctrines. Nāgeśa points out that P.1.1.69 is based on vyakti-vāda "doctrine of individuals," and on distinctiveness of pitch, nasality and quantity.[83] The principle of universal-mention, on the other hand, presupposes that a sound, by nature, stands for its universal, which naturally covers varieties differing in pitch, nasality and quantity. What is intended is a universal, and an individual is given simply because there is no other way of expressing the universal.[84]

3.17. Even if we decide to follow universal-mention and omit /a-Ṇ/ from P.1.1.69, we still do not achieve simplicity of description. The condition apratyayaḥ "non-affixal" in P.1.1.69 says that affixal sounds cannot stand for their homogeneous sounds. Nāgeśa points out that we still need this condition in universal-mention.[85] This is comparable to Kātyāyana's treatment of P.1.1.70 (taparas tat-kālasya) which says that a vowel followed by the marker /T/ stands only for homogeneous varieties of the same quantity.[86] Kātyāyana says that this rule operates even in universal-mention.[87] Patañjali explains that a vowel without /T/ may cover all co-universal (sajātīya) varieties. To restrict this, wherever we need, to varieties of the same quantity, we must use the marker /T/.[88] Nāgeśa realizes similarity between this argument and the restriction made by the condition apratyayaḥ in P.1.1.69.[89]

3.18. Finally, we should investigate some of the subtle problems created by universal-mention, which can certainly be avoided by a proper interpretation of Pāṇini's savarṇa-grahaṇa. In the final interpretation of P.1.1.69, only the /a-Ṇ/ sounds as they are listed in the Śiva-sūtras have the capacity of representing their homogeneous sounds. Thus, /a/ can represent varieties of /ā/ and /ā3/, but /ā/ cannot represent either /a/ or /ā3/.[90] By P.1.1.70 (taparas tat-kālasya) a vowel followed by /T/ stands only for homogeneous sounds of the same quantity. Thus, in the case of /a-Ṇ/ sounds, this rule becomes restrictive, while it becomes prescriptive for non-/a-Ṇ/ sounds.[91]

In universal-mention, in principle, any instance stands for its universal and that universal covers all co-universal varieties. Thus, the difference between /a-Ṇ/ and and non-/a-Ṇ/ sounds would be obliterated. If every vowel can represent, through its universal, all co-universal varieties, then the meta-element /T/ becomes universally restrictive (niyāmaka), and does not remain prescriptive (vidhāyaka) in any case. Thus /ā/ could also represent eighteen co-universal varieties, like /a/.

Bhartṛhari and Kaiyaṭa do realize this problem.[92] They claim that /ā/ would not stand for /a/, because /ā/ involves additional effort. If /a/ and /ā/ both can represent all co-universal varieties, then why would one use /ā/

instead of /a/? This is a very good practical argument, but it has no philosophical value.

3.19. Nāgeśa quotes a view held by some of the earlier grammarians. These grammarians think that /a/ expresses the pervading universal (vyāpaka-jāti), but /ā/ expresses only a pervaded universal (vyāpya-jāti). This pervaded universal /ā/-ness covers only long varieties.[93] But actually this does not work.

For instance, P. 7. 2. 84 (aṣṭana ā vibhaktau) prescribes the replacement /ā/ for the final /n/ of aṣṭan under certain conditions. Historically, the condition apratyayaḥ "non-affixal" in P. 1. 1. 69 (aṇ-udit savarṇasya cāpratyayaḥ) restricts only affixes from homogeneous-representation, and does not apply to substitutes.[94] Thus, if /ā/ can cover six co-universal varieties, including the nasal varieties, then by P. 1. 1. 50 (stāne'ntaratamaḥ), a nasal /ā̃/ would be substituted for the nasal /n/ of aṣṭan. Kātyāyana himself realized this difficulty. He answered it by pointing out that /ā/ is a non-/a-Ṇ/ sound, and hence it cannot stand for its homogeneous sounds by P. 1. 1. 69. Therefore, only a non-nasal /ā/ will be substituted for /n/ in aṣṭan.[95] But this solution would not really work in the procedure of universal-mention, if /ā/ were to stand for a pervaded universal (vyāpya-jāti), covering all the long varieties.

3.20. There is another example which shows Pāṇini's preciseness of formulations, which would be totally disturbed in universal-mention. P. 3. 1. 111 (ī ca khanaḥ) prescribes the substitute long /ī/ for /n/ in the root khan and also an affix KyaP. Thus we have khan + KyaP leading to kha+ ī + ya, and finally to kheya. It seems strange that Pāṇini should give long /ī/ as the substitute, instead of giving short /i/. Even Bhaṭṭoji Dīkṣita felt that Pāṇini should have given short /i/.[96] As it is mentioned earlier, historically, substitutes in Pāṇini's grammar could represent their homogeneous sounds. Even Kātyāyana realized this fact, but it was later obscured by discussions in Patañjali.[97] If Pāṇini were to give short /i/ as the substitute for /n/

in khan, this short /i/ being an /a-Ṇ/ sound would represent its homogeneous varieties, including nasal varieties. Thus, /n/ would be substituted by a nasal /ĩ/, finally leading to an undesirable nasal /ẽ/ in khẽya*. Since Pāṇini realized this, he gave long /ī/ as the substitute for /n/. This is not an /a-Ṇ/ sound and hence it cannot represent any homogeneous sounds. Thus, there is no possibility of obtaining the undesirable form khẽya*. If we accept universal-mention, then /ī/ could also cover its co-universal varieties and that would lead to the above mentioned problem.

3.21. From the above given analysis of universal-mention, it will be clear that it is not sufficient to replace Pāṇini's homogeneous-representation, unless a grammarian accepting this theory is prepared to build another structure of rules which would properly control its over-extensions. Kātyāyana seems to have given only a rough hypothesis. However, Kātyāyana's theory did not go unnoticed in the history of Sanskrit grammar. He had two illustrious followers, namely Candragomin and Śākaṭāyana. These two grammarians tried to develop Kātyāyana's suggestions in different ways. Their grammars will be studied later in Chapter XII.

CHAPTER IV

PATAÑJALI'S PROPOSAL OF PRAYATNA-BHEDA

4.1. Pāṇini's rule P.1.1.9 (tulyāsya-prayatnaṁ savarṇam) says that two sounds having the same points of articulation and internal effort are mutually homogeneous. Then he formulates P.1.1.10 (nājjhalau) which denies mutual homogeneity to sounds denoted by the shortforms /a-C/ and /ha-L/. No vowels denoted by /a-C/ are homogeneous with any consonants denoted by /ha-L/. Since Pāṇini formulates this rule, we must assume that at least some vowels and consonants have the same internal effort. The tradition believes that, according to Pāṇini, vowels and ūṣmans, i.e./ś/, /ṣ/, /s/ and /h/ are vivṛta "open."[98] There are many Śikṣās and other texts which do not subclassify these two groups according to their internal effort.[99] Thus, /ā/ and /h/ are both kaṇṭhya "produced in the throat" and open. Similarly, /i/ and /ś/ are both palatal and open. Thus these sounds would be mutually homogeneous, unless prevented by P.1.1.10 (nājjhalau).[100]

4.2. Kātyāyana and Patañjali discuss problems concerning the interpretation of P.1.1.10. In the prima facie view (pūrva-pakṣa), it is assumed that homogeneous-representation (P.1.1.69) applies to the terms /a-C/ and /ha-L/ in P.1.1.10. Kaiyata explains that, if P.1.1.69 is applied to P.1.1.10, then /i/ included in /a-C/ could stand for its homogeneous sounds including /ś/.[101] Similarly, /a/ could stand for /h/. Normally, an exclusion rule applies first, and then the general rule applies. However, in this case, the negation rule has yet to come into being. We cannot deny homogeneity of /a-C/sounds with /ha-L/ sounds, before interpreting these very terms, and there that denial cannot apply. Now if /i/ in /a-C/ stands for /ś/, and /ś/ also occurs in /ha-L/, then /ś/ would be non-homogeneous with itself. Similarly, /h/ included in /ha-L/ is an /a-Ṇ/ sound, and hence by P.1.1.69, it could stand for all varieties of /a/. This would result in non-homogeneity of all the varieties of /a/ with each other and with themselves.[102]

4.3. Kātyāyana realized this problem. Thus, he says: "In the prohibition [of homogeneity] between /a-C/ and /ha-L/ sounds, the prohibition [of homogeneity] of /ś/ [with /ś/ obtains], since [/ś/ is both] an /a-C/ sound and a /ha-L/ sound."[103] Patañjali explains that /ś/ is an /a-C/ sound because it is represented by /i/, and it is a /ha-L/ sound because it is so listed in the group.[104] P.8.4.65 (jharo jhari savarṇe) prescribes deletion of a sound included in the group /jha-R/, if it is followed by a homogeneous sound from the same group, and preceded by any consonant. Patañjali points out that non-homogeneity of /ś/ with itself would prohibit deletion of /ś/ followed by /ś/.[105]

4.4. To this difficulty, Kātyāyana offers two solutions. Here, we shall only be concerned with the first solution: "The desired result is achieved, since [/ś/] is not an /a-C/ sound."[106] This statement is given without any supporting reasons.[107] However, we have an explanation from Patañjali:

> The desired result is achieved. How? [It is achieved], since [/ś/] is not an /a-C/ sound. Why is [/ś/] not an /a-C/ sound? [Consider the following:] The articulator of stops is in contact [with the point of articulation]. [The articulator] of semi-vowels is in slight contact. [The articulator] of ūṣmans is with a gap, i.e. open. Here the word "slight" continues. [The articulator] of vowels is also open. Here the word "slight" is not continued.[108]

By subclassifying ūṣmans as īṣad-vivṛta "slightly open" and vowels as vivṛta "open," Patañjali avoids homogeneity of /i/ and /ś/. Thus /i/ cannot stand for /ś/, and hence the undesired non-homogeneity of /ś/ with /ś/ does not result.

4.5. Patañjali's subclassification of vivṛta "open" removes the particular problem, but at a great cost. It makes P.1.1.10 (nājjhalau) totally redundant. If ūṣmans and vowels differ in their internal effort, then actually there is no possibility whatsoever of any vowel ever being homogeneous with any consonant. Thus, there is no need for Pāṇini to make any rule such as P.1.1.10. Kaiyaṭa realizes that Patañjali's suggestion leads to the rejection of P.1.1.10.[109] This realization is also shared by later grammarians like Bhaṭṭoji Dīkṣita.[110] But some of the later texts like the Laghu-siddhānta-kaumudī of Varadarāja adopt this subclassification in their phonetic description.[111]

The tradition clearly attributes this subclassification to Patañjali.[112] Actually, some later grammarians ascribe to Patañjali a sevenfold classification of internal effort by incorporating four subdivisions of vivṛta, i.e. īṣad-vivṛta "slightly open," vivṛta "open," vivṛta-tara "more open and vivṛta-tama "most open."[114] These distinctions are seen also in several other Śikṣās and Prātiśākhyas.[115]

Patañjali himself uses these distinctions to avoid homogeneity of /a/ [which is presumed to be open within the grammar] with /e/ and /o/ which are said to be more open.[116] There are again differences of opinion in this respect. Nāgeśa holds that these subclassifications must be accepted to give a phonetic explanation of why /e/ and /o/ are not homogeneous with /ai/ and /au/.[117] Otherwise, one must say that they are not homogeneous simply because Pāṇini lists them separately in the Śiva-sūtras.

4.6. Some of the later commentators show a clear awareness of the historically Pāṇinian view in this matter. Thus, Bhaṭṭoji Dīkṣita says that ūṣmans and vowels have the same internal effort.[118] Hari Dīkṣita warns us that we should not believe that Pāṇini intends the distinctions given by Patañjali.[119] Nāgeśa declares that the subclassifications of "open-ness" are not distinctive as far as homogeneity is concerned, and this is indicated by the fact that Pāṇini gives P.1.1.10.[120] In one place Nāgeśa thinks that P.1.1.10 echoes Patañjali's subclassifications,[121] but later comes back and says that these distictions constitute a virtual rejection of P.1.1.10.[122]

4.7. Historically, the question we may ask is if Patañjali invented this subclassification, or he just adopted an already established doctrine. Franz Kielhorn says:

> Patañjali, in his comments on the vārttika: siddham anactvāt on P.1.1.10, appears (in the words: spṛṣṭaṁ karaṇaṁ sparśānām/ īṣat-spṛṣṭam antaḥsthānām/ vivṛtam ūṣmaṇām/ svarāṇāṁ ca vivṛtam) to quote a Śiksā which may have resembled the Āpiśali, --unless indeed the rules given by him should have been quoted from the Atharvaveda Prātiśākhya I, 29-32 (spṛṣṭaṁ sparśānāṁ karaṇam/ īṣat-spṛṣṭam antaḥsthānām/ ūṣmaṇāṁ vivṛtaṁ ca/ svarāṇāṁ ca)."[123]

The Āpiśali-śikṣā-sūtras which have come down to us read as follows: spṛṣṭa-karaṇāḥ sparśāḥ/ īṣat-spṛṣṭa-karaṇā antaḥsthāḥ/ īṣad-vivṛta-karaṇāḥ ūṣmāṇaḥ/ vivṛta-karaṇāḥ svarāḥ/... saṁvṛto'kāraḥ/.[124] Comparing this text with the text quoted by Patañjali, it is clear that he has not quoted the Āpiśali-śikṣā-sūtras. There is a definite resemblance between the text quoted by Patañjali and the Atharvaveda Prātiśākhya. Thieme actually holds that Patañjali is quoting the APr, and hence must be later than the APr.[125]

It is, however, not clear if the APr exactly intends what Patañjali's interpretation seems to speak. On the APr I.31 (ūṣmaṇāṁ vivṛtaṁ ca), Whitney says:

> The final ca of the rule indicates, according to the commentators, that īṣat-spṛṣṭam is also to be inferred from the previous rule: in the formation of the spirants, the organ is both in partial contact and open --a rather awkward way of saying, apparently, that its position is neither very close nor very open.[126]

The APr thus may not exactly be speaking of Patañjali's īṣad-vivṛta, but it certainly differentiates spirants from vowels in their internal effort.

4.8. This brings us to a new possible historical link. We have been using the name "Atharvaveda Prātiśākhya," along with Thieme and others, for a text, which actually bears the title Śaunakīyā Caturādhyāyikā, in the solitary Berlin MS from which it was edited by Whitney. Whitney gave it the title of APr. But new manuscripts bearing the title "APr" have come up, which are quite different from Whitney's APr. Important to us is the discovery of a manuscript titled Kautsa-vyākaraṇa by Sadashiv L. Kātre, in 1938 [ref. "Kautsa-Vyākaraṇa: A Detailed Notice," New Indian Antiquary, Vol. I, 1938-9, pp. 383-396]. This article gives all deviations of this Kautsa-vyākaraṇa from Whitney's APr. Despite some minor divergences, these two texts are identical. This is extremely important. If this Kautsa is identical with Kautsa who is Pāṇini's disciple [ref: Mahābhāṣya on P.3.2.108: upasedivān kautsaḥ pāṇinim], that could substantially add to our knowledge of the historical development of the Pāṇinian tradition.

4.9. Hypothetically accepting Kautsa's identity as a student of Pāṇini, we may speak of some continuous historical development. Pāṇini did not subclassify vivṛta "open," and thus has composed P.1.1.10. Then came his disciple, Kautsa, who in his Prātiśākhya did subclassify spirants and vowels. Then, we find Kātyāyana giving two alternatives to solve problems in P.1.1.10, i.e. a) anactvāt "since spirants are not vowels," and b) vākyāparisamāpter vā "incompletion of a sentence." As we shall see later, the second alternative is based on retaining P.1.1.10, which implies that vowels and spirants have the same effort. The first alternative, however, distinguishes spirants from vowels. What is not clear is the ground on which this distinction is made. It is possible that Kātyāyana was aware of the distinctions made by Kautsa. We may find some tentative support to conclude that Kātyāyana knew the difference concerning internal effort of vowels and spirants. Thieme has almost conclusively proved the identity of Kātyāyana, the Vārttikarkāra, and Kātyāyana, the author of the Vājasaneyi Prāriśākhya [see: n. 284]. The definition of savarṇa in the VPr [see: 10.5.2] is virtually identical with P.1.1.9, and yet there is no homogeneity of any vowels with spirants, since, as Uvaṭa points out, vowels are aspṛṣṭa "without contact" and spirants are ardha-spṛṣṭa "with halfway contact." With the same assumption, perhaps, Kātyāyana differentiated vowels and spirants in his vārttika: anactvāt on P.1.1.10. However, realizing that this is not Pāṇini's view, he offered the other explanation: vākyāparisamāpter vā. Finally, Patañjali came out with explicit discussion of this problem. Thus, this suggestion of prayatna-bheda can be ascribed to Patañjali, only in the sense that he came out with this explicit discussion for the first time in the Pāṇinian tradition.

4.10. Anyway, Patañjali does not stand alone in differentiating the internal effort of spirants from that of vowels. The Yajus recension of the Pāṇiniya-śikṣā (verse 30) considers vowels to be aspṛṣṭa "without contact" and spirants to be nema-spṛṣṭa "with halfway contact."[127] But the preceding verse itself considers vowels and spirants to be vivṛta "open."[128] The Pāṇinīya-śikṣā-sūtras say that spirants may be considered either īṣad-vivṛta or vivṛta.[129] These sūtras which are probably of a late origin seem to record both the traditions. The Āpiśali-śikṣā-sūtras, without option, consider spirants to be īṣad-vivṛta.[130] This has prompted certain scholars to consider this Śikṣā to be post-Pāṇinian.[131] Uvaṭa's commentary on the VPr,[132] the Yājñavalkya-śikṣā[133] and the Varṇa-ratna-pradīpikā-śikṣā of Amareśa[134] consider spirants to be ardha-spṛṣṭa "with halfway contact." The terms nema-spṛṣṭa and ardha-spṛṣṭa seem to combine the notion of the APr that spirants are both īṣat-spṛṣṭa "with slight contact" and vivṛta "open." The term īṣad-vivṛta seems to have originated with Patañjali's discussion.

CHAPTER V

A NON-TRADITIONAL APPROACH

5.1. By a non-traditional approach, I intend the following axioms: a) A rule can apply to itself, and b) a rule can apply to another rule, even if the first presupposes the second. In the present context, this would mean that P.1.1.69 applies to itself, and it also applies to P.1.1.10. In the Pāṇinian tradition, no one has adopted this view, which amounts to a criticism of the notion of vākyāparisamāpti "incompletion of a sentence," a procedure adopted by Kātyāyana and the rest of the Pāṇinian tradition. The details of this procedure will be discussed in the following chapter, but basically it says that P.1.1.69 cannot apply to itself, nor to P.1.1.10. S. P. Chaturvedi (1933) launched a heavy criticism of this traditional way of interpreting Pāṇini. He says that the procedure of vākyāparisamāpti "which is propounded by Bhāṣyakāra Patañjali...should be regarded as ekadeśi-bhāṣya and not as a siddhānta-bhāṣya" [Chaturvedi (1933), p. 168]. He further says:

> This doctrine cuts at the very root of the Pāṇinian system and its acceptance will lead to many complications. The Aṣṭādhyāyī of Pāṇini is a whole interconnected work. For the formation of a single word, we have to apply sūtras from various parts of the work. Each sūtra should be interpreted in the light of what we know from the other sūtras. It is wrong to maintain that at the time of interpretation of nājjhalau-tulyāsya-prayatnaṁ savarṇam (I.i.9, 10), we connot take help from the sūtra aṇuditsavarṇasya cāpratyayaḥ (I.i.69), its meaning being still unknown to us according to vākyāparisamāptinyāya. When we interpret the pratyāhāra 'ac' in nājjhalau, we should do so as we interpret other pratyāhāras in the Aṣṭādhyāyī. [Chaturvedi (1933), p. 170]

With this argument, Chaturvedi criticizes Bhaṭṭoji Dīkṣita and proposes that either we should apply P.1.1.69 to P.1.1.10 and abandon vākyāparisamāptinyāya or accept the subclassification of vivṛta "open" [Chaturvedi (1933), p. 173]. p. 173]. As we shall later discuss in detail, Chaturvedi's argument is wrong on several counts. The vākyāparisamāpti precedes Patañjali and is found in Kātyāyana, who uses it in many contexts as the only explanation of apparent problems in Pāṇini's rules. [Sec. 6.14-15]

No other scholar has openly accepted a view like Chaturvedi's, but there are many cases of implied acceptance. For instance, S. C. Vasu translates P.1.1.69 as:

> The letters of the pratyāhāra a-Ṇ, i.e. the vowels and semi-vowels, and a term having u for its indicatory letter refer to their own form as well as to their homogeneous letters, except when they are used as pratyayas.[135]

With this goes the comment:

> The pratyāhāra a-Ṇ in this sūtra includes all the vowels (underlining mine) and liquids.[136]

This is clearly applying P.1.1.69 to P.1.1.69. Let us also glance at Vasu's translation of P.1.1.10.

> There is, however, no homogeneity between vowels and consonants.[137]

Colebrook, Böhtlingk and Renou have exactly parallel translations.[138] The term /a-C/ in P.1.1.10 cannot mean all vowels, unless P.1.1.69 is applied to P.1.1.10. Without its application, /a-C/ would stand only for /a/, /i/, /u/, /ṛ/, /ḷ/, /e/, /o/, /ai/ and /au/ as they are listed in the Śiva-sūtras. This would indicate that these scholars have applied P.1.1.69 to P.1.1.10.

5.2. Recently, S. D. Joshi has provided some discussion of P.1.1.69 and its interpretation. Kaiyaṭa quotes an older maxim: grahaṇān-grahaṇe grahaṇābhāvaḥ, which is rendered by S. D. Joshi as: "(One can) not (apply the principle of) grahaṇa (i.e. P.1.1.69) to the term /a-Ṇ/ in the grahaṇa rule (itself)."[139] In a footnote to this, he says: "The pratyāhāra /a-Ṇ/ includes all vowels (underlining mine), semi-vowels and /h/."[140] This is quite similar to Vasu's comment and implies that Joshi is applying P.1.1.69 to itself. In fact, S. D. Joshi is quite aware of the exact meaning of the traditional maxim and of some of the effects of not accepting it. This is what he has to remark:

> The quotation is probably from the lost part of Bhartṛhari's Mahābhāṣya-Dīpikā. The term /aṆ/ in P.1.1.69 refers only to those vowels which are included in the pratyāhāra /aṆ/. The rule P.1.1.69 states that these vowels represent their homorganic varieties also. Now if P.1.1.69 is applied in P.1.1.69 itself, it would give the meaning that the vowels included in /aṆ/ and their savarṇa (homorganic) varieties stand for their savarṇa varieties. This means that the vowels long /ā/ etc. also represent the corresponding short varieties.[141]

The reader is not sure if S. D. Joshi prefers applying the rule to itself, as his footnote would have us believe, or he is simply explaining what would happen if the rule applies to itself. In view of this confusing state of affairs, we need to go into a detailed examination of this alternative. Some of the alleged examples of a rule applying to itself are P.1.3.3 (hal-antyam) and P.7.3.119 (ac ca gheḥ). We shall discuss these cases critically and study the question of a rule applying to itself in more general terms.

5.3. P.1.3.3 (hal-antyam) literally means: "The final hal is termed it." Does the term hal in the rule stand for the Śiva-sūtra: /ha-L/, or does it represent the shortform /ha-L/? The rule which forms shortforms, i.e. P.1.1.71 (ādir antyena sahetā), says: "The initial sound, along with the final it sound, stand for the initial sound and the sounds which are in between." This rule presupposes the definition of it, i.e. P.1.1.3. On the other hand, if /ha-L/ in P.1.3.3

is to be a shortform, it presupposes P.1.1.71. This is a case of interdepencence.[142] Kātyāyana's final solution to this problem runs as: "[The desired result is established] alternatively by [considering hal in P.1.3.3 to be] a mention [of both the Śiva-sūtra: /ha-L/ and the shortform /ha-L/] by a single-remainder transformation (ekaśeṣa)."[143] Patañjali says that hal in the rule, by single-remainder, stands for two words of the same shape.[144] For instance, the dual rāmau is derived, in Pāṇini's system, from two singulars, i.e. rāmaḥ and rāmaḥ, which have the same phonetic shape and the same case, by P.1.2.64 (sarūpāṇām ekaśeṣa eka-vibhaktau). Kaiyaṭa believes that the first word /ha-L/ is a genitive Tatpuruṣa compound meaning "/l/ near /ha/" (hasya laḥ). The second word /ha-L/ is a shortform.[145] Thus the first interpretation of P.1.3.3 is: "The sound near /ha/, /l/, is it." Then by P.1.1.71, we can form the shortform /ha-L/ beginning with /h(a)/ in the Śiva-sūtra: /h(a)/ /y(a)/ /v(a)/ /r(a)/ /Ṭ/ and ending in the marker /L/ of the Śiva-sūtra: /h(a) / /L/. This covers all consonants. With this shortform /ha-L/. we come back to P.1.3.3. Now the rule means that all consonants occurring at the end of given units are termed it. Nāgeśa doubts Kaiyaṭa's interpretation of genitive compound,[146] and thinks that Patañjali has actually opted for repeating the rule. This is the interpretation of Bhaṭṭoji Dīkṣita.[147]

This repetition of the rule and separate interpretation of the two instances of P.1.3.3 is designed to avoid mutual dependence with P.1.1.71, as well as for avoiding the so-called application of P.1.3.3 to itself. What we have are two rules with the same wording, and not one and the same rule being applied to itself. It is clear that the two interpretations of P.1.3.3 do not apply to each other, and also they do not apply within themselves.

5.4. Another alleged instance is P.7.3.119 (ac ca gheḥ). In the rule, we have the form gheḥ, genitive singular of the stem ghi-. The technical term ghi- stands for nominal stems ending in short /i/ and /u/, excluding sakhi- and those nominals which are termed nadī (P.1.4.7 (śeṣo ghy asakhi)). The word ghi- itself fulfills all the conditions for the technical designation ghi-. The commentators admit that only because ghi- is termed ghi-, can we have guṇa replacement of /i/ in ghi in the form gheḥ by P.6.1.111 (gher ṅiti).[148] Thus the technical term ghi applies to ghi- itself.

5.5. This is quite different from saying that a rule applies to itself. We have to make a distinction between the expression of a rule and its contents. If the theoretical contents of a rule apply to themselves, then it is a case of a rule applying to itself. However, if the contents of a rule apply to the expression of itself, then this is a different kind of dependence. As linguistic utterances, there is actually no difference between the expression of a grammatical rule and a sentence in a drama. The traditional grammarians have squarely dealt with this problem. For instance, in terms of contents, P.6.1.101 (akaḥ savarṇe dīrghaḥ): "If an /a-K/ sound is followed by a homogeneous sound, both are replaced by a long variety" is dependent on P.1.1.9 (tulyāsya-prayatnaṁ savarṇam) which defines homogeneity. However, in the expression of P.1.1.9, we have a sandhi of tulya and āsya, which depends on the contents of P.6.1.101. Bhaṭṭoji discusses this example and points out that as linguistic utterances illustrating a certain grammatical feature, there is no difference between the expressions tulyāsya and daṇḍāḍhaka.[149] Thus, P.7.3.119 is not an example of a rule applying to itself.

5.6. Some grammarians held that sandhi rules do not apply to the Śiva-sūtras because the sandhi rules have yet to come into being. The expression of sandhi rules depends on shortforms, which depend on the Śiva-sūtras. Nāgeśa points out that this is a false argument. The rule which applies in upendra should also apply in /a-i-u-Ṇ/. The reason there is no sandhi is that it would create a lot of confusion in identifying the sounds in the list. This is the real reason.[150]

5.7. We have already considered the undesirable effects of applying P.1.1.69 to P.1.1.10, in Sec. 4.2-3. Here we shall discuss the effects of applying P.1.1.69 to itself.

We already have some hints from S. D. Joshi. Here we have also to consider P.1.1.70 (taparas tatkālasya). This rule says: "A sound marked with /T/ stands only for the homogeneous varieties of the same quantity." If we do not apply P.1.1.69 to itself, then we have the following:

[A] [1] /a/ stands for eighteen varieties.
[2] /ā/ stands for itself.
[3] /aT/ stands for six short varieties.
[4] /āT/ stands for six long varieties.

If we apply P.1.1.69 to itself, then we have the following:

[B] [1] /a/ stands for eighteen varieties.
[2] /ā/ stands for eighteen varieties.
[3] /aT/ stands for six short varieties.
[4] /āT/ stands for six long varieties.

This shows the difference between the two alternatives. The alternative [B] is very much like Kātyāyana's theory of universal-mention. If /ā/ or any non-/a-Ṇ/ sound could represent its homogeneous varieties, that creates problems which are common with Kātyāyana's universal-mention. [cf. Sec. 3.18].

5.8. There are also other implications of applying P.1.1.69 to itself. In this alternative, the difference between /a-Ṇ/ sounds and non-/a-Ṇ/ sounds is obliterated. The same would apply to sounds marked with /U/, and sounds represented by sounds marked with /U/. Non-/a-Ṇ/ vowels and semi-vowels would be capable of representing their homogeneous sounds. Similarly, sounds marked with /U/ and sounds represented by such sounds would also be capable of representing their homogeneous sounds. Just as /ā/ could represent all the eighteen varieties, similarly /kh/ could also represent /k/, /kh/, /g/, /gh/ and /ṅ/. The same would happen to other series of stops.

5.9. Though this is obviously not what Pāṇini intended, such an implication seems to follow from V̇. N. Misra's translation of P.1.1.69:

> A member of the /a-Ṇ/$_2$ group (vowel, semi-vowel and /h/) or of the groups /kU/, /cU/, /ṭU/, /tU/, /pU/, stands for itself as well as for its homorganic correspondents, but only when it is not a component of a suffix.[151]

Misra speaks of the group /a-Ṇ/$_2$ as "vowel, semi-vowel and /h/" and not just sounds as listed in the Śiva-sūtras. Thus, he is certainly applying P.1.1.69 to itself. Misra goes even further. The other part of his translation could mean two things. It may mean that each of the groups /kU/ etc. stands for itself and its homorganic correspondents, or any member of any of these groups stands for itself and for its homorganic correspondents. Both of these are inaccurate statements.

5.10. All the above discussed implications of applying P.1.1.69 to itself would come to mean that all vowels, semi-vowels and stops are capable of representing their homogeneous varieties. If this were Pāṇini's intention, he could have formulated the shortform /a-Y/ to cover all these sounds and could have formulated P.1.1.69 as: ay savarṇasya cāpratyayaḥ. Actually such an interpretation of P.1.1.69 would seriously put Pāṇini's entire grammar in jeopardy. This searching analysis would show that the alternative of applying P.1.1.69 to itself is neither historically Pāṇinian, nor theoretically effective, and hence must be abandoned.

CHAPTER VI

BACK TO PĀṆINI

6.1. After considering the un-Pāṇinian alternatives, we now come back to an interpretation, which in all probability is Pāṇinian. On P.1.1.10, Kātyāyana first presents a prima facie view that P.1.1.69 applies to P.1.1.10. The problems resulting from this have been discussed in Sec. 4.2. To solve these problems, Kātyāyana offers two solutions. The first solution and its interpretation by Patañjali are also discussed in Sec. 4.3-4. The second solution given by Kātyāyana initiates the procedure of vākyāparisamāpti "incompletion of a sentence." Kātyāyana says: "[The desired result that /ś/ is homogeneous with itself, and is not homogeneous with /i/ is established] alternatively by [adopting the procedure of] incompletion of a sentence."[152] On this Patañjali gives the following explanation:

> What is this incompletion of a sentence? First there is the teaching of sounds [in the Śiva-sūtras]. [The definition of] the term it [in P.1.3.3] follows the teaching of sounds. [The definition of] a pratyāhāra "shortform" [i.e. P.1.1.71] follows [the definition of] the term it. [The definition of] the term savarṇa "homogeneous" [in P.1.1.9] follows [the definition of] shortforms. [The definition of] savarṇa-grahaṇa "homogeneous-representation" [in P.1.1.69] follows [the definition of] the term "homogeneous." By this complete and interlinked sentence, there is representation of homogeneous sounds elsewhere [but not within any link of this sentence].[153]

The Pāṇinian procedure of homogeneous-representation is built up of five stages, each of which is dependent on the previous stage, and all the five stages are linked together like clauses of a complex sentence. To some extent, this linking could be compared with an inferential process, where the product of a previous inference becomes the premise of the next inference. The Naiyāyikas consider stages within an inference to be like clauses of a sentence, and hence the expression of a full inference used to convince others (parārtha) is called a "five-limbed sentence" (pañcāṅgika-vākya).[154] Representation of homogeneous sounds is the cumulative effect of this ordered sequence of rules, and the procedure does not apply to any rule within the closed group.

6.2. Patañjali says that the definition of the term savarṇa "homogeneous" follows the definition of shortforms. This is at first confusing. P.1.1.9 (tulyāsya-prayatnaṁ savarṇam) does not involve any shortforms, and does not depend on the definition of shortforms (P.1.1.71). However, as Bhaṭṭoji Dīkṣita points out, P.1.1.10 needs to be interpreted before P.1.1.9. P.1.1.10 (nājjhalau) literally means: "The sounds denoted by the shortforms /a-C/ and /ha-L/ are not mutually homogeneous." This rule involves two shortforms. According to the Pāṇinian tradition, an exception rule is to be interpreted before interpreting the general rule. The same sequence belongs to their application.[155] If we first have mutual homogeneity of /a-C/ and /ha-L/ sounds by P.1.1.9, and then deny it by p.1.1.10, it would be like asking a man who has already eaten not to eat.[156] Thus, the definition of homogeneity indirectly depends on the definition of shortforms. We cannot interpret P.1.1.69 before interpreting P.1.1.9, since we cannot interpret the procedure of homogeneous-representation before defining "homogeneous." This ordered dependence of rules is the essence of incompletion of a sentence, for any rule within the structure.[157]

6.3. The reason why P.1.1.69 cannot apply to P.1.1.10 is that we cannot understand P.1.1.69 before interpreting P.1.1.9, and P.1.1.9 cannot be interpreted before interpreting P.1.1.10. Thus, in a way, P.1.1.69 does not exist, while interpreting P.1.1.10.[158] Hari Dīkṣita points out that what counts is the logical or cognitive sequence of rules in terms of their dependency requirement.[159] Thieme explains this situation:

> Bezüglich der in Pān. 1. 1. 10 (nājjhalau "ein 'ac' und ein 'hal' sind nicht gleichlautig") genannten pratyāhāra hat zwar 1. 1. 69 nicht statt, da erst nachdem die Definition der 'Gleichlautigkeit' vollständig gegeben ist, der Ausdruck savarṇasya in 1. 1. 69 verstanden werden kann. An anderen Stellen der Grammatik, wo ein pratyāhāra genannt wird, hat jedoch 1. 1. 69 statt, und nennen die in den pratyāhāra enthaltenen Laute auch ihre 'gleichlautigen' Partner, z. B. das in akaḥ in 6. 1. 101 enthaltene /i/ auch langes /ī/.[160]

Thus, P. 1. 1. 69 does not apply to P. 1. 1. 10.

6. 4. Similarly, P. 1. 1. 69 cannot apply to itself. Bhartṛhari explains the logic behind this:

> However, here in P. 1. 1. 69, there is no homogeneous-representation by P. 1. 1. 69. What is the reason? In this rule (i. e. P. 1. 1. 69), the relation of a sound with the designated items (i. e. homogeneous sounds) is not yet established. [Thus] the rule of homogeneous-representation does not apply to the shortform /a-Ṇ/ in the same rule, because [a] the procedure of representation has not yet come about, [b] there is no other rule of such representation, and [c] an action [of a thing] is contradicted with respect to the same [thing].[161]

Thus, while interpreting a statement, we cannot take for granted its own meaning. Otherwise, we would be involved in the fallacy of circularity. Finally, Bhaṭṭoji Dīkṣita points out two historical aspects of this procedure. In this procedure, both P. 1. 1. 10 and P. 1. 1. 69 are necessary, and vowels and spirants have the same internal effort.[162] Compared to other alternatives, these aspects make this alternative more historically true to Pāṇini's system.

6.5. At this point, we have to dive deeper into some of the most fundamental aspects of Pāṇini's theory of homogeneity. He felt the necessity of adopting this procedure of homogeneous-representation, because the features of pitch, nasality and quantity are basically distinctive. On P.1.1.1 (vṛddhir ād-aic), Kātyāyana says: "The marker /T/ is attached to /ā/ [In P.1.1.1] to obtain [representation of] homogeneous sounds [of the same quantity]. Since pitch is a distinctive feature, [the non-/a-Ṇ/ sound /ā/ cannot by itself stand for any of its homogeneous sounds]."[163] The sound /ā/ as uttered by Pāṇini must have had some pitch, and it must be distinct from /ā/ sounds with a different pitch. Thus, /ā/ with a certain pitch, by itself, cannot stand for /ā/ with a different pitch. Since /ā/ is a non-/a-Ṇ/ sound, P.1.1.69 cannot help it. Thus, addition of the marker /T/ is the only solution.

Patañjali, on the other hand, holds a different view. He counters Kātyāyana's explanation with the following comment:

> The only correct view is that [for Pāṇini] the features [of pitch etc.] are not distinctive. What is the basis for such a view? The reason is that [Pāṇini] specifically states a certain vowel to be highpitched in P.7.1.75 (asthi-dadhi-sakthy-akṣṇām anaṅ udāttaḥ). If the features were distinctive, then he might have simply uttered the highpitched vowel.[164]

If these features are not distinctive, it does not matter with what feature Pāṇini pronounced /ā/ in P.1.1.1; it will still represent other varieties of /ā/, without P.1.1.69. Patañjali clearly says: "Thus, the marker /T/ in P.1.1.1 is simply to remove doubts,"[165] and has no prescriptive function as interpreted by Kātyāyana.

6.6. Despite Patañjali's arguments, Kātyāyana's view has a richer significance. It represents the historical truth as far as Pāṇini's original system is concerned. Pāṇini needed homogeneous-representation, because basically, pitch, nasality and quantity are distinctive. This has been brought out by Kātyāyana: "Because of the difference of [sounds on account of] pitch, nasality and quantity, [Pāṇini made the rule that] an /a-Ṇ/ sound represents its homogeneous sound."[166] Kātyāyana consistently maintains his view throughout. A sound cannot stand for another sound with different features, unless such a capacity is invested by P.1.1.69, or by the marker /T/. Bhartṛhari testifies that this was Pāṇini's view.[167] The later tradition mostly follows Patañjali's view, but some grammarians have exhibited a historical attitude. Nāgeśa points out that Pāṇini's rule P.1.1.69 is made with a view that features are distinctive and that a sound basically stands only for itself (vyakti-vāda).[168] Nīlakaṇṭha Dīkṣita says that the maxim abhedakāḥ guṇāḥ "Features are not distinctive" is not universally valid, because of Pāṇini's inclusion of the /a-Ṇ/ sounds in P.1.1.69.[169]

6.7. In fact, both the so-called opposite views do not contradict each other, if understood in a specific manner. Pāṇini starts with the real pronounced sounds of the object language, where the features of pitch, quantity etc. are phonemically distinctive. For instance, the final sounds in śyāma and śyāmā are phonemically different. Similarly, the two Vedic words, i.e. bráhman and brahmán are phonemically distinct from each other. This is the level Kātyāyana is talking about, when he considers these features to be distinctive.

However, those features which are phonemically distinctive are not necessarily so in morphophonemics. For instance, both /a/ and /ā/ in śyāma and śyāmā take the same guṇa replacement /e/, if they are followed by /i/ in iti, yielding śyāmeti. Thus, the feature of quantity is not distinctive with reference to this morphophonemic operation. Similarly, in a large number of rules in Pāṇini's grammar, these features are morphophonemically non-distinctive. This is what Patañjali intends to say. Nāgeśa rightly interprets Patañjali's view to mean that the features like pitch do not cause non-homogeneity of sounds.[170] Thus, Kātyāyana's view belongs to a pre-homogeneity stage, while Patañjali's view, in this moderate interpretation, belongs to a post-homogeneity stage.

In fact, Patañjali seems to agree with Kātyāyana, when he says: "The designation 'homogeneous' is founded on the difference [between sounds, in features other than the point of articulation and internal effort]. If it were to apply [to sounds] where there is total identity [of features], the designation 'homogeneous' would serve no purpose."[171]

6.8. Thus, there is no contradiction in saying that a feature such as pitch is phonemically distinctive, while it is morphophonemically non-distinctive. This has been achieved by Pāṇini through his conception of savarṇa "homogeneous" and savarṇa-grahaṇa "homogeneous-representation." Each /a-Ṇ/ sound in the Śiva-sūtras is phonemically distinct from other homogeneous sounds, because of the difference of pitch, nasality and quantity. However, through the procedure of homogeneous-representation, it becomes morphophonemically non-distinct from other homogeneous sounds. Thus a morphophonemic operation prescribed with respect to /a/ also applies to /ā/, unless prevented by /T/.

When Pāṇini wanted certain sounds to be marked with distinct features even in morphophonemics, he used special devices like the condition apratyayaḥ "non-affixal" in P.1.1.69, the marker /T/ defined by P.1.1.70 to limit the quantity of the represented homogeneous sounds, and specific mention of accentual features in rules such as P.7.1.75. Thus, homogeneous-representation is a process of selecting features which are common to a group of sounds undergoing identical morphophonemic operations, and of keeping aside the phonemically distinctive features which are morphophonemically not pertinent.

6.9. After this question, we need to investigate a still deeper question. This is the basic notion of identity and difference between sounds. Can a sound /a/, say low-pitched, non-nasal and short, stand for another low-pitched, non-nasal and short /a/, without the help of P.1.1.69? For instance, is /a/ in /a/-/i/-/u/-/Ṇ/ able to cover /a/ in P.7.4.32 (asya cvau), without P.1.1.69? Are the two /a/-s identical or are they different? P.1.1.69 is prescribed with reference to /a/ in /a/-/i/-/u/-/Ṇ/, and if this /a/ is different from /a/ in P.7.4.32 (asya cvau), then P.1.1.69 may not apply to /a/ in P.7.4.32. Kātyāyana, on the first Śiva-sūtra, does foresee this objection: "In the secondary references, there would be no representation of homogeneous sounds, because they might not be regarded to be /a-Ṇ/ sounds." In the course of a long winding discussion, Kātyāyana proposed three solutions to this problem. They are as follows:

[A] The desired result is established, since there is only one single real /a/ sound.[173]
[B] The desired result is established, since there is universal-mention.[174]
[C] [The desired result is established] alternatively by relying on identical features [of different sounds].[175]

The explanation [B], the procedure of universal-mention, has already been discussed at length. It is historically un-Pāṇinian, since it constitutes a total rejection of P.1.1.10 and a partial rejection of P.1.1.69.[176] In what follows, we shall discuss the other two alternatives and search for a clue in Pāṇini's rules.

6.10. ONTOLOGICAL IDENTITY THEORY. The alternative [A] says that the sound /a/ in /a/-/i/-/u/-/Ṇ/ and in P.7.4.32 is a numerically identical single real sound, which is manifested time and again. The same real sound appears in the Śiva-sūtra, secondary references and verb-roots etc.[177] This view is based on the dichotomy between a real eternal sound, and its various non-eternal manifestations. In order that two manifestations should represent the same real sound, they must have identity with respect to all distinctive features. However, Kaiyaṭa says that the difference of pitch belongs to the manifesting sounds and not to the real sound.[178] It is doubtful if Kātyāyana meant this. The arguments offered by Kātyāyana to defend identity of a real sound through different manifestations are very similar to those found in Śabara.[179] It is possible that Kātyāyana developed this theory of identity of a real sound on the basis of Vyāḍi's doctrine of Vyakti-vāda, which he quotes extensively. The standard example is that of the sun. The same sun at the same time happens to be seen in different places. The other example is that of Indra. Indra, being invoked simultaneously by a hundred different sacrificers, appears in all those different places at the same time. These arguments are used to extablish the unitary character (ekatva) and eternality (nityatva) of the real sounds. The manifesting sounds, however, are infinite and are non-eternal. Thus, there are eighteen real /a/ sounds.[180] There is no necessary relation between eternality and unitary character of a sound. Bhartṛhari says that there were some philosophers who held that sounds were eternal and unitary, while others held that they were unitary but not eternal.[181]

Kaiyaṭa is aware that P.1.1.69 is formulated on the basis of vyakti-vāda "doctrine of individual."[182] Nāgeśa also acknowledges that this is the solution for applying P.1.1.69 to /a/ in P.7.4.32 (asya cvau).[183] This doctrine of eternal real sound-individuals, like the doctrine of eternal sound-universals, is dependent on a great deal of metaphysical argumentation. Kātyāyana probably took it from the early school of Vyāḍi's Mīmāṁsā, and it is later seen adopted with much more sophistication in Jaimini's Mīmāṁsā.

6.11. FEATURAL IDENTITY THEORY. Kātyāyana also presents the opposite doctrine, namely that /a/ in /a/-/i/-/u/-/Ṇ/ and in P.7.4.32 are actually two different sounds, and that each instance constitutes a different sound. The two /a/ sounds have to be different sounds, since they could be separated by time, by other sounds and be simultaneously in different places.[184] Patañjali gives the example daṇḍa agram to show two /a/ sounds separated by time, and the example daṇḍaḥ to show two /a/ sounds separated by other sounds. If/a/ were only one real sound, it could not be seen simultaneously in different words. Devadatta cannot be simultaneously in the cities of Srughna and Madhurā.[185] Though /a/ sounds in /a/-/i/-/u/-/Ṇ/ and P.7.4.32 are different sounds, they do not differ in any distinctive features, and hence are featurally identical with each other. Though there is no real identity, as in the previous view, still there is featural identity. On the basis of this featural identity, both are considered to be /a-Ṇ/ sounds. The examples given by Patañjali are very interesting. One of the examples is: "We eat the same rice [here], which we used to eat in the Magadhas."[186] Obviously it is not the same rice, but the varieties of rice do not differ in any essential features. Bhartṛhari further clarifies the philosophical basis of this alternative:

> How is this a solution? Some grammarians explain as follows: Even if there is no universal property (ākṛti), still there is no problem. Just as there is no universal property in different coins; but you have a coin in the city of Mathurā and it is still an item of money.[187]

In terms of grammar, this means that a low-pitched, short, non-nasal /a/ naturally covers /a/ with the same features. This view does not presume any universals. It also does not presume eternal sound-individuals. Thus, it is philosophically a non-commital view, and depends more on common sense. This featural identity is much more exacting than the conditions of homogeneity. Homogeneity requires identity of only two distinctive features, while the argument here requires total featural identity. The sounds with such total identity of distinctive features may, however, differ in features such as speed (vṛtti). Features like these are considered to be phonemically non-distinctive by Kātyāyana.[188]

6.12. There are certain hints in Pāṇini's grammar which indicate that Pāṇini favoured the non-ontological alternative of total featural identity (rūpa-sāmānya), instead of committing himself to either eternal sound-individuals or eternal sound-universals. The rule P.1.1.68 (svaṁ rūpaṁ śabdasyāśabda-saṁjña) says that a word in grammar stands for its own form or phonetic shape (rūpa), and not for its conventional meaning, unless it is a technical term in grammar (śabda-saṁjñā). Here, Pāṇini has utilized the notion of rūpa "phonetic shape or form" of a word. Pāṇini also uses the notions of sarūpa "with identical phonetic shape" and asarūpa "with different phonetic shape." [P.1.2.64 (sarūpāṇām ekaśeṣa eka-

vibhaktau) and P.3.1.94 (*vā'sarūpo'striyām*)]. The words *rāma*$_1$ "Rāma, the son of Daśaratha" and *rāma*$_2$ "Paraśurāma, the son of Jamadagni" differ in meaning and yet they are *sarūpa* "with identical shape." However, *rāma* and *ramā* are *asarūpa* "with different phonetic shape." Similarly the affixes /aṆ/ and /Ka/ are *sarūpa*, because markers do not cause difference in the phonetic shape of the affix. In all these cases, the features of quantity etc. are distinctive. Thus, /á/ and /á/ are *sarūpa* "with identical phonetic shape," but /á/ and /ā́/, or /á/ and /ā́/ are not with identical phonetic shape. Thus, we may say that if two sounds are *sarūpa* "with identical phonetic features," then we do not need homogeneous-representation for one to cover the other. This is the direct implication of P.1.1.68. However, if two sounds are *asarūpa* "without having all identical phonetic features," and if they have the same point of articulation and internal effort, then they are homogeneous with each other, and by the procedure of homogeneous-representation (P.1.1.69) one may cover the other. There seem to be thus two principles in Pāṇini's grammar, i.e. *sārūpya* "total featural identity" and *sāvarṇya* "homogeneity, or identity of two features."

This may indicate that Kātyāyana's third alternative in fact represents the view held by Pāṇini. This is also a justification for Kātyāyana's view that, in Pāṇini, the features of quantity etc. are basically distinctive, and hence Pāṇini needed the procedure of homogeneous-representation.[189] Kātyāyana says that difference in speed (*vṛtti*) does not affect duration of real sounds (*varṇa*), which are fixed in their duration (*avasthitāḥ*).[190] This indicates that the difference in quantity does differentiate sounds from one another, while speed does not. This is clearly understood by Kaiyaṭa who says that short, long and extra-long sounds are basically different sounds, and are manifested by different physical sounds. Hence, the difference in quantity is real difference.[191] Kumārila, in his *Śloka-vārttika*, quotes this view: "Some held that [short], long and extra-long are in fact different sounds (*varṇāntaratvam evāhuḥ kecid dīrgha-plutādiṣu*)."[192]

6.13. Bhartṛhari has developed further the philosophy of language, which is seen only in its infancy in the works of Kātyāyana and Patañjali. However, Bhartṛhari sometimes soars beyond the empirical grammatical conception of language. Bhartṛhari says that the real sound (sphoṭa) in /a/, /ā/ and /ā3/ is the same.[193] The duration-difference pertains to the primary manifesting sounds (prākṛta-dhvani), and not to the real sound (sphoṭa). However, the duration-difference of the primary manifesting sounds is imposed (upacaryate) on the real sound. The difference in speed is attributed to secondary manifesting sounds (vaikṛta-dhvani), which are prolongations of the primary manifesting sounds. The difference of speed is not imposed on the real sound. Bhartṛhari also notes that some thinkers identified the level of real sounds with what he considers to be primary manifesting sounds. In that case, the short, long and extra-long sounds are different real sounds. This seems to be the view of Kātyāyana and, perhaps, of Pāṇini also.

On the level of empirical linguistics, however, Bhartṛhari's views are not in any real contradiction with Kātyāyana. In fact, Bhartṛhari's real sound (sphoṭa) stands on a supra-mundane level and is not a part of analytical grammar. The level of analytical grammar is reflected in Bhartṛhari's primary manifesting sounds, whose distinctions of quantity are imposed on the timeless real sound. This imposition has a functional value in grammar. It shows that these features of quantity etc. are not distinctive on the supra-mundane level of real sounds, but are distinctive on the level of analytical grammar. On the other hand, the distinctions of speed, belonging to secondary manifesting sounds, are not imposed on the real sound. This shows that they are not distinctive for analytical grammar. Thus, there may be a difference between Bhartṛhari and Kātyāyana on the level of sphoṭa "real sounds," but they fully agree on the fact that features such as quantity are basically distinctive in Pāṇini's grammar.

6.14. This procedure of Pāṇinian homogeneous-representation radically differs from Kātyāyana's proposal for universal-mention. In universal-mention, a term, by nature, stands for the type or universal, while Pāṇini lists the sounds and then states the rule P.1.1.69, whereby the sounds listed are terms standing both for themselves and sounds homogeneous with them. Thus, we have a basic division of sounds, i.e. a) sounds which are directly listed in the Śiva-sūtras, and b) sounds which are represented by the listed sounds. Only the listed /a-Ṇ/ sounds and consonants marked with /U/ stand for their homogeneous sounds, while the represented sounds (i.e. non-/a-Ṇ/ sounds) are not capable of representing their homogeneous sounds. Thus, /a/ stands for all the eighteen homogeneous sounds, while /ā/ stands for itself. Here "itself" naturally covers those varieties or instances which are totally identical in distinctive features with /ā/. In a number of instances, Kātyāyana shows that the non-/a-Ṇ/ sounds in Pāṇini just stand for themselves. These are some of the cases:

[A] On P.1.1.1 (vṛddhir ād-aic), Kātyāyana says that the marker /T/ added to /ā/ is necessary for the coverage of homogeneous varieties of the same quantity, since pitch is distinctive, and without /T/, /ā/ would not cover varieties differing in pitch.[194]

[B] The Śiva-sūtra /a/-/i/-/u/-/Ṇ/ contains an open (vivṛta) /a/. In P.8.4.68 (a a), open /a/ is replaced with a closed /a/. The second /a/ being a closed /a/ is not an /a-Ṇ/ sound. Kātyāyana is afraid that this closed /a/ might not cover any homogeneous varieties. To resolve this problem, he proposes that /T/ should be added to this closed /a/, so that it can cover six short closed varieties.[195]

[C] Kātyāyana points out that /ā/ in P.7.2.84 (aṣṭana ā vibhaktau) which is a substitute for /n/ in aṣṭan is a non-/a-Ṇ/ sound and hence it cannot represent its nasal homogeneous varieties. Thus, there is no undesired possibility of /n/ being substituted by a nasal /ā̃/.[196]

All these cases show that for Kātyāyana the non-/a-Ṇ/ sounds in Pāṇini are incapable of representing their homogeneous sounds, and this is the result of the procedure of Vākyāparisamāpti.

6.15. In these cases, Kātyāyana is not proposing a new theory of his own, but is trying to answer objections against Pāṇini by explaining Pāṇini's own position. Even the addition of /T/ proposed in [C] above is in accordance with the procedure of Vākyāparisamāpti. Many of the Vārttikas of Kātyāyana are not codanās "objections" or "new injunctions," but are rather anvākhyānas, in Thieme's words, "explanation(s) of the purpose of Pāṇini's rule as given by a teacher to a student, who left to himself, might or might not have missed the point."[197] For a historical insight into the Vārttikas of Kātyāyana, Thieme proposed the following:

> The explanations said to be 'recited' by Kātyāyana are, of course, meant to be memorized by the students. They are part of the scholastic training. Yet, important as they are for the correct understanding of Pāṇini, they are routine answers of anonymous origin, they may even be imagined to go back to Pāṇini himself. Kātyāyana recites them because he did not invent but only repeats them as part of the exegetic tradition. They must, to say it again, be clearly distinguished from those vārttikas that contain a vacana, an original 'teaching,' where Kātyāyana places himself on the same level with Pāṇini and opposes or adds his own scientific formulation to that of the Aṣṭādhyāyī. A vacana, too, is meant, of course, to be 'recited' by teacher and pupil, but it has a much higher dignity: in this instance, the teacher does not merely 'recite,' he 'speaks' as an individual, a self-thinking, creative scholar.[198]

Kātyāyana's explanation of problems in Pāṇini's grammar on the basis of the procedure of vākyāparisamāpti seems to be a part of the routine exegetical tradition which precedes Kātyāyana, and may go back to Pāṇini himself. On the other hand, Kātyāyana's proposal of universal-mention or of splitting the internal effort of vowels from spirants belong to himself.

CHAPTER VII

PROBLEMS IN VĀKYĀPARISAMĀPTI

7.1. A TRADITIONAL APPROACH

7.1.1. In the view of vākyāparisamāpti, P.1.1.69 does not apply to the shortforms /a-C/ and /ha-L/ in P.1.1.10, and hence the sounds denoted by these shortforms cannot further represent their homogeneous sounds.[199] This makes /a-C/ and /ha-L/ mutually exclusive classes and thereby avoids problems like /ś/ being non-homogeneous with itself [ref: Sec. 4.2-3]. But the following also results:

[1] /ā/ and /ā3/ are still homogeneous with /h/.
[2] /ī/ and /ī3/ are still homogeneous with /ś/.
[3] /ṝ/ and /ṝ3/ are still homogeneous with /ṣ/.
[4] /ḷ3/ is still homogeneous with /s/.[200]

According to the Pāṇinian tradition, this is the ineveitable logical conclusion of the procedure of vākyāparisamāpti.

7.1.2. This has created many problems for the traditional grammarians. For instance, P.6.1.101 (akaḥ savarṇe dīrghaḥ) literally means: "Whan an /a-K/ sound [i.e. /a/, /i/, /u/, /ṛ/ and /ḷ/] is followed by a homogeneous sound, both are replaced by a homogeneous long sound." By P.1.1.69, /a-K/ stands for all the varieties of the denoted sounds. P.1.1.10 also applies to /a-K/ sounds, so that it does not represent any consonants.[201] Let us see what happens in the example kumārī śete. Here /ī/ is an /a-K/ sound. It is represented by /i/ included in /a-K/. Though by P.1.1.10, /i/ is not homogeneous with /ś/, /ī/ is still homogeneous with /ś/. Thus, in kumārī śete, an /a-K/ sound is followed by a homogeneous sound, and both /ī/ and /ś/ together would be replaced by /ī/. So finally we might derive the undesirable form kumāryete*. Similarly, from kanyā hasati, we might derive the undesirable form kanyāsati*. Surprisingly, this point has not been noted by Kātyāyana and Patañjali.

Bhartṛhari noticed this difficulty for the first time and answered it by relying on the continuation of the word aci in this rule.[202] With the addition of this word, P.6.1.101 means: "when a homogeneous /a-C/ sound follows." Though /ś/ is homogeneous with /ī/, it is not a homogeneous /a-C/ sound, since /i/ in /a-C/ is not homogeneous with /ś/ and will not represent /ś/. Looking at the text of the Aṣṭādhyāyī, we find aci in P.6.1.77 (iko yaṇ aci). The gap between P.6.1.77 and P.6.1.101 is too wide to justify continuation of aci, unless it is continued through all the intervening rules. The word aci does not continue through all of these intervening rules. This makes Bhartṛhari's suggestion historically very doubtful. However, if it is accepted, it solves the problem in P.6.1.101. This solution has been followed by all the later commentators.[203] Bhaṭṭoji Dīkṣita and Nāgeśa say that we need not continue aci in P.6.1.101, if we accept subclassification of vivṛta "open."[204] Otherwise, they approve Bhartṛhari's proposal.

7.1.3. Bhartṛhari's solution does not solve all the problems. If /ā/ and /ī/ are homogeneous with /h/ and /ś/, is it possible that /ā/ and /ī/ could stand for /h/ and /ś/? This does not happen because, /ā/ and /ī/ are non-/a-Ṇ/ sounds, and hence they cannot stand for any homogeneous sounds. Even /āT/ and /īT/ cannot stand for /h/ and /ś/, because the marker /T/ enables a sound to stand for homogeneous sounds of the same quantity. Similarly, /ś/ cannot stand for /ī/, because /ś/ is a non-/a-Ṇ/ sound, and it is not marked with /U/. The only loophole left is that /h/ is an /a-Ṇ/ sound, and it would be able to stand for /ā/ and /ā3/.

7.1.4. The realization of the problem that /h/ is an /a-Ṇ/ sound and that it might undesirably represent /ā/ and /ā3/ is seen in the commentaries on the Kāśika-vṛtti. P.8.3.59 (ādeśa-pratyayayoḥ, iṇ-koḥ from 57) says that /s/ is replaced by /ṣ/, if /s/ is either a substitute or a part of an affix, and if it is preceded by /i-Ṇ/ sounds or by /kU/ sounds (i.e.

/k/ series of stops). The shortform /i-Ṇ/ is formed with /Ṇ/ in /l(a)-Ṇ/, and hence it covers /h/ which might stand for /ā/ by P.1.1.69. The Kāśikā-vṛtti, on P.8.3.57 (iṇ-koḥ), gives dāsyati as a counter example. This creates a prima facie problem, which is answered by the Nyāsa of Jinendrabuddhi as follows:

> How is this counter-example justified, while /h/ included (in /i-Ṇ/) stands for /ā/ by P.1.1.69? The sound /ā/ is homogeneous with /h/, because they have the same point of articulation and internal effort. As the sounds /a/, /kU/ (/k/-series), /h/ and /ḥ/ are produced in throat (kaṇṭhya), these two have the same point of articulation. As the internal effort of spirants and vowels is 'open,' their internal effort is also the same. Thus, by the rule P.8.3.57 (iṇ-koḥ), the retroflex substitute [/ṣ/ for /s/] obtains [in dāsyati], because P.1.1.10 does not prohibit the designation 'homogeneous' [to /ā/ and /h/]. If this is the problem, there is no difficulty, because he (Pāṇini) uses [the word vayasyāsu] in P.4.4.127 (vayasyāsu mūrdhno matup), where he does not change /s/ after /ā/ to /ṣ/. From this it is inferred that /h/ does not represent /ā/. Otherwise, he would not have made use of the form vayasyāsu.[205]

Thus, in the view of the Nyāsa, /h/ and /ā/ are homogeneous, but as it can be inferred from Pāṇini's own usage, /h/ does not stand for /ā/. The other commentary, Padamañjarī of Haradatta, gives a different explanation:

> Just as homogeneity of /ī/ and /ś/ is not prohibited [by P.1.1.10], so also of /ā/ and /h/. So what? Would there be a possibility of the substitution of /ṣ/, because /h/ would stand for /ā/? There is no problem. The sound /h/ is vivṛta 'open,' but /ā/ is vivṛta-tara 'more open.'...This justifies [Pāṇini's] usages like vayasyāsu."[206]

While Patañjali would have /h/ to be slightly open and /ā/

to be open, Haradatta has /h/ open and /ā/ more open. The effect is the same. This works well, but is obviously un-Pāṇinian, since it would make P.1.1.10 without purpose.

7.1.5. Then comes Bhaṭṭoji Dīkṣita, whose subtle analysis brings out more problems due to homogeneity of /h/ and /ā/. He gives about ten examples where this might create problems.[207] He also goes a step further and points out that /h/ would also stand for /ā3/ and would create problems in some cases.[208] In his Śabda-kaustubha, Bhaṭṭoji discusses at length various solutions to this problem. Along with the solutions of universal-mention and subclassification of openness, he proposed the following new solution: In the view of vākyāparisamāpti, we have to imagine an insertion of /ā/ in P.1.1.10. By combining /ā/ and /ā3/, we get /ā/. Then we split nājjhalau as na āc-halau, where /āc/ is to be explained as /ā/+/ā3/+/aC/. Thus this rule specifically denies homogeneity of /ā/ and /ā3/ with consonants, and gets rid of all the problems.[209] Bhaṭṭoji mentions P.3.3.163 (kāla-samaya-velāsu tumun) where the term velāsu occurs. If /ā/ and /h/ were homogeneous for Pāṇini, he would have used the expression velāṣu*. Bhaṭṭoji takes this usage as a sanction for his insertion of /ā/ in P.1.1.10.[210]

7.1.6. Later grammarians like Hari Dīkṣita and Nāgeśa are faced with evaluating Bhaṭṭoji's suggestion. Both of them realize that they have two alternatives.[211] We may either have an independent rule saying that, in Pāṇini, /ā/ and /h/ are not mutually homogeneous, or we may accept Bhaṭṭoji's insertion of /ā/ in P.1.1.10. With their typical traditional outlook, they feel that adding a rule to Pāṇini's grammar involves the fault of prolixity, while Bhaṭṭoji's explanation has the merit of brevity.

Actually, P.1.1.10 could be interpreted as Bhaṭṭoji does by following the normal rules of sandhi. But this interpretation is still far from being historically valid. However, we have to accept Bhaṭṭoji's inference from velāsu in P.3.3.163 that Pāṇini did not want /h/ to represent /ā/. Bhaṭṭoji's suggestion solves the problems pointed out by him, but then the whole picture of homogeneity still remains very much distorted. Neither Bhartṛhari nor Jinendrabuddhi and Bhaṭṭoji can avoid homogeneity of /ī/ with /ś/ etc. All that they do is to try to avoid practical problems. With all respect to these great grammarians, one still feels doubtful, if this distorted picture of homogeneity was intended by Pāṇini. Or might there be another interpretation which is lost to us?

7.1.7. Looking at the problem from within the Pāṇinian tradition, this is what we can say. The procedure of vākyāparisamāpti was the procedure of Pāṇini. It was so realized by Kātyāyana and was utilized to answer many objections to Pāṇini's formulations. This procedure apparently did not pose any problems of its own either for Kātyāyana or for Patañjali, and they show no awareness of any loopholes in it.

This, however, does not mean that for Pāṇini, Kātyāyana and Patañjali, it was fine if, for instance, /h/ represented /ā/. Jinendrabuddhi and Bhaṭṭoji have given valid inferences from Pāṇini's own usages to the contrary. In Kātyāyana's theory of universal-mention, long vowels and ūṣmans have different universals. Patañjali, as we have seen, subclassifies open-ness and avoids homogeneity of vowels with consonants. Patañjali makes a clear statement: "The ūṣmans and /r/ have no homogeneous sounds [other than themselves]."[212] K. V. Abhyankar comments:

> This is an axiomatic assertion of the Bhāṣyakāra, based on a careful observation and scrutiny of words and letters used in the language. Grammar is to follow language, language is not to follow grammar.[213]

This comment implies that Patañjali's statement, though true, does not follow from Pāṇini's rules. Whether this is true can only be decided if we ever unearth a pre-Kātyāyana commentary on Pāṇini.

7.2. A NEW APPROACH

7.2.1. The discussion in the previous section puts us into a serious problem. The silence of the great Pāṇinians on problems of vākyāparisamāpti may be an indication that for them there were no problems with P. 1. 1. 10, and that there was probably some normal explanation of P. 1. 1. 10. Unfortunately, the works of Kātyāyana and Patañjali deal mainly with problems in Pāṇini's grammar, and they did not concern themselves with those rules which to them were perfectly normal and without problems. This task was left to the conventional Vṛttis. Some of these commentaries did exist even before Patañjali, but they are now lost to us. The first rule-to-rule commentary that is available to us is the Kāśikā-vṛtti, which in some respects preserves the older traditions,[214] but is itself a very late work, and is influenced by the grammar of Candragomin.[215] It is quite possible that many normal explanations were already lost by the time of the Kāśikā-vṛtti.

7. 2. 2. Let us look at the modern interpretations of P. 1. 1. 10. The earliest interpretation of P. 1. 1. 9 and P. 1. 1. 10 that we have goes back to Colebrook:

> P. 1. 1. 9: Letters articulated near the same organ of speech and with the same aperture for the voice, are homogeneous; P. 1. 1. 10: but a vowel and a consonant are not so.[216]

S. C. Vasu translates P. 1. 1. 10 as follows:

> There is however no homogeneity between vowels and consonants, though their place and effort be equal.[217]

Louis Renou's translation runs as:

> Les phonêmes 'a. . . c' (=les voyelles) et 'ha. . . l' (=les consonnes) (même étant dans les conditions requises sous 9) ne sont pas (homophones entre elles).[218]

Otto Böhtlingk renders P. 1. 1. 10 as:

> Ein Vocal (ac) und ein Consonant (hal) sind einander nicht homogen.[219]

No scholar says anything as to how the meaning that he gives is derived, though the intuitively given meaning is what the rule ought to teach. Instead of just depending on intuition, the Pāṇinian grammarians tried to give their own explanations. We may disagree with their explanations, but it at least shows that there lies a rule which still needs a rational explanation.

7.2.3. Another partial hypothesis about P.1.1.10 has occurred to me. We shall briefly discuss it here. The argument is as follows. If a=b and a≠c, then obviously b≠c. Similarly, if /a/ is homogeneous with /ā/, and is not homogeneous with /h/, then it should naturally follow that /ā/ is not homogeneous with /h/.

On the face of it, this seems quite sound. However, this is not exactly the case with Pāṇini's rules. By P.1.1.9, we get the following three statements:

[1] /a/ is homogeneous with /ā/.
[2] /a/ is homogeneous with /h/.
[3] /ā/ is homogeneous with /h/.

These statements are quite independent of each other and each case fulfils the conditions of homogeneity laid down in P.1.1.9. The statement [3] is not deduced from [1] and [2], but stands on its own grounds. Now by P.1.1.10, we get denial of the statement [2]. Since the other two statements are in no way dependent on [2], the denial of [2] cannot in any way lead to the denial of either [1] or [3]. The statements [1] and [3] still fulfill the conditions of P.1.1.9, and there is nothing in Pāṇini's rules to stop [3] from being true, except of course the inferences of Jinendrabuddhi and Bhaṭṭoji. Though such inferences have a definite practical value, the system as such still remains faulty on account of its loopholes.

7.2.4. In what follows, an explanation is offered, which by

no means is claimed to be the historical explanation, but, in a modest way, to be an explanation which is more probable than the others seen before.

Before going to P.1.1.10, let us go back to P.1.3.3 (hal-antyam). The circularity in this rule can be removed only by reading the rule twice and giving a different interpretation to each reading. This case has been discussed in detail in Sec. 5.3. It has also been critically studied by Thieme.[220] This solution goes back to Kātyāyana, and it is quite possible that it even precedes him.

The same procedure may be extended to P.1.1.10. This removes all the problems in the procedure of vākyāparisamāpti. For the sake of interpretation, the order of rules should be as follows:

[1] na ac-halau P.1.1.10A.
[2] P.1.1.69.
[3] P.1.1.10B.

If interpreted in this order, the second reading, i.e. P.1.1.10B, gives us the final meaning of the rule, just as the second reading of P.1.3.3 gives its final meaning.

P.1.1.10A means: "The /a-C/ sounds, as listed in the Śiva-sūtras, are not homogeneous with /ha-L/ sounds." With this we interpret P.1.1.69: "The /a-Ṇ/ sounds and sounds marked with /U/ stand for their homogeneous sounds, unless they are affixes." By this rule, /a/ can stand for all its homogeneous sounds, but not for /h/, since P.1.1.10A has already denied homogeneity of /a/ and /h/. We then use P.1.1.69 to interpret P.1.1.10B, which then means: "Sounds represented by /a-C/ and /ha-L/ sounds are not mutually homogeneous." Here, /a/ in /a-C/ stands for all varieties of /a/, including /ā/, but not for /h/. Thus, finally, P.1.1.10B means to say: "No vowels are homogeneous with any consonants." In this interpretation, the picture of homogeneity becomes straightened out.

7.2.6. Though we may not be able to say that this is the

historically true interpretation, this very procedure seems to have been implicitly followed by all the modern scholars, whose translations are given earlier. All of them clearly interpret P. 1. 1. 10 as denying homogeneity between the classes of all vowels and all consonants. These classes cannot be obtained without applying P. 1. 1. 69 to P. 1. 1. 10. However, if we apply P. 1. 1. 69 to P. 1. 1. 10 before denying homogeneity of /a-C/ sounds with /ha-L/ sounds, then the classes represented by /a-C/ and /ha-L/ overlap. None of the scholars intends such overlapping. This means they implicitly applied P. 1. 1. 69 to P. 1. 1. 10 after non-homogeneity of /a-C/ and /ha-L/ sounds was already established. Thus it seems that these scholars implicitly considered P. 1. 1. 10 on two different levels, and without ever clarifying their intuition, they arrived at the right conclusion. An interpretation similar to this might have existed in the early centuries of Pāṇinian interpretation. However, no historical claims can be made for lack of any real substantiating evidence.

CHAPTER VIII

RESTRICTIONS ON HOMOGENEOUS-REPRESENTATION

8.1. In this chapter, we shall discuss the question of the interpretation of the condition apratyayaḥ in P.1.1.69 and certain problems related with P.1.1.70. I have devoted a long article to these problems. However, as these considerations are very important in understanding the function and implementation of homogeneity in Pāṇini's rules, we shall discuss here the main arguments. For the details, the reader is referred to the original article. ["Pāṇinian Procedure of Taparakaraṇa: A Historical Investigation," Zeitschrift für vergleichende Sprach-forschung, Band 86, Heft 2, 1972, pp. 207-254.]

8.2. By P.1.1.69, the non-affixal sounds denoted by the shortforms /a-Ṇ/ and sounds marked with /U/ stand for themselves and their homogeneous sounds. The expression apratyayaḥ "non-affixal" occurs in two other rules of Pāṇini and five vārttikas of Kātyāyana in the sense of "non-affix" or "excluding affixes."[221] Kātyāyana has no doubt about its meaning, nor any objections to raise.

Patañjali, however, reinterprets P.1.1.69 and derives a general maxim: bhāvyamānena savarṇānāṁ grahaṇaṁ na "There is no representation of homogeneous sounds by a sound which is itself introduced by a rule." [MB, Vo. I, Sec. I, p. 370-1.] Henceforth we shall refer to this maxim as Maxim [1]. Patañjali tries to show that Pāṇini could not have meant "affix" by the term pratyaya in P.1.1.69. An affix is a meaning-bearing unit and it will not represent its homogeneous sounds, simply because they will not convey the same meaning. Then, a prima facie solution is given to this question. Some sounds are directly known (pratīyante), while other homogeneous sounds are made known or represented (pratyāyyante) by the sounds which are directly known. Thus, apratyayaḥ may mean that the represented sounds do not represent their homogeneous sounds. But Pāṇini need not say this, since a long /ā/ would not represent the short variety, because it requires an additional effort for its pronounciation. It also may not represent the extra-long varieties, because the long variety itself is a non/a-Ṇ/ sound. Thus the condition apratyayaḥ apparently seems to be redundant and hence Patañjali takes it to be an indication (jñāpaka) of the above mentioned Maxim [1].

The term bhāvyamāna in the Maxim [1] is rendered as "introduced elements." If a rule is: "If preceded by A and followed by D, B is replaced by C," then C is the introduced element, while A, B and D are not introduced elements. They are conditioning elements and substituendum. In Patañjali's argument, the term "introduced elements" refers to affixes, substitutes and augments. The later term for bhāvyamāna is vidhīyamāna.

8.3. Kaiyaṭa on this discussion almost misunderstands Patañjali. For Patañjali, the condition apratyayaḥ does not mean "non-introduced elements," but is simply an indication of the Maxim [1]. Kaiyaṭa says that pratyaya means vidhīyamāna, because the verbs pratīyate and vidhīyate have the same meaning [MB-P, Vol. I, Sec. I, p. 370; SK, p. 3]. Nāgeśa points out that this is quite untenable:

> In fact, the literal meaning of the Bhāṣya is that Pāṇini implies the Maxim [1], by allowing a portion [of the introduced elements, namely the affixes, to be without the capacity of homogeneous-representation]. What Kaiyaṭa says is doubtful, since pratīyate is not found used in the meaning of vidhīyate. [MB-P-U, Vol. I, Sec. I, p. 371.]

8.4. Patañjali's argument deviates considerably from Pāṇini's original scheme, and the Maxim [1] is Patañjali's addition. We shall see later that this suggestion might actually be pre-Patañjali, but post-Kātyāyana. Patañjali holds that in Pāṇini's rules, substitutes (ādeśa) and augments (āgama) along with affixes (pratyaya) lack the capacity to represent their homogeneous sounds. However, it is doubtful if this was Pāṇini's own intention, since he uses the marker /T/ with about fifty substitutes[222] in restrictive and prescriptive functions. As the word pratyaya simply stands for affixes, P.1.1.69 must be effective with all non-affixal /a-Ṇ/ sounds, including substitutes and augments. This is the understanding of the Kāśikā-vṛtti.[223] So is Louis Renou's rendition:

> Les phonèmes /'a-ṇ'/ (=voyelles et semi-voyelles) et ceus â exposant /u/--désignent les homophones (en même temps que leur forme propre), excepté si ce sont des affixes.[224]

8.5. These two views about apratyayaḥ in P.1.1.69 affect the interpretation of P.1.1.70 (taparas tat-kālasya). There are two major interpretations of P.1.1.70:

> Interpretation [A]: If the term /a-Ṇ/ in P.1.1.69 is carried over into P.1.1.70, then it comes to mean that /a-Ṇ/ sounds followed by /T/ represent the homogeneous varieties of the same quantity. Here, as in P.1.1.69, the term /a-Ṇ/ stands only for the sounds as they are listed in the Śiva-sūtras. Thus, /T/ has restrictive function (niyāmakatva) with respect to /a-Ṇ/ sounds, but has no function with respect to non-/a-Ṇ/ sounds. Since Pāṇini uses /T/ with a large number of non-/a-Ṇ/ sounds,[225] this interpretation appears insufficient.

> Interpretation [B]: The term /a-Ṇ/ in P.1.1.69 is not continued into P.1.1.70. Thus, P.1.1.70 means that any vowel followed by the marker /T/ represents homogeneous sounds of the same quantity. In the case of /a-Ṇ/ vowels, this rule becomes restrictive (niyāmaka), while in the case of non-/a-Ṇ/ sounds, the rule becomes presecriptive (vidhāyaka). Without /T/, a non-/a-Ṇ/ sound can stand only for itself, and cannot cover other varieties of the same quantity.

Of these two interpretations of P.1.1.70, [B] seems to be the historically Pāṇinian interpretation, since this alone explains the cases of non-/a-Ṇ/ sounds with the marker /T/ in Pāṇini's rules.

8.6. Taking into account the major divergent interpretations, it is possible to discern two prominent views concerning the function of the marker /T/.

> View [A]: apratyayaḥ = "non-introduced elements." The introduced elements, i.e. affixes, substitutes and augments do not represent their homogeneous sounds, and hence there is no need to attach a restrictive marker /T/ to these elements. In the case of non-introduced elements, namely conditioning elements, the /a-Ṇ/ and non-/a-Ṇ/ sounds with the marker /T/ stand for homogeneous sounds of the same quantity.
>
> View [B]: apratyayaḥ = "non-affixal." Excepting the affixes, all the /a-Ṇ/ sounds as given in the Śiva-sūtras are capable of representing their homogeneous sounds by P.1.1.69. The /a-Ṇ/ and non-/a-Ṇ/ sounds with /T/ stand for homogeneous sounds of the same quantity. Without /T/, /a-Ṇ/ sounds represent all their homogeneous sounds, while the non-/a-Ṇ/ sounds represent only themselves.

Of these two views, the View [A] is held by almost the whole tradition of Pāṇinians beginning with Patañjali, or rather with Vyāḍi, while the View [B] is what Pāṇini must have intended and is so understood by Kātyāyana. This has been conclusively demonstrated after studying every rule with /T/, in Deshpande [1972].

8.7. If we accept the View [A] or the Maxim [1], then no substitutes are capable of any representation, since every substitute is an introduced element, and hence there is no need to attach the marker /T/ to restrict homogeneous-representation. Patañjali [MB, Vol. I, Sec. I, p. 370] considers the Maxim [1] to be necessary to avoid representation of homogeneous sounds in P. 2. 3. 3 (idama iś).[226] However, there are several arguments which go against Patañjali's view. There are about fifty examples of substitutes with /T/ in Pāṇini's rules, against only about twenty cases of vocalic substitutes without /T/.[227] These statistics themselves stand as a proof for the unhistoricity of the Maxim [1]. Pāṇini could not have attached the marker /T/ to so many substitutes without any significance. The significance of /T/ with substitutes has to be explained according to P. 1. 1. 70, and not according to P. 6. 1. 185 (tit svaritam), since they are not affixes.[228] In a number of rules such as P. 7. 4. 66 (ur at),[229] it is clear that the substituenda are long vowels, while the substitutes are short vowels, and Pāṇini rightly thinks that, in the absence of /T/, the non-affixal substitutes will represent their homogeneous sounds. Then only the long vowels will be effected as the substitutes by P. 1. 1. 50 (sthāne'ntaratamaḥ) "In the place [of a substituendum] a most-similar substitute is effected." Thus, the marker /T/ has a positive restrictive function with these substitutes. Sometimes, even the Kāśikā-vṛtti accepts this restrictive function of the marker /T/ with substitutes.[230]

8. 8. On P. 7. 2. 84 (aṣṭana ā vibhaktau), Kātyāyana says: "In the case of [the substitution of] /ā/ for [the final /n/ of] aṣṭan, jan etc., pathin and mathin, there is a possibility of a nasal [/ā/ being substituted], because it is most similar [to the nasal substituendum /n/]."[231] This objection is answered as follows: "[The desired result that only a non-nasal /ā/ will be substituted for nasal /n/] is achieved, since [the substitute /ā/ is] a non-/a-Ṇ/ sound, [and hence it does not represent any homogeneous varieties]."[232] This shows that, for Kātyāyana, a substitute does represent its homogeneous sounds, if it is an /a-Ṇ/ sound. This shows that the Maxim [1] is of post-Kātyāyana origin.[233] Kātyāyana himself uses /T/ in his vārttikas with substitutes. For instance, /T/ is attached to the substitute /i/ in vt 6 on P. 7. 3. 1, (vahīnarasyed-vacanam), and to the substitute /ī/ in vt 1 on P. 8. 2. 17, (īd rathinaḥ).

8. 9. Patañjali accepts the Maxim [1] first, and then to

explain a single rule, he has to introduce another maxim, henceforth Maxim [2], which runs as: bhāvyamāno'py ukārah savarṇān gṛhṇāti: "An introduced /u/ sound also represents its homogeneous sounds."[234] This is an exception to Maxim [1]. Once the Maxim [1] is accepted, then /T/ attached to /u/ in rules such as P.6.1.131 (diva ut) and P.6.1.111 (ṛta ut) becomes technically redundant. This has been taken as an indication by Patañjali and later grammarians for Maxim [2]. Then it is used to explain that the substitute /u/ in P.7.2.80 (adaso'ser dād u do maḥ) is without /T/ and hence it desirably represents its homogeneous sounds.

All this deductive logic sounds very convincing, if one accepts validity of Maxim [1]. The unhistoricity of that maxim has already been pointed out. If an occurrence of /T/ with an introduced /u/ indicates that an introduced /u/ can represent its homogeneous sounds, then by the same line of argument, the occurrence of /T/ with introduced /a/, /i/, /ṛ/, /ā/, /ī/, /ū/, /e/, /o/ and /au/, in Pāṇini's rules,[235] should also indicate that these also represent their homogeneous sounds. It is a fact that Pāṇini uses /T/ with all these introduced sounds. This cuts at the very root of Maxim [1]. Similarly, if one accepts Maxim [2], it creates very intricate problems which are neither discussed nor solved by Patañjali.[236]

Once the View [B] is accepted as truly the Pāṇinian view, all the difficulties disappear. For Pāṇini, the /a-Ṇ/ substitutes are capable of representing their homogeneous sounds, as they are non-affixes. Similarly, the marker /T/ with substitutes has its normal restrictive and prescriptive functions. In the rule P.6.1.131 (diva ut), Pāṇini attaches /T/ to /u/, since only short /u/ is intended to be the substitute. In P.7.2.80 (adaso'ser dād u do maḥ), he does not attach the marker /T/ to /u/, since representation of long /ū/ is desired. There is nothing exceptional about this rule.

8.10. There is a clear possibility that these two maxims may in fact belong to pre-Patañjali times. Maxim [1] is identical with Maxim 30[237] and Maxim [2] is identical with Maxim 31[238] in a text called Paribhāṣā-sūcana, which is ascribed to Vyāḍi. According to the tradition, Vyāḍi is the first author on the paribhāṣās "maxims." The style of this work is very similar to the Mahābhāṣya, but it never refers to Patañjali. This would be strange if Vyāḍi were posterior to Patañjali. We can certainly agree with K. V. Abhyankar when he argues that Vyāḍi, the author of the Paribhāṣā-sūcana, is not posterior to Patañjali.[239] However, K. V. Abhyankar also regards this Vyāḍi to be prior to Kātyāyana. Kātyāyana certainly refers to a grammarian named Vyāḍi.[240] But the author of the two maxims could not be pre-Kātyāyana, since there is no trace of these maxims in the vārttikas of Kātyāyana, and Kātyāyana's explanations clearly go against them.[241] It is possible that there were several persons named Vyāḍi.

8.11. That Patañjali's innovations are historically un-Paṇinian does not deprive him of his significant contribution which lies in his attempts to bring uniformity and simplicity of description in Pāṇini's grammar. Representation of homogeneous sounds is not at all needed in any of the rules prescribing affixes, augments and substitutes, except in P. 7. 2. 80. On the other hand, Pāṇini has to use the marker /T/ to stop such representation in many cases. This prompts Patañjali to make Pāṇini's system more uniform. He almost suggests that /T/ is not necessary after any substitutes, and it could be eliminated, if we say that substitutes do not represent any homogeneous sounds. Such representation is needed only in one rule. If varieties differing in pitch, accent etc. are needed, they can be obtained by considering these features to be non-distinctive.

However, a critical distinction must be made between any attempts of simplifying Pāṇinian procedures and those of understanding them as they stand in their own right. Worth noting is S. D. Joshi's remark:

> This will prevent us from committing the same mistake which was made by Patañjali and the commentators following after him, when they read later developed theories into Pāṇini and Patañjali respectively.[242]

Patañjali's suggestion was certainly valuable as a reform in Paṇini's grammar. Some of the later systems like Jainendra-Vyākaraṇa follow Patañjali's suggestion and incorporate it into their rules. [ref: N. 358.]

CHAPTER IX

VYĀḌI ON HOMOGENEOUS-REPRESENTATION

9.1. The name Vyāḍi is more known, in the Pāṇinian tradition, for the now lost magnificent Saṁgraha, an encyclopedic work on grammar, than for the Paribhāṣā-sūcana, a compendium of grammatical maxims, which is more-over similar to the well known Paribhāṣenduśekhara of Nāgeśa. The great antiquity of this work, its probable pre-Patañjali date, increases its importance for the history of Pāṇinian interpretation. As we have already seen, this work is probably post-Kātyāyana in origin, or at least parts of it are of post-Kātyāyana origin. This historical place of Vyāḍi's Paribhāṣāsūcana enhances the value of its comments on homogeneity and its function in Pāṇini's grammar.

9.2. The Maxim 55 in this text runs as: udit sva-vargam eva gṛhṇāti, na savarṇa-mātram: "A sound marked with /U/ stands only for the members of its varga 'group of homorganic stops,' and not for all the homogeneous sounds."[243] Vyāḍi's commentary on this maxim gives the reasoning behind this statement:

> A sound marked with /U/ stands only for its varga, and not for all its homogeneous sounds. How is this known? [We know this], because he [Pāṇini] independently mentions /s/ in the rule P.1.3.4 (na vibhaktau tu-s-māḥ), while the mention of /tU/ would have been sufficient [to include /s/]. What is the purpose in indicating this [maxim]? In the rule P.8.2.30 (coḥ kuḥ), the mention of /cU/ does not cover /ś/, and hence [/ś/] does not happen [to undergo the substitution] by /kU/ sounds. Thus, the correct form viḍ is derived.[244]

This statement of Vyāḍi needs to be carefully analysed in order to get at its implications. It means to say that unless we restrict a sound marked with /U/ to stand only for its varga, it will stand for all its homogeneous sounds. As Vyāḍi's examples indicate, /tU/ might cover /s/, and /cU/ might cover /ś/. This implies that Vyāḍi does not want /tU/ and /cU/ to stand for /s/ and /ś/ respectively, but, according to him, by Pāṇini's definition of homogeneity, /t/ and /c/ are respectively homogeneous with /s/ and /ś/. No other grammarian in the tradition ever suspected that P.1.1.9 could lead to such homogeneity of /t/ and /s/, and /c/ and /ś/.

9.3. According to Vyāḍi, however, P.1.1.9 somehow leads to homogeneity of /t/ and /s/, /c/ and /ś/. The internal effort of /t/ and /c/ is, according to all the traditions, spṛṣṭa "with contact." Depending on the interpretation we accept, /s/ and /ś/ are either vivṛta "open" or īṣad-vivṛta "slightly with a gap, slightly open." Thus, /t/ and /c/ differ from /s/ and /ś/, in respect of internal effort. They, however, share the same point of articulation. Thus, /t/ and /s/ are dental, while /c/ and /ś/ are palatal.

This leaves us with only two alternatives: either,

[A] Vyāḍi considered that P.1.1.9 only requires two sounds to have the same point of articulation, or

[B] for him, stops and spirants had the same internal effort.

The term āsya-prayatna in later days did only stand for internal efforts, but there is no conceivable way to interpret it to mean only sthāna: "point of articulation." Thus, the alternative [A] cannot be right as a correct description of the Pāṇinian conception of homogeneity. The alternative [B] also has no support either in the Pāṇinian tradition or elsewhere.[245]

9.4. Patañjali does not mention this maxim of Vyāḍi. In the later tradition of Paribhāṣā-works, three authors have commented on this maxim. The reading in Sīradeva's Bṛhat-paribhāṣā-vṛtti is somewhat different from Vyāḍi's reading: udit savarṇaṁ gṛhṇāti, na savarṇa-mātram:

"A sound marked with /U/ stands only for its homogeneous sounds, but not for all homogeneous sounds."[246] On the face of it, this does not make any sense. However, Sīradeva's explanation is worth noting:

> By P. 1. 1. 69, a sound marked with /U/ stands only for those homogeneous sounds, which share [the same] point of articulation and internal effort, and not for all homogeneous sounds. Thus, in the rule P. 8. 2. 30 (coḥ kuḥ), the mention of /kU/ does not include /h/. The indication [for this maxim] is provided by the [separate] mention of /s/, in spite of that of /tU/, in P. 1. 3. 4 (na vibhaktau tu-s-māḥ). This fact, which actually follows naturally is explained through an indication (jñāpaka), for the sake of easy comprehension.[247]

Like Vyāḍi's work, Sīradeva is also ambiguous as to what conception of homogeneity is being rejected. The examples of Sīradeva are parallel to Vyāḍi's examples.

9. 5. Haribhāskara Agnihotrin has the same reading as Sīradeva, but his explanation goes a step ahead:

> A sound marked with /U/, by P. 1. 1. 69, stands only for those homogeneous sounds, which are identical with respect to the point of articulation and internal effort, and not for all those homogeneous sounds which only share the same point of articulation. [This is established either] by the indication of the separate mention of /s/, along with /tU/, in P. 1. 3. 4, or by the fact that P. 1. 1. 69 teaches the designation 'homogeneous' only of a sound which shares the [same] point of articulation and internal effort.[248]

Thus, the wrong notion of homogeneity, according to Haribhāskara Agnihotrin, is conditioned only by identity of the point of articulation, but he does not think that it is an interpretation of P. 1. 1. 69. Thus, this notion of homogeneity as being identical with the notion of sasthāna "homorganic, with the same point of articulation" is of some non-Pāṇinian origin. It is possible that some grammarians before Vyāḍi tried to bring this notion into Pāṇini's grammar, and that Vyāḍi's maxim was an attempt to prohibit application of such a notion of homogeneity. Within the Pāṇinian tradition, however, we do not need this maxim.

9.6. Nīlakaṇṭha Dīkṣita gives the final blow to this maxim. He gives the same interpretation, but includes it among those maxims, which are classed as spurious and baseless. This is what he says:

> Since this maxim is not seen in the Mahābhāṣya, and since the designation 'homogeneous' is made [by P.1.1.69] of only those sounds which are qualified [by both, the same point of articulation and internal effort], this [maxim] is spurious.[249]

With all respect for Vyāḍi's name, we must agree with Nīlakaṇṭha Dīkṣita's assessment.

PART TWO

NON-PĀṆINIAN TRADITIONS

CHAPTER X

PRĀTIŚĀKHYAS ON SAVARṆA

10.1. In the intitial stages of Indological research, Martin Haug arrived at the conclusion that the Śikṣās are decidedly older than the Prātiśākhyas, and that the doctrines contained in the former were incorporated and further developed in the latter.[250] A. C. Burnell agrees with Haug and further says: "The Śikṣās and Prātiśākhyas represent, so far, one side of the oldest form of the Aindra Grammar--the phonetic analysis of the language."[251] These scholars held that the views expressed in these texts preceded Pāṇini's grammar, which is supposed to have superceded the now lost Aindra School of Grammar.

Franz Kielhorn, with ample new evidence, proved conclusively that the Śikṣās that have come down to us are certainly posterior to the Prātiśākhyas.[252] He is not ready to consider these texts as either pre-Pāṇinian or productions of a school of grammarians.[253] Paul Thieme rightly accepts a high antiquity of the branch of the Śikṣā literature, but as far as the Śikṣā texts available to us are concerned, his views agree with those of Kielhorn. Thieme says: "They are all of them, young, elaborations of the definitions laid down in the Prātiśākhyas."[254] This prompts us to consider the conception of savarṇa in the Prātiśākhyas, before passing on to the Śikṣās and other non-Pāṇinian systems of grammar. Without delving into the debatable question of the relative chronology of the Prātiśākhyas, we shall briefly study their conception of savarṇa, and its implementation.[255] The question whether the Prātiśākhyas are pre-Pāṇinian or post-Pāṇinian is still highly debated, and yet there is no doubt that the Prātiśākhyas do represent a grammatical tradition, which is certainly pre-Pāṇinian.

10.2. THE ṚGVEDA-PRĀTIŚĀKHYA

10.2.1. The RPr considers the long and short corresponding vowels [e.g. /a/, /ā/; /i/, /ī/; /u/, /ū/; /ṛ/, /ṝ/] to be savarṇas, and no featural definition of this term is given. It says that when a short vowel is mentioned, it stands for the short and long savarṇa sounds.[256] This seems to exclude consonants, extra-long vowels, diphthongs and /ḷ/ from the scope of the term savarṇa.[257] Though this conception does not seem to cover the groups of homogranic stops, the RPr does have the notion of varga "group of five homorganic stops."[258]

10.2.2. After this, the RPr uses the term savarṇa only once, and that also in the context of consonants. The term savarṇa-pūrva "preceded by a savarṇa" is used in the context of stops.[259] The example given by Uvaṭa is yad devāḥ, where /d/ in devāḥ is preceded by /d/, which is a savarṇa "identical varṇa." If it were preceded even by /n/, still it would not fulfill the condition. This means that /d/ is savarṇa only with /d/, and not with any other sound.

10.2.3. Thus, for the RPr, /a/, /i/, /u/ and /ṛ/ are respectively savarṇa with /ā/, /ī/, /ū/ and /ṝ/, and /d/ is savarṇa with /d/. Looking at these examples, we might be able to dig out a general conception of savarṇa, which basically seems to mean "belonging to the same varṇa." The term varṇa functions on two levels. Its primary meaning is just a "sound." In its extended meaning, it stood for an abstraction, which may be characterized as "the real sound" or "class of sounds sharing some essential features." Thus, in the primary sense of the term, /a/ and /ā/ are different varṇas "sounds," but in the extended sense, they both belong to the same varṇa. The origin of this extended notion of varṇa can be traced in the idea that a long vowel is essentially the same as the short vowel, but which has been prolonged. Thus quantity, nasality and pitch were in some sense added features to a given common factor. It was this common factor which came to be designated by the term varṇa. Then the term savarṇa can be explained as directly based on this extended notion of varṇa. Thus, /a/ and /ā/ are savarṇas "belonging to the same varṇa." This extended notion of varṇa, however, did not change very much with consonants. Thus, the term savarṇa used with respect to consonants stood moreover for "identity of the sound." The sounds /k/ and/kh/ did not belong to the same varṇa, and hence could not be grouped under the conception of savarṇa. This was the reason for having the concept of varga "group of homorganic stops" side by side with the concept of savarṇa "belonging to the same varṇa."

Of course, the RPr adopted this background notion of savarṇa to its own needs, and restricted it to simple vowels. There also it excluded /ḷ/ and extra-long vowels. This is based on the praticular needs of this particular system. The RPr uṣed the term in the context of consonants in the sense of "identity of varṇa." Thus, from this particularized conception of savarṇa, we have to infer the background conception.

10.2.4. Though there is no comprehensive rule of homogeneous-representation like P.1.1.69, ṣtill we find the following system of representation in the RPr:

[1] A short simple vowel also stands for its long varieties.
[2] No other vowel can stand for other varieties.
[3] The terms /ka/-varga etc. stand for the respective groups of homorganic stops.
[4] Otherwise, a consonant stands for itself.

The RPr seems to be in a more primitive stage compared to other Prātiśākhyas, where these things are stated in the form of explicit rules.

10.2.5. The concept of savarṇa is not used very frequently by the RPr, and many rules are formulated with terms like sasthāna "having the same point of articulation," where other Prātiśākhyas use the term savarṇa. For instance, the rule of the substitution of a long vowel for two consecutive simple homogeneous vowels is formulated with the term sasthāna "homorganic."[260]

Since the term savarṇa is used in a very limited sense, and is not defined in featural terms, there are no problems such as P.1.1.10. There is no concept of mutual homogeneity of /ṛ/ and /ḷ/. There seems to be no problem of how to make /a/ and /ā/ savarṇas of one another. There are two reasons for this. The first reason is that savarṇa is not featurally defined, but depends on the impressionistic and conventional notion of varṇa. The other reason is that the RPr considers all vowels including /a/ to be aspṛṣṭa "without contact."[261]

10.3. THE TAITTIRĪYA-PRĀTIŚĀKHYA

10.3.1. The TPr contains more points of interest than the RPr. The rule TPr (1.3) says: "The corresponding two sounds, short and long, are homogeneous (savarṇa)."[262] As the commentary Tribhāṣya-ratna explains, the sequences such as /a/-/a/, /a/-/ā/, /ā/-/ā/, and /ā/-/a/ are sequences of homogeneous vowels.[263] This definition applies only to the simple vowels (samāna), and there are nine of these according to the TPr, i.e. /a/, /ā/, /ā3/; /i/, /ī/, /ī3/; /u/, /ū/ and /ū3/.[264] Thus, this conception of savarṇa is restricted to short and long /a/, /i/ and /u/. The TPr (1.4) says that a simple vowel preceding an extra-long vowel is not savarṇa with the latter.[265] This prevents the undesired lengthening.

The commentary points out that the only purpose of the term savarṇa is to formulate a rule for savarṇa-dīrgha "homogeneous lengthening." This is the rule TPr (x.2) (dīrghaṁ samānākṣare savarṇa-pare) "If a simple vowel is followed by a homogeneous sound, then both are replaced by the corresponding long vowel."[266] The exclusion of /ṛ/ from the scope of the term savarṇa is quite understandable, because "in fact, no case occurs in the Vedic text in which two of them are fused into one."[267]

10.3.2. The commentator says that "the term (savarṇa) is self-explanatory. Homogeneity means similarity. Thus there should be no suspicion of /a/ being regarded homogeneous with /i/ etc., since they have different points of articulation and internal effort."[268] The description of savarṇa sounds here seems to be quite influenced by the notions in the Pāṇinian system (P.1.1.9). However, such a general conception is not intended by the TPr.

10.3.3. Though there is no rule in the TPr based on homogeneity like P.1.1.69, still the TPr has its own devices:

Rule (i.16): A sound followed by the affix -kāra is the name of that sound.
Rule (i.20): A short vowel, with the word -varṇa after it, is the name of the three vowels [short, long and extra-long].
Rule (i.27): The first mute, followed by the word -varga is the name of the series.[269]

Thus, /a/-kāra stands only for a short /a/, /ā/-kāra stands for only long /ā/, but /a/-varṇa stands for /a/, /ā/ and /ā3/. But there is no such a thing as /ā/-varṇa. This corresponds to the non-/a-N/ vowels in Pāṇini, in some respects. Similarly, only /ka/-varga can stand for the whole series, but /k/ by itself cannot. This is also similar to Pāṇini's treatment of the sounds marked with /U/. While the TPr keeps the notions of savarṇa and grahaṇa quite apart, Pāṇini builds an inter-dependent procedure of savarṇa-grahaṇa.

In the TPr, there is neither /ṛ/-varṇa, nor /ḷ/-varṇa. Whitney rightly says:

> As our treatise acknowledges no protracted /ṛ/, and neither a long nor a protracted /ḷ/, it does not admit the compounds /ṛ/-varṇa and /ḷ/-varṇa: of the other three it frequently avails itself.[270]

In this respect, the procedure of the TPr differs from Pāṇini's, as the latter does bestow the capacity to stand for their savarṇas on /ṛ/ and /ḷ/, by P.1.1.69.

10.3.4. The problem of homogeneity in the TPr is made complex by the fact that it keeps on using the term savarṇa, even in the context of consonants. In the context of syllabification, the TPr (xxi.7) (nāntaḥsthā-param asavarṇam) says: "If a consonant is followed by a semi-vowel and is asvarṇa 'non-identical' with that semi-vowel, then it does not belong to the preceding vowel, [but belongs to the following vowel]."[272] On this rule, the commentary Tribhāṣya-ratna explains the word asavarṇa with vilakṣaṇa "different."[272] Whitney explains this usage as follows:

> 'Dissimilar' is simply explained by vilakṣaṇa, 'of diverse characteristics, different,' it excludes from the operation of the rule doubled semi-vowel itself, and would also exclude the nasal semi-vowel into which /n/ and /m/ are converted before /l/, and /m/ before /y/ and /v/ (v.26, 28), if these occurred where the rule could apply, which is not the case.[272]

If asavarṇa can thus mean "different," savarṇa should then mean "non-different, the same." The TPr does use the term savarṇa in this sense. For instance, the TPr (xiv.23) (savarṇa-savargīya-paraḥ) says: "A sound followed by the same sound (savarṇa), or by a sound of the same series of stops (savargīya) is not duplicated."[274] Here the term savarṇa stands for identity of form, and not just identity of the point of articulation and internal effort. This rule draws for us the important distinction between savarṇa "identity of a sound" and savargīya "belonging to the same series of homorganic stops." Thus, /p/ and /p/ or /y/ and /ỹ/ are savarṇas, but /k/ and /kh/ are only savargīyas "belonging to the same series."[275] In the Pāṇinian conception of savarṇa, which is far more expanded, this distinction is dissolved. There, the savargīyas are also savarṇas.

10.3.5. The distinction between savarṇa and savargīya affects the rule-formation of the TPr. Where Pāṇini can have just one rule, the TPr needs two rules:

[1] TPr (v.27) (makāraḥ sparśa-paras tasya sasthānam anunāsikam): "The sound /m/, when followed by a stop, becomes a nasal of the same point of articulation with it."

[2] TPr (v.28) (antaḥsthā-paraś ca savarṇam anunāsikam): "Followed by a semi-vowel, /m/ becomes an identical nasal [semi-vowel]."[276]

The reason why the TPr needs these two rules is quite clear. According to its conception, /y/ and /ỹ/ are savarṇas "the same sound," but /t/ and /n/ are not. They are only sasthānas "sharing the same point of articulation." With his expanded notion of savarṇa, Pāṇini needs only one rule, i.e. 8.4.58 (anusvārasya yayi para-savarṇaḥ).

10.3.6. An overview of the TPr shows that its conception of savarṇa is basically the same as that of the RPr, discussed in Sec. 10.2.3. It is based on the expanded notion of varṇa, which can be clearly seen in the convention of affixing -varṇa to short vowels to stand for long and extra-long varieties. In this extended notion of varṇa, the features of quantity, nasality and pitch seem to become non-distinctive for inclusion in a varṇa. Such a background conception of varṇa is used in the notion of savarṇa "identity of a varṇa." Such a general notion of savarṇa is then restricted to particular needs of our treatise. As far as vowels are concerned, the TPr restricts the notion of savarṇa only to short and long /a/, /i/, and /u/, while the RPr, as already shown, included long and short /ṛ/ also. This would indicate that the same background conception of savarṇa was adopted for their particular needs by different works.[277]

10.4. THE ATHARVAVEDA-PRĀTIŚĀKHYA

10.4.1. The text which we shall consider under the name APr is the Śaunakīyā Caturādhyāyikā edited by Whitney, which is the same as the Kautsa-Vyākaraṇa [see: Sec. 4.8]. In this text, the term savarṇa occurs only once. The APr (iii.42) (samānākṣarasya savarṇe dīrghaḥ) says: "A simple vowel followed by a savarṇa vowel becomes long [along with the following]."[278] This rule is not too different from the TPr (x.2) (dīrghaṁ samānākṣare savarṇa-pare), except in the conventions of rule-formation. The TPr expresses the substitute in accusative case, while the substituenda are expressed in the nominative case. This is the convention of the older tradition, which is later continued by the *Kātantra* grammar. This is quite different from Pāṇini's grammar, where the substitute is expressed in the nominative and the substituenda are expressed in the genitive case. [P. 1. 1. 49 (*ṣaṣṭhī sthāne-yogā*).] The *APr* has followed the same convention. But this single rule by itself would not help us understand the general notion of *savarṇa* in the *APr*.

10.4.2. On the *APr* (i. 27), the unnamed commentary supplied by Whitney quotes a verse from some ancient *Śikṣā*: *samānāsya-prayatnā ye te savarṇā iti smṛtāḥ.*[279] This line means to say that those sounds which are produced with a like effort [at a point in] the mouth are styled homogeneous. The expression of this definition is notably identical with P. 1. 1. 9 (*tylyāsya-prayatnaṁ savarṇam*). The definition of this *Śikṣā* could not really be interpreted by taking the term *āsya-prayatna* to stand just for internal effort, and hence, this definition becomes quite identical with Pāṇini's rule, and probably belongs to a very ancient date. At the same time, it must be pointed out that this is not the notion of *savarṇa* in the *APr*. Whitney comments:

> The term *savarṇa* 'similar,' applied to sounds differing in quantity only, and not in quality, is used but once in our treatise (iii. 42), and is not defined by it: The cited definition is almost the same with that of Pāṇini (i. 1. 9): that of the *Vāj Pr*. (i. 43) is more explicit: the other treatises, like our own, employ the word without taking the trouble to explain.[280]

10.4.3. We are left to ourselves to figure out the conception of *savarṇa* in the *APr*. Could it be more like the *RPr* and *TPr*, or more like P. 1. 1. 9? A close study of the *APr* shows that the former is the case. Though the *APr*, unlike *TPr*, does not define the conventions of the usage of *-kāra*, *-varṇa* and *-varga*, behaviorally we can see that the same distinctions hold true in the *APr*. The affix *-kāra* appended to a vowel makes it stand for itself. For instance, /a/-*kāra* in the *APr* (ii. 92) excludes /ā/.[281] The affixation of

-varṇa helps short simple vowels to stand for their varieties differing in quantity. Thus, we have /a/-varṇa, /i/-varṇa, /u/-varṇa, /ṛ/-varṇa etc.[282] But the long simple vowels and diphthongs always go with -kāra, e.g. /ā/-kāra (iii.38), /ī/-kāra (i.74), /ū/-kāra (i.74), /e/-kāra (i.34), /o/-kāra (i.34), /ai/-kāra (i.41) and /au/-kāra (i.41). With consonants, if there is affixation of -akāra, they stand for themselves; but the sound /k(a)/, /c(a)/ etc. affixed with -varga stand for the respective series of homorganic stops. We also see that, unlike Pāṇini, but like the RPr and the TPr, the APr widely uses the concept of sasthāna "having the same point of articulation," where Pāṇini uses savarṇa.[283] This would show that the notion of savarṇa in the APr must be similar to that in the RPr and TPr. For other reasons, we may agree with Thieme and Liebich that "the author of the AVPr. did draw upon Pāṇini's grammar,"[284] but we do not have to identify the two conceptions of savarṇa.

10.4.4. Since the notion of savarṇa in the APr is more like the two other Prātiśākhyas, based on identity of varṇa, conventional and impressionistic, it is not faced with many problems, which Pāṇini was faced with. Thus, there is no problem similar to P.1.1.10.[285] The APr considers the short /a/ to be closed (saṁvṛta), and other vowels to be open (vivṛta).[286] Still it does not create problems similar to P.8.4.68 (a a).[287] If the notion of the APr were like P.1.1.9, there would have been all these problems. The very fact that there are no problems like this in the APr is a negative proof that its notion of savarṇa is different from Pāṇini's. The VPr, which defined savarṇa like P.1.1.9, is faced with all these problems, and had to make specific efforts to get out of them.

10.5. THE VĀJASANEYI-PRĀTIŚĀKHYA

10.5.1. The VPr goes under two other names, i.e. Śukla-yajuḥ-prātiśākhya and Kātyāyana-prātiśākhya. There is a pointed controversy whether the same Kātyāyana wrote vārttikas on Pāṇini and this Prātiśākhya.[288] We shall not deal with this vexed question here, but will limit our inquiry to comparing and contrasting various definitions of savarṇa.

10.5.2. The VPr (i.43) defines savarṇa as follows: samāna-sthāna-karaṇāsya-prayatnaḥ savarṇaḥ: "A sound which has the same point of articulation, articulator and the internal effort [with another sound] is termed savarṇa 'homogeneous' [with respect to that other sound]."[289] This is clearly a featural definition. Of the three conditions, the first two, i.e. the points of articulation and articulators, are discussed in detail in the VPr.[290] However, the āsya-prayatnas or internal efforts are not discussed by the VPr. If we follow Uvaṭa's commentary, there are six āsya-prayatnas: saṃvṛta "closed" for /a/, vivṛta "open" for other vowels, aspṛṣṭatā "lack of contact" for vowels, spṛṣṭatā "contact" for stops, īṣat-spṛṣṭatā "slight contact" for semi-vowels and ardha-spṛṣṭatā "half-way contact" for spirants and anusvāra.[291]

Since vowels and spirants have different internal efforts, they are not savarṇas of each other, and thus there is no need for any rule like P.1.1.10. However, /a/ is closed, while other vowels are open, and hence /a/ would not be homogeneous with /ā/. The VPr is aware of this problem and explicitly says (i.72) that they should be treated as if they are homogeneous (savarṇa-vat).[292] "It contains in words what is implied in the procedure of Pāṇini; who has used the ingeneous device of pronouncing in his grammar a sound different from what it is like in the actual language."[293] Pāṇini pronounces /a/ as an open sound in his grammar, so that it should be homogeneous with the open /ā/ and /ā3/. In the final rule of his grammar, P.8.4.68 (a a), he reinstates the closed /a/. This is the final operation in any derivation, and hence we never get open /a/ in the object language.

10.5.3. There is apparently a problem still left in. The sounds /i/ and /e/ are produced in the same point of articulation (tālavya "palatal")[294] and their articulator is the middle of the tongue,[295] and both are open sounds. Similarly, /u/ and /o/ are both labial (oṣṭhya),[296] and their articulator is also the lips.[297] These two are also open sounds. Thus, /i/ would be homogeneous with /e/, and /u/ would be homogeneous with /o/. However, this does not seem to be intended by the VPr. This could be avoided, perhaps, by considering /i/ and /u/ as vivṛta "open" and /e/ and /o/

as vivṛta-tara "more open," as has been done by many Śikṣās and Prātiśākhyas.[298]

10.5.4. The definition of the VPr needs to be compared with P.1.1.9 and Kātyāyana's vārttika on it. P.1.1.9 conditions homogeneity by āsya-prayatna, which in Kātyāyana's days came to stand only for internal effort. However, if homogeneity is conditioned by internal effort alone, then the sounds /j/, /b/,/g/, /ḍ/ and /d/ could also be homogeneous. With such an objection, the Vārttikakāra Kātyāyana rephrases P.1.1.9 as follows: siddhaṁ tv āsye tulya-deśa-prayatnaṁ savarṇam "The correct result is established by stating that a sound is homogeneous [with another sound, if they share] the same point of articulation and internal effort in the mouth." [For details: Sec. 2.4.] This reformulation speaks of two conditions, while the definition of the VPr has added identity of the articulator as the third condition. Thieme considers P.1.1.9 to be "concise, but not precise," the VPr definition to be "not concise, but precise" and the vārttika reformulation to be "both precise and concise."[299]

10.5.5. In his "Pāṇini and the Veda," Thieme says that according to Patañjali "the place of articulation (deśa) is formed by the passive (sthāna) and active organ (karaṇa)."[300] If this is the meaning of the word deśa in the vārttika, then both the vārttika and the VPr (i.43) would be quite synonymous with each other.

This is doubtful. In fact, Patañjali does not explain the word deśa with any other word. Instead of accepting Kātyāyana's reformulation, which leads to breaking up Pāṇini's rule, Patañjali proposes to reinterpret Pāṇini's words as they stand. Thus, he interprets the word āsya as meaning not just mouth, but as something that lies in the mouth [āsye bhavam]. Then he asks the question: "What is it that lies in the mouth?" The reply is: sthānaṁ karaṇaṁ ca "The point of articulation and karaṇa."[301] This passage was taken by Thieme as an interpretation of the word deśa. The term karaṇa here is explained by Kaiyaṭa as standing either for internal effort or for the active organ.[302] It can be conclusively proved that here Patañjali only intends internal effort. This is what Patañjali says:

> If the designation _savarṇa_ were simply based on some similarity with some difference, then such a designation would be obtained for /ś/ and /ch/, /ṣ/ and /ṭh/, and /s/ and /th/. These [sounds in each pair] have identity in all other respects, except _karaṇa_.[303]

The sounds /ś/ and /ch/ have the same articulator, but they differ only in their internal effort. The same is true of the other pairs. Thus, the term _karaṇa_ in this context can only stand for internal effort. Thus, Thieme's explanations need to be revised.

10.5.6. Thus the term _deśa_ in Kātyāyana's _vārttika_ stands only for _sthāna_ "point of articulation." Thieme himself, from quite different considerations, comes to accept this view in his later writings:

> Formerly ["Paṇini and the _Veda_," p. 92, n. 3], I suggested that Kātyāyana's _deśa_ was meant as a comprehensive term for _sthāna_ and _karaṇa_. I do not uphold this conjecture: it is hard to believe that Kātyāyana could have expected to be understood when introducing such usage without further explanation. It is more probable that (in contradistinction to the view taken in the _Vāj_. _Prat_.) he thought of the mentioning of _karaṇa_ in the definition to be dispensable, since the definition is, indeed, unambiguous without it. In fact, the definition of the _vārttika_ conforms to the pattern of a true _lakṣaṇa_, which is not a characterizing description, but a restrictive characterization, as was lucidly set forth by A. Foucher, "Compendium des Topiques" (Paris 1949) pp. 8 ff.[304]

Whether we agree with Thieme's views on the relationship of the two texts, i.e. the _vārttika_s and the _VPr_, or we disagree with him, his characterization of the _vārttika_ definition is quite significant.

10.5.7. Now, we enter into a problem which needs to be critically analysed. Thieme says: "A full and complete analysis of what Pāṇini obviously meant by the expression āsya-prayatna is given in Vāj. Pr. I.43."[305] He also thinks that the term karaṇa "articulator" in the VPr definition is not essential, and therefore, Kātyāyana took it out in the vārttika on P.1.1.9.

Whether karaṇa "articulator" as the third condition is non-essential needs to be tested by referring to the usage of the VPr. According to the VPr, nāsikā "nose" is an articulator of the nasal sounds.[306] If the difference of articulator is to cause non-homogeneity, then /a/ and /ã/, /y/ and ỹ/, /k/ and /ṅ/ would be non-homogeneous. For Pāṇini, these sounds are obviously homogeneous, and he uses the term savarṇa in the context of these sounds. Thus, in the sequences /ṁ/-/y/, and /ṁ/-/k/, /ṁ/ changes into /ỹ/ and /ṅ/ respectively, such that /ỹ/ and /ṅ/ are para-savarṇas "homogeneous with the following sounds."[307] But the VPr uses the term para-sasthāna "having the same point of articulation with the following sound," in this very context.[308] It also says that /m/, followed by a stop, changes into the fifth of the series of the following.[309] Even here, the term savarṇa is not used. Is it, then, possible, that for the VPr, /y/ and /ỹ/ are only sasthāna, but not savarṇa? Similarly, is it possible that /k/ and /ṅ/ belong to the same series, but are not savarṇa?

10.5.8. Despite the arguments in the previous section, it is hard to believe that nasality causes hon-homogeneity in the VPr. If /a/ is not homogeneous with /ã/, then we may not be able to apply the VPr (iv. 50) (siṁ savarṇe dīrghaḥ)[310] to a sequence like /a/-/ã/ to derive /ā̃/. We cannot say that such a combination is not desired by the VPr, because the very next rule says: (VPr iv.51) (anunāsikavaty anunāsikam) "In case the following vowel is a nasal, [the resulting vowel] is nasal."[311] This clearly allows that kind of combination. Similarly, we cannot say that /y/ and /ỹ/ are not homogeneous. The rule VPr (iv.110) (savarṇe) says: "[Doubling does not take place] when a homogeneous consonant follows."[312] The example given by Uvaṭa includes the sequences /ȳy/ and /v̄v/, where there is no duplication.[313]

Thus, in summary, we must say that inclusion of karaṇa in the definition is not carried to its logical conclusions, and hence, in view of the requirements, it is unnecessary. Thieme is certainly right in regarding it to be dispensable. That karaṇa "articulator" is dispensable is clearly stated, later, by Hemacandra [ref: Sec. 12.7.2].

10.5.9. Uvaṭa, on the VPr (i.43), says that even the sounds /ṛ/ and /ḷ/ can be combined in a savarṇa-dīrgha, if an example is found in the Vedic usage.[314] This, actually, seems to be an extension of Kātyāyana's vārttikas into the VPr, but has no basis. The sounds /ṛ/ and /ḷ/ have different points of articulation, and articulator, and hence they cannot be homogeneous.[315] Nor is their homogeneity imposed by the VPr. In fact, Uvaṭa himself indicates that /ḷ/ never figures initially or finally in the object language.[316] Thus, there is no possibility of such savarṇa-dīrgha.

10.5.10. Though the conception of savarṇa in the VPr seems to be identical in scope with P.1.1.9, the VPr does not utilize this conception as extensively as it is used by Pāṇini. The VPr still follows the tradition of the Prātiśākhyas in formulating its rules. Thus, there is no rule of savarṇa-grahaṇa like P.1.1.69, and the VPr follows other Prātiśākhyas in their conventions of -kāra, -varṇa and -varga. The usage of -kāra, in the expressions like /a/-kāra, /ka/-kāra etc. is clearly defined.[317] The VPr defines that a short vowel stands for long and extra-long vowels, and a first consonant of a series stands for the series in the section where points of articulation are explained.[318] This is somewhat similar to P.1.1.69, but this is restricted to a very small number of rules. The VPr continues to utilize affixation of -varṇa and -varga. It still uses terms like sasthāna, where its own conception of savarṇa could have been used. Thus, the VPr resembles Pāṇini's grammar only in its definition of savarṇa, but not in its implementation.

10.5.11. Finally the question that we ought to ask is whether the VPr needs the kind of definition of savarṇa it has given to account for its own usage of this term. The rule VPr (iv. 110) (savarṇe) requires /y/, /v/ and /l/ to be homogeneous with their nasal counter-parts. The third and last rule using the term savarṇa is the VPr (iii. 8) (pratyaya-savarṇam mudi śākaṭāyanaḥ). This rule says that /ḥ/ followed by /s/, /ś/ or /ṣ/ changes to a sound homogeneous with the following. Here /s/, /ś/ and /ṣ/ are required to be homogeneous with themselves. These are the only three rules in the VPr which use the notion of savarṇa.

If we look at the examples closely, it will be instantly clear that they can be savarṇas simply because they show identity of the varṇa, and fit well in the notion of savarṇa of the other Prātiśākhyas. Thus, the definition of savarṇa in the VPr is unnecessarily over-extensive, and compared to its own requirements, it is quite superfluous. It may be the case, that the author of this Prātiśākhya came under a heavy influence of Pāṇini's grammar, and hence gave the expanded definition of savarṇa. However, while writing his rules, he faithfully followed the tradition of the other Prātiśākhyas.

10.6. THE SĀMAVEDA-PRĀTIŚĀKHYAS

10.6.1. There are four texts which go under the general category of the Sāmaveda-prātiśākhyas, i.e. the Ṛk-tantra attributed to the pre-Pāṇinian Śākaṭāyana, the Sāma-tantra ascribed to Audavraji, the Puṣpasūtra ascribed to Puṣparṣi, and the Akṣaratantra. Of these four texts, only the Ṛk-tantra has general discussion of phonetics, while the other texts are concerned more with the particular problems of Sāman-recitation. The Ṛk-tantra shows the tendency of shortening the grammatical terms, e.g. māsa for samāsa, rga for varga, gha for dīrgha etc. The term savarṇa is never used in any of these texts. The term sva is used in the Ṛk-tantra occasionally for identity of an element [e.g. kānt sve, Ṛk-tantra 155, kān-śabdaḥ sve pratyaye sakāram āpadyate/ kāṁs kān ha jayati, comm. p. 34] . The Ṛk-tantra [25, sparśaḥ sve] says that a stop followed by a sva belongs to the preceding vowel. Here sva seems to cover sounds of the same varga [see: Notes to Ṛk-tantra, by Surya Kanta,

p. 14, n. 25]. Within a particular section of the Ṛk-tantra, a stop stands for its varga [sparśe ṛgasya, Ṛk-tantra 13, sparśa-grahaṇe vargasya grahaṇaṁ vijñeyam, comm. p. 7]. Thus, /k/, /c/, /ṭ/, /t/ and /p/ stand for the respective vargas in the rules [4] jihvā-mūle ḥkṛ, [5] tāluni ścye, [6] mūrdhani ṣaṭau, [7] dante tslāḥ and [9] oṣṭhe voḥpū [see: Ṛk-tantra, pp. 5-6]. In one case, /ṛ/ seems to stand for /ṝ/ [jihvā-mūle ḥkṛ, Ṛk-tantra 4, jihvā-mūlīyasthā jihvā-mūla-sthānāḥ kakāra-ṛkāra-ṝkārāḥ, comm. p. 5]. In some rules, /e/ and /o/ seem to stand also for /ai/ and /au/ [tāluni ścye, Ṛk-tantra 5, tālu-sthānāḥ śakāra-cakāra-yakāra-ikāra-īkāra-ekārāḥ, comm; and oṣṭhe voḥpū, Ṛk-tantra 9, oṣṭhya-sthānā vakāra-okāra-aukāra-upadhmānīya-pakāra-ukāra-ūkārāḥ, comm, p. 6]. The commentary seems to be somewhat inconsistent in including /au/ in rule 9, but in not including /ai/ in rule 5. It is important to note that Śākaṭāyana, who is supposedly pre-Pāṇinian, accepts vowels and spirants to be both open [vivṛtaṁ svaroṣmaṇām, 1.3, p. 3]. The same tradition might have continued up to Pāṇini forcing him to construct P.1.1.10 (nājjhalau). But in contrast to Pāṇini, Śākaṭāyana accepts /a/ and /ā/ to be both open, or rather more open [vivṛtataram akāraikārau-kārāṇām, 1.3, p. 3]. [Note: In this statement, akāra seems to cover ākāra also.]

10.6.2. The Puṣpa-sūtra has nothing parallel to savarṇa. It uses the term sva [= svakīya] in connection with sāmans belonging to a group [see: Puṣpa-sūtra, Einleitung, p. 507]. Expressions with -kāra and -varṇa are quite frequent, and the notion of savargīya "belonging to the same varga" is occasionally used [Puṣpa-sūtra, pp. 636, 639, 667]. The Sāma-tantra ascribed to Audavraji is very important from the point of view of ancient grammatical terminology, but it has no notion of savarṇa. It uses the term ga for varga [see: na ga-prathama-cu, 3.5.6., na varga-prathamādir mandram āpadyate, comm., Sāma-tantra, p. 89]. In one place, /ṭ/ seems to stand for ṭa-varga [see: au ṭi, 5.5.9., p. 156]. Unfortunately I have not been able to obtain the Akṣara-tantra, but from its description, it seems to be very much similar to the Sāma-tantra. Thus, as far as the notion of savarṇa is concerned, the Prātiśākhyas of the Sāmaveda have many unfinished ideas, but no conclusive development. In some ways, they may reflect a more ancient state of grammatical development, compared to the Prātiśākhyas belonging to the other Vedas. However, the exact dates of these texts are not as yet definitely known. The Mātrālakṣaṇa, an ancillary text of the Sāmaveda, uses the term savarṇa once (1.9) in the context of homorganic varieties of /a/, /i/, /u/ and /ṛ/. [Mātrālakṣaṇa, ed. B. R. Sharma, Kendriya Sanskrit Vidyapeetha, Tirupate, 1970.] However, nothing is known about the author or the date of this text.

CHAPTER XI

ŚIKṢĀS ON SAVARṆA

11.1. As it has been already discussed in Sec. 10.1., the class of the Śikṣā-texts is extremely old to have been mentioned in the Upaniṣads, and it is older than the Prātiśākhyas and Pāṇini. However, it must be remembered that the Śiksā texts which are available to us today are certainly not these old Śikṣās, but are all younger than the Prātiśākhyas and Pāṇini [see: Sec. 10.1].

11.2. The main purpose of the Śikṣās is phonetics, pure and applied, and not grammar. Thus, the Śikṣās extensively deal with the articulatory process in all its aspects and classify sounds accordingly. These phonetic considerations have been utilized by the grammarians to define certain grammatical categories. The notion of savarṇa is based on these phonetic considerations, but serves a purpose which is more grammatical. The difference in phonetic considerations can lead to problems in the definition and implementation of savarṇa. When one reads through the available Śikṣā texts, one comes across different notions of savarṇa, which may be put together and studied carefully. What follows is an attampt in this direction. At this stage, we shall not see how phonetics here affects the notion of savarṇa elsewhere, but rather what the Śikṣās themselves have to say on this notion.

11.3. The metrical version of the Pāṇinīya-śikṣā does not use the term savarṇa, but the Pāṇinīya-śikṣā-sūtras contain two statements involving this term. They are as follows: [1] "The spirants and /r/ have no savarṇas," and [2] "A member of a varga (group of homorganic stops) is savarṇa with other members of the same varga."[319] The first statement is identical with a statement found in the Mahābhāṣya, and its significance has been discussed in

Sec. 7.1.9. The Pāṇinīya-śikṣā-sūtras seem to have taken this statement from Patañjali.[320] They appear to be post-Patañjali, because we find that the rule (3.6) says: "the spirants have their articulator with a slight gap," while the rule (3.7) says: "or they might be regarded open."[321] This seems to be an attempt to accomodate views of both Pāṇini and Patañjali. Similar rules are also to be found in the Śikṣā-sūtras ascribed to Āpiśali.[322] [For a different view, see n. 124.]

11.4. The Varṇa-ratna-pradīpikā-śikṣā of Amareśa apparently presents quite a strange notion of savarṇa. It says:

> Whatever is the point of articulation (sthāna) and articulator (karaṇa) of a sound, [if it is the same with another sound, then] it should be accepted as savarṇa [with respect to the other sound]. [Their] internal effort (āsya-prayatna) may, however, be different.[323]

Thus, identity of the point of articulation and the articulator defines homogeneity, and the internal effort is not to be taken into account. This Śikṣā clarifies the reason for adopting such a view:

> Let there be homogeneity of long /ā/ and short /a/, despite the difference of internal effort. Therefore, [homogeneity] is thus defined.[324]

The short /a/ sound is closed, while the long /ā/ is open, and hence there might not be homogeneity of these two sounds, if internal effort is one of the conditions.

For this very problem, Pāṇini pronounces open /a/ in his grammar, and reinstates the closed sound /a/ at the end of his grammar (P.8.4.68). The VPr makes a special rule to consider /a/ and /ā/ as if they are homogeneous. [Sec. 10.5.2.] These measures seem to be very careful, but modifying the general definition as is done by the Varṇa-ratna-pradīpikā-śikṣā creates a lot of problems. For instance, this conception could make /i/, /c/-series,

/y/ and /ś/ homogeneous with each other. However, it is not clear how this conception was meant to be utilized, because the term is used only once again, where /ś/, /ṣ/ and /s/ are required to be homogeneous with themselves.[325] This Śikṣā also defines a convention that a sound affixed with -varṇa stands for its homogeneous sounds.[326]

11.5. The Prātiśākhya-pradīpa-śikṣā comments on the rules of the VPr containing the term savarṇa, without really explaining the term.[327] On one occasion, the term savarṇa is rendered by sadṛśa "similar."[328] This Śikṣā advocates homogeneity of /ṛ/ and /ḷ/, quoting the vārttika of Kātyāyana (ṛ-ḷ-kārayoḥ savarṇa-vidhiḥ) (on P.1.1.9). This homogeneity is used to interpret a rule from the Pratijñā-sūtra. The Pratijñā-sūtra prescribes that /ṛ/ should be pronounced as /re/. Thus, kṛṣṇa and ṛtviya are to be pronounced as kreṣṇa and retviya. The Śikṣā extends this rule to /ḷ/ and says that kḷpta should be pronounced as klepta.[329]

The Keśavī-śikṣā of Keśava Daivajña says that a rule that applies to /r/ also applies to /l/, because they are savarṇa "homogeneous."[330] This is a somewhat different context. This rule requires that the svara-bhakti of /r/ in some places is pronounced as /re/. Thus the word barhiṣe is pronounced as barehiṣe. The Keśavī-śikṣā extends this to /l/, and says that valhāmasi should be pronounced as valehāmasi.

11.6. F. Kielhorn quotes the definition of savarṇa given by the Vyāsa-śikṣā: tulya-rūpaṁ savarṇaṁ syāt "Sounds with identical form are savarṇas."[331] Unfortunately, I have not been able to reach the original text of this Śikṣā, which has been published in the Journal of the University of Madras (1929).[332] Heinrich Lüders' study "Die Vyāsa-śikṣā, besonders in Ihrem Verhaltnis zum Taittirīya-Prātiśākhya," [Göttingen, 1894] is very detailed, and provides some help on the conception of savarṇa in the Vyāsa-śikṣā. In his "Inhaltsübersicht der Śikṣā," Lüders provides the following description:

Verse (5): "Definition von varga," and "Bildung des

Namens eines varga."
Verse (10): "Definition von savarṇa."
Verse (13): "Bildung der Namen von Vokalen mit varṇa, mit kāra und t."
Verse (14): "Bildung der Namen von Konsonanten mit -akara."[333]

This system looks very much like the Prātiśākhyas, and hence the definition of savarṇa (tulya-rūpaṁ savarṇam) seems to stand basically for identity of a varṇa.

That the Vyāsa-śikṣā is very much in the tradition of the Prātiśākhyas can be determined by studying several of its rules which involve the notion of savarṇa. The verse (166) is described as: "Behandlung des /i/-Vokals und des /u/-Vokals vor nicht homogenen (asavarṇa) Vokalen."[334] This seems to be the change of /i/ to /y/ and /u/ to /v/ before a-savarṇa "non-homogeneous" vowels. The verse (172) is described as: "Verschmelzung der ersten acht Vokale mit einem folgenden gleich-artigen."[335] This is parallel to VPr (iv.50, siṁ savarṇe dīrghaḥ), APr. (iii.42, samānākṣarasya savarṇe dīrghaḥ) and TPr (x.2, dīrghaṁ samānakṣare savarṇa-pare); and it is different from P.6.1.101 (akaḥ savarṇe dīrghaḥ) in its structure. The verse (269) is described as: "Zugehörigkeit des Konsonanten vor ungleich-artigem Halb-volkal."[336] This rule discusses the syllabic relationship of a consonant with the following asavarṇa semi-vowel, and it is comparable to the TPr (xxi.7, nāntaḥsthā-param asavarṇam) [Sec. 10.3.4]. Lüders has systematically brought home the point that this Śikṣā is almost a versified version of the TPr. Thus, the notion of savarṇa in the Vyāsa-śikṣā is generally not different from the Prātiśākhya-type of definition.[337]

11.7. An unnamed commentary on the APr quoted by Whitney cites a verse from a Śikṣā text: samānāsya-prayatnā ye te savarṇā iti smṛtāḥ, and comments "the cited definition is almost the same as that of Pāṇini" [ref: Sec. 10.4.2]. Literally this line says that two sounds having the same āsya-prayatna are savarṇas. The use of the term āsya-prayatna, in this verse, is of historical significance.

No text, other than P.1.1.9, uses the term āsya-prayatna to stand for both the points of articulation and internal effort. But this Śikṣā uses the term to stand for both of these conditions, like Pāṇini. If it were to stand only for the internal effort, that would be quite a novel conception of homogeneity. Thus, this Śikṣā seems to be very ancient and perhaps older than all those texts which use the term āsya-prayatna to stand just for internal effort. It may even be pre-Pāṇinian. Thus, Pāṇini was not alone in his usage of the term āsya-prayatna to stand for both the point of articulation and internal effort.

The Nāradīya-śikṣā belonging to the Sāma-veda uses the term savarṇa twice. It says that /m/ followed by /y/, /v/ or /l/ changes to a para-savarṇa "sound homogeneous with the following."[338] This does not help us get a clear notion of savarṇa, since this rule could be formulated in the Pāṇinian conception of savarṇa as well as in the Prātiśākhya conception. The term savarṇa is also used with respect to yama (e.g. nasal /k̃/, /g̃/ etc. found in Vedic). This yama is said to be savarṇa "homogeneous" with the preceding sound.[339] The commentary of Bhaṭṭa Śobhākara on this verse explains savarṇa by sadṛśa "similar."[340] In the Pāṇinian grammar, yamas do not play any important role. They are not listed in the Śiva-sūtras, nor are they considered to be homogeneous with any consonants. Bhartṛhari says that the yamas are neither represented through homogeneous representation, nor through universal-mention.[341] The Nāradīya-Śikṣā seems to use the term in a very general sense of identity of the varṇa and similarity.

11.8. The concept of savarṇa in some of the Śikṣās seems to come very close to the Pāṇinian conception. The Śaiśirīya-śikṣā says that a word-final /m/, followed by a stop, changes into a nasal sound homogeneous (savarṇa) with the following stop [antya-sthāne makāro'yam pūrvaḥ sparśe padāntagaḥ/ udaye tat-savarṇaḥ syāt sarvasminn anunāsikaḥ//, verse 281, Journal of Vedic Studies, Vol. II., No. 2., 1935, p. 15]. This verse makes /n/ and /t/ homogeneous with each other, which is very similar with Pāṇini's procedure. A similar usage of the term savarṇa is seen in the Vyāsa-śikṣā [see: n. 337] and Sarva-sammata-śikṣā [see: sparśānāṁ yavalānāṁ ca makāraḥ pūrva-sthitaḥ/ teṣām avāpnuyāt śliṣṭe savarṇam anunāsikam//, verse 16; the commentary of Alamūcu Mañcibhaṭṭa on this verse says: samāno varṇaḥ savarṇaḥ, tulya-sthāna-karaṇaḥ; Bhandarkar Oriental Research Institute, Poona, MS. No. 383 of 1883-84, folio 7]. The Kauṇḍinya-śikṣā uses a triple distinction of terms: savarṇa in the context of savarṇa-dīrgha, sarūpa "with identical form" for "identity of sound" and savargīya "belonging to the same stop-series." [See: na sarūpa-savargīya-paro varṇo dvir ucyate, verse 68; savarṇa-dīrgha in verses 87 and 89. Prof. K. V. Abhyankar, Poona, has a copy of this Śikṣā made from the single MS which exists in a private collection in Hyderabad. This is planned to be published in the Annals of the Bhandarkar Oriental Research Institute.] The Śikṣādhyāya of the Bharatabhāṣyam by Nānyabhūpāla says that some scholars considered /l/, /h/ and /r/ to be savarṇas of each other because they have the same point of articulation and internal effort. It also refers to Nārada's opinion that /u/ is savarṇa with /v/ and /ś/ is savarṇa with /s/ [Bharatabhāṣya, Śikṣādhyāya, verses 48-9, p. 21]. The context indicates that the term has been used for nothing more than "similar sounds."

CHAPTER XII

NON-PĀṆINIAN GRAMMARS ON SAVARṆA

12.1. A comprehensive study of the conception of savarṇa cannot be complete without considering its definitions and implementation in the non-Pāṇinian systems of Sanskrit grammar. There is an extensive published literature of these systems, and they have drawn some attention of scholars. Among the studies on these systems, noteworthy are Liebich's translation of the Kātantra ["Das Kātantra," Zur Einführung in die indische einheimische Sprachwissenschaft I, Heidelberg, 1919] and his Konkordanz Pāṇini-Candra [Breslau, 1928]. Also noteworthy is A. C. Burnell's Essay on the Aindra School of Sanskrit Grammarians [Mangalore, 1875].

Many scholars have devoted articles to non-Pāṇinian systems of Sanskrit grammar, but Franz Kielhorn is perhaps unique in this field in having worked with so many different systems, even before they were published. His articles include: 1) "Indragomin and other Grammarians" [Indian Antiquary, vol. 15, 1886, pp. 181-3]; 2) "On the Jainendra-Vyākaraṇa" [Indian Antiquary, vol. 10, 1881, pp. 75-9]; 3) "The Chāndra-Vyākaraṇa and the Kāśikā-Vṛitti" [Indian Antiquary, vol. 15, 1886, pp. 183-5]; 4) "On the Grammar of Śākaṭāyana" [Indian Antiquary, vol. 16, 1887, pp. 24-8]; 5) "Scheinbare Citate von Autoritäten in grammatischen Werken" [Festgruss Böhtlingk, 1888, pp. 52-3]; 6) "A Brief Account of Hemachandra's Sanskrit Grammar" [Wiener Zeitschrift, vol. 2, 1888, pp. 18-24]; 7) "Malayagiri's Saṁskṛit Grammatik" [Göttinger Nachr., 1892, pp. 318-327]; and 8) "Die Śākatāyana-Grammatik" [Göttinger Nachr., 1894, pp. 1-14].

Also noteworthy are the following articles: 1) "Das Cāndra-Vyākaraṇa," Bruno Liebich [Nachrichten von der Königl. Gesellschaft der Wissenschaften zu Göttingen, Phil. Hist. Klasse, 1895]; 2) "The Text of the Jainendra-Vyākaraṇa and the Priority of Candra to Pūjyapāda," K. B. Pathak [Annals of the Bhandarkar Oriental Research Institute, vol. 13, 1931-2]; 3) "Ist Candragomin der Verfasser der Cāndra-vṛtti?" R. Birwé [Mélanges d'Indianisme à la mémoir de Louis Renou, Paris, 1968]; 4) "Über die Grammatik Kātantra," Otto Böhtlingk [ZDMG, Vol. 41, 1887]; 5) "Kātantra und Kumāralāta," Heinrich Lüders [BSB, Phil. Hist. Kl., 1930, also included in Philologica Indica, Göttingen, 1940]; 6) "Moggallānas Saddalakkhaṇa und das Cāndra-Vyākaraṇa," Otto Franke [Journal of the Pali Text Society, Vol. 53, 1903]; 7) "Das Verhältnis von Candra's Dhātupāṭha zu den Pāli Dhātupāṭhas, Otto Franke, [Ibid.]; 8) "A Glimpse into the Kāśakṛtsna School of Sanskrit Grammar," G. B. Palsule [Proceedings and Transactions of the All India Oriental Conference, 17th Session, 1953]; 9) "The Technical Terms of the Harināmāmṛta-Vyākaraṇa of Jīva Gosvāmin," G. B. Palsule [CASS Studies, No. 2., University of Poona, Poona, 1974]; 10) "Kāśakṛtsna," K. C. Chatterjee [Indian Historical Quarterly, Vol. VIII, 1932]; 11) "A Note on Āpiśali," V. Pisani [Journal of the Oriental Institute, Baroda, Vol. 5, 1956]; 12) "Aspects of pre-Pāṇinian Sanskrit Grammar," Batakrishna Ghosh [B. C. Law Comm. Volume]; 13) "The Relation of Pāṇini's Technical Devices to his Predecessors," Mangala Deva Shastri [Proceedings of the 4th All India Oriental Conference, 1926]; 14) "Les 'innovations' de la grammaire de Candragomin," Louis Renou [Études de Grammaire Sanskrite, Paris, 1936]; 15) The Sanskrit Dhātupāṭhas, a Critical Study, G. B. Palsule [Poona, 1961], (a comparative study of the Dhātupāṭhas of the various systems of Sanskrit Grammar); 16) Geschichte und Kritik der einheimischen Pāli-Grammatik und -Lexicographie, Otto Franke [Strassburg, 1902], (contains material on various systems of Sanskrit Grammar in comparison with Pāli grammatical systems); 17) Robert Birwé's extensive introduction to the edition of the Śākaṭāyana-vyākaraṇa [Bhāratīya Jñānapīṭha Prakāshan, Banaras, 1971], (which discusses a great many historical problems); and 18) Ācārya Hemacandra aur unakā Śabdānuśāsana: Eka Adhyayana, Nemichandra Shastri [Banaras, 1963].

Apart from such specialized studies, general accounts of these systems are found in Colebrooke's "On the Sanskrit and Prakrit Languages" [Asiatic Researches, Vol. VII, 1803, pp. 199-231]; Belvalkar's Systems of Sanskrit Grammar [Poona, 1915]; K. V. Abhyankar's Introductory Volume [Vol. VII] (Prastāvanā-Khaṇḍa) to his father's complete Marāthī translation of the Mahābhāṣya [Poona, 1954]; Yudhisthir Mimamsaka's Vyākaraṇa-śāstrakā Itihāsa [Ajmer, 1961-2] in three volumes; and Gurupada Haldar's Vyākaraṇa Darśanera Itihāsa [Calcutta, 1350 Bengali Era, 1943 A.D.]. Several texts in several editions on these non-Pāṇinian systems have been published in India and abroad, and there is enough material available for a comparative study. In our study of the conception of savarṇa in these systems, we shall follow approximately the order of systems given in the "Chronological Conspectus of the Different Schools" in S. K. Belvalkar's Systems of Sanskrit Grammar. Though this "Conspectus" could certainly be improved, we shall not deal here with matters of pure chronology.

12.2. ĀPIŚALI ON SAVARṆA Pāṇini refers to Āpiśali in P.6.1.94 (vā supy āpiśaleḥ). Though Āpiśali's grammar has not come down to us, there are Śikṣā-sūtras ascribed to him. These do not provide a definition of savarṇa, but use the term twice. This Śikṣā says that the spirants and /r/ have no homogeneous sounds, and that a member of a varga is homogeneous with other members of the same varga.[342] From these two statements we are left to infer Āpiśali's conception of savarṇa. Since /k/, /kh/, /g/, /gh/ and /ṅ/ are considered to be savarṇas, the point of articulation must be one of the conditions. However, it could not be the only condition, because, in that case, /k/ would be homogeneous with /h/. This has been denied by this text. Thus, /k/ and /h/ are not savarṇas. This might indicate that internal effort was also included in the definition of savarṇa. According to this Śikṣā, the spirants are īṣad-vivṛta "slightly open," while stops are spṛṣṭa "with contact."[343]

Since spirants are slightly open, and vowels are open, there is no need of any rule such as P.1.1.10 (nājjhalau). It also speaks of saṁvṛta "closed" short /a/.[344] This would create the problem of non-homogeneity of /a/ with /ā/, That would indicate that Āpiśali must have had some way to get around this difficulty. This close similarity with Pāṇini's grammar makes us wonder why Pāṇini did not follow Āpiśali in considering spirants to be slightly open? That would have spared him the trouble of formulating P.1.1.10. Most of the later grammars have accepted this subclassification. It is somehow hard to think that this subclassification existed before Pāṇini and yet Pāṇini took the trouble of formulating P.1.1.10. It may be that the Śikṣā ascribed to Āpiśali is actually a late work in that tradition, which accepted the classification made by Patañjali. [For a different view, see: n. 124.] There is yet no decisive evidence to prove that this text is older than Pāṇini.

12.3. THE KĀTANTRA AND KĀŚAKṚTSNA-VYĀKARAṆA

12.3.1. Burnell believed that terms like savarṇa were taken by Pāṇini from the Aindra School of grammar.[345] Burnell also believed that the Kātantra system reflects this ancient school.[346] The Kātantra takes for granted its list of sounds (varṇa-samāmnāya), where the first fourteen sounds [i.e. /a/, /ā/, /i/, /ī/, /u/, /ū/, /ṛ/, /ṝ/, /ḷ/, /ḹ/, /e/, /o/, /ai/, /au/] are vowels; and of these the first ten are termed samāna "simple vowels."[347] Then the term savarṇa is introduced: Kāt (1.1.4) "Of these [simple vowels], two by two are savarṇa with each other."[348] Liebich explains this term as "von gleicher Kaste."[349] In fact, more than "Kaste," the term savarṇa is related to the linguistic meaning of varṇa. Then the term is used in the following rules. Kātantra (1.2.1) says: "A simple vowel followed by a homogeneous vowel is lengthened and the following vowel is deleted."[350] Though the procedure here is different from the single-substitute (ekādeśa) procedure followed by the Prātiśākhyas, still it is terminologically closer to them than to Pāṇini. The rules (1.2.8-11) say that before an asavarṇa vowel, the /i/-vowels, /u/-vowels, /ṛ/-vowels and /ḷ/-vowels are respectively changed to

/y/, /v/, /r/ and /l/, and the following sound is not deleted.[351] The rule (3.4.56) says that /i/-vowels and /u/-vowels of the first element of the root-reduplication are replaced by /iy/ and /uv/, before an asavarṇa vowel.[352] These are the only occurrences of the term savarṇa in the Kātantra-vyākaraṇa. Thus, we might say that the notion of savarṇa here is quite in the tradition of the Prātiśākhyas, except that it is extended here to /ḷ/ and /ḹ/.[353] But the Prātiśākhyas use this concept of savarṇa also with consonants, in the sense of "identity of varṇa." The Kātantra does not use this term with respect to consonants. The conventions of using the affixation of -kāra, -varṇa and -varga are the same as in the Prātiśākhyas.

12.3.2. The original Kātantra system makes independent rules for /ṛ/ and /ḷ/ and thus there seems to be no notion of their homogeneity.[354] However, as Eggeling points out: "Between 4 and 5, the Laghuvṛtti adds two sūtras, or rather vārttikas (a) ṛkāra-ḷkārau ca and (b) vargyaḥ sva-vargyeṇa."[355] This seems to be a later introduction in the Kātantra under influence of Kātyāyana's vārttikas. These two statements mean that /ṛ/ and /ḷ/ are homogeneous with each other, and that members of a varga are homogeneous with each other. The second statement seems to bring the Kātantra notion of savarṇa closer to Pāṇini's notion. This is also a late attempt. The commentary of Trilocanadāsa on this system points out that homogeneity of /ṛ/ and /ḷ/ is established on the basis of worldly usage of these sounds.[356] This conception of Trilocanadāsa is refuted by the Laghubhāṣya by saying that people do not identify /ṛ/ and /ḷ/.[357]

12.3.3. The Kātantra-paribhāṣā-sūtra-vṛtti of Bhāvamiśra contains the following maxim: varṇa-grahaṇe savarṇasyāpi grahaṇam.[358] This is an explanation of the affixation of -varṇa to short simple vowels, so that they also stand for the long varieties. This is the principle of grahaṇa "representation" followed by the Kātantra system.

12.3.4. We may here refer briefly to the grammar of Kāśakṛtsna. In 1952, A. N. Narasimhia published the

Kāśakṛtsna-Śabdakalāpa-Dhātupāṭha of Cannavīrakavi [Sources of Indo-Aryan Lexicography: 5, Deccan College, Poona, 1952]. It contains a Dhātupāṭha ascribed to Kāśakṛtsna, with a brief Sanskrit and Kannada commentary. This commentary quotes a few rules of Kāśakṛtsna's grammar. [For a survey of views on Kāśakṛtsna's date, see my review of S. D. Joshi and J. A. F. Roodbergen, Vyākaraṇa-Mahābhāṣya, Karmadhārayāhnika, Publications of the Centre of Advanced Study in Sanskrit, University of Poona, Class C, No. 6, 1971 (review forthcoming in Orientalistische Literaturzeitung, Leipzig).] G. B. Palsule (1953) has presented an interesting study of Kāśakṛtsna's grammar based on the above mentioned Dhātupāṭha and the rules found in the commentary thereon. Kāśakṛtsna is most probably post-Pāṇinian and pre-Kātyāyana [Palsule (1953), p. 350]. We have to mention Kāśakṛtsna in the context of the Kātantra system, because "excepting one or two solitary cases Kāśakṛtsna agrees entirely with the Kātantra in the matter of the technical terms" [Ibid., p. 352]. Kāśakṛtsna uses the terms like samāna, nāmin, varga, sandhyakṣara, -kāra, which show that he belongs to the general class of the Aindra type, which is seen in the Prātiśākhyas and the Kātantra. Yudhisthir Mimamsaka (1961-2, Vol. I, p. 113) claims that the Kātantra is in fact a summary of Kāśakṛtsna's grammar. This question still needs to be investigated further.

12.4. THE JAINENDRA-VYĀKARAṆA

12.4.1. The Jainendra-vyākaraṇa of Devanandin defines the term sva [= savarṇa] as: (1.1.2) "[A sound is termed] sva 'homogeneous' [with respect to another sound, if they share] the same point of articulation and internal effort."[359] This is quite parallel to P.1.1.9. The Mahāvṛtti of Abhayanandin on this rule gives extensive details of phonetics and also of the scope of the term sva. According to the Mahāvṛtti, spirants are slightly open, and vowels are open.[360] This follows Patañjali's subclassification. Thus there is no need of a rule like P.1.1.10. Similarly, there is no question of how /a/ and /ā/ can become homogeneous. Abhayanandin says that the view [of the Pāṇinians] that /a/ is closed in the object language, but is open in grammar is false. There should be no difference of pronounciation in the object language and grammar.[361] He explains that /r/ and spirants have no homogeneous sounds, but members of a varga are homogeneous among themselves.[362] All this is quite parallel to the Pāṇinian conception.

12.4.2. This system has a procedure which is identical with Pāṇini's savarṇa-grahaṇa (P.1.1.69). The rule (Jain.1.1.72) says: "An /a-Ṇ/ sound and a sound marked with /U/ stands for itself and for its homogeneous sounds, except if it is an introduced sound (bhāvya) or is marked with /T/."[363] This rule combines several things in the Pāṇinian system. It combines P.1.1.69 with P.1.1.70 and the maxim: bhāvyamānena savarṇānāṁ grahaṇaṁ na [Sec. 8.2]. This shows that while constructing his grammar, Devanandin attempted to follow the late phase of Pāṇinian interpretation. Patañjali's suggestions are followed verbatum. The correspondence of this system with Pāṇini is so strong, that for almost every Pāṇinian rule with savarṇa, we find a rule with sva.[364] Due to the acceptance of Pāṇini's Śiva-sūtras with some minor modifications, with almost the same system of markers and metatheoretic conventions, rules of the Jainendra grammar look like a revised edition of Pāṇini's system.[365] To add to this, this system accepts homogeneity of /ṛ/ and /ḷ/, following Kātyāyana.[366]

12.5. THE CĀNDRA-VYĀKARAṆA

12.5.1. The system of Cāndra-vyākaraṇa of Candragomin follows Kātyāyana's suggestion of universal-mention, instead of following Pāṇini's homogeneous-representation. While commenting on his modified version of the Śiva-sūtras, Candragomin says that these sounds are intended to stand for their universals.[367] Thus, there is no definition of savarṇa nor is there any procedure like P.1.1.69.

12.5.2. Kātyāyana himself thought that even in universal-mention, a rule of representation would have to be retained for the classes of stops. Thus, he suggested that only /a-Ṇ/ sounds should be omitted from P.1.1.69, retaining the rule udit savarṇasya. [Sec. 3.16.] But this would make it necessary to have a definition of homogeneity like P.1.1.9. Candragomin found a better way out. He ruled that the initial sound of a varga, marked with /U/, stands for the respective varga (1.1.2).[368] Thus he resorted to the older notion of varga, which Pāṇini had replaced with his expanded definition of savarṇa. He reformulated Pāṇini's rules in such a way that he could avoid using the term savarṇa.[369] Instead, he made use of the older terms like sasthāna, which are self-expressive (anvartha) and do not need any definition.[370] Candragomin has shown independence in not following Patañjali, but in following Kātyāyana's suggestions. As we shall see later, there were other systems which followed Kātyāyana's suggestions, but Candragomin was the pioneer in this direction.

One thing, however, is not very clear. Why did Candragomin accept the theory of universals, which is not accepted by any Buddhist school of philosophy? The Jain grammarians, right at the outset, say that their grammars are based on the Jain doctrine of anekānta "many-faced nature of reality." Thus, they accept individualism (vyakti-vāda) and universalism (ākṛti-vāda) as the need be. But Candragomin apparently has accepted a non-Buddhist philosophical theory. It is possible that he accepted only the conceptual-reality of these universals.

12.6. THE ŚĀKAṬĀYANA-VYĀKARAṆA

12.6.1. Under this name, we shall consider the work of the Jain Śākaṭāyana, who is clearly post-Pāṇinian. The grammar of the pre-Pāṇinian Śākaṭāyana is now lost to us, unless he is the author of the Ṛk-tantra. The system of Śākaṭāyana also tries to fuse together the Pāṇinian notion of homogeneity with Kātyāyana's notion of universal-mention.

On his modified version of the Pāṇinian Śiva-sūtras, Śākatāyana says in his Amoghavṛtti that the vowels listed here also stand for long, extra-long and nasal varieties, since they share the same universal (sāmānya = ākṛti).[371] This is quite parallel to Kātyāyana's proposal of universal-mention. A short vowel stands for long and extra-long varieties sharing the same universal, unless it is either an introduced sound (bhāvya)[372] or marked with /T/.[373] This rule is somewhat similar to Jainendra (1.1.72), in accepting the maxim of introduced sounds, and incorporating it into the rules of grammar. But the Jainendra does not accept universal-mention.

12.6.2. At the same time, Śākaṭāyana gives a comprehensive definition of sva (= savarṇa), which is quite parallel to P.1.1.9. Homogeneity is conditioned by identity of the point of articulation and internal effort.[374] The discussion of this definition in the Amoghavṛtti involves certain problems. It considers /a/ to be closed and /ā/ and /ā3/ to be open.[375] It is clear as to how Śākaṭāyana tried to get around this problem. Since there is universal-mention, he does not need them to be homogeneous. The Amoghavṛtti says that the sound /i/ etc. have eighteen varieties, while about the /a/-vowels, it says that /a/-kāra is six-fold, while the long and extra-long varieties are twelve in all.[376] The reason behind this separation is not clearly stated. The only conceivable way seems to be that even if /a/ and /ā/ are not homogeneous, still they share the same universal. This would overcome many problems. The spirants are classified as slightly open, and vowels are classified as open, and hence there is no need of a rule like P.1.1.10.[377] This system follows Patañjali in his subclassification, and the conclusion is also stated that /r/ and spirants have no homogeneous sounds.[378]

12.6.3. Though Śākaṭāyana accepts universal-mention for vowels, he does not accept it for stops. The universal of /k/ does not cover /kh/, /g/, /gh/ and /ṅ/. This is quite parallel to Kātyāyana's understanding [Sec. 3.16]. Thus, he makes the rule (1.1.2) that a sound marked with /U/ stands for its svas "homogeneous sounds."[379] While Candragomin's rule (Cāndra. 1.1.2, utā sva-vargasya) is based on the notion of varga, Śākaṭāyana's rule, like P.1.1.69, is based on the notion of homogeneity. However, the Amoghavṛtti seems to redefine the rule in terms of the notion of varga.[380]

Śākaṭāyana consistently carried out Kātyāyana's suggestion for homogeneity of /ṛ/ and /ḷ/. He accepts their homogeneity repeatedly in his grammar, and reformulates the Śiva-sūtra ṛ-ḷ-K by ṛ-K.[381] He clearly says that the rules which apply to /ṛ/ also apply to /ḷ/, and offers the fictional examples of /ḷ/, which are so commonplace in the later Pāṇinian tradition.[382]

12.6.4. Though Candragomin and Śākaṭāyana both tried out Kātyāyana's suggestion for universal-mention, in a way, Śākaṭāyana is closer to the spirit of Kātyāyana. Candragomin made a vigorous effort to get rid of the notion of savarṇa, but Śākaṭāyana replaces only certain parts of savarṇa-grahaṇa. This is very similar to Kātyāyana, who suggests removal of only /a-Ṇ/ sounds from P.1.1.69, and retaining udit savarṇasya. Thus, Śākaṭāyana retained the term sva in many rules, while Candragomin tried to get rid of it.[383] The commentary Cintāmaṇi of Yakṣavarman and the Prakriyā-saṁgraha of Abhayacandrasūri follow the interpretations given by the Amoghavṛtti and have very little new to add.

12.7. THE HEMACANDRA-ŚABDĀNUŚĀSANA

12.7.1. Hemacandra's Śabdānuśāsana with his auto-commentary Bṛhad-vṛtti represent a peculiar fusion of the Pāṇinian notion of homogeneity and the rest of the technical terminology which mostly comes from the Kātantra system. Nemichandra Shastri has pointed out this mixed nature of Hemacandra's technical terminology,[384] though his extensive comparisons have not touched the details of Hemacandra's conception of sva and its application in his system.

12.7.2. Hemacandra defines sva "homogeneous" as: (1.1.17) "[A sound is termed] sva [with reference to another sound, if it has] the same point of articulation and internal effort."[385] This definition is clearly identical with P.1.1.9. Hemacandra's Bṛhad-vṛtti presents a very extensive and systematic account of phonetics. Hidden in the comments of the Bṛhad-vṛtti, there lies, perhaps, a historical suggestion that Hemacandra based his definition not on P.1.1.9, but rather on the VPr (i.43, samāna-sthāna-karaṇāsya-prayatnaḥ savarṇaḥ). Hemacandra uses the term sthāna for the points of articulation, and āsya-prayatna for internal effort. Of the three conditions of the VPr, Hemacandra omitted the second condition, i.e. karaṇa "articulator." The Bṛhad-vṛtti says: "Karaṇa 'articulator' which is the root, middle, forward and the tip of the tongue does not differ when the point of articulation and internal effort are identical."[386] This comment of Hemacandra actually supports Thieme's conclusion that karaṇa in the definition of the VPr is logically superfluous [Sec. 10.5.6].

12.7.3. Hemacandra quotes extensively from the Āpiśali-śikṣā-sūtras. He accepts Patañjali's subclassification of "open."[387] Thus there is no need of a rule like P.1.1.10. Similarly, Hemacandra subscribes to the view that short /a/ is open, and says that according to others, short /a/ is closed.[388] Thus, for him there is no problem of /a/ being non-homogeneous with /ā/.

12.7.4. However, there is no rule exactly parallel to Pāṇini's homogeneous-representation (P.1.1.69) in Hemacandra. On the contrary, he follows the Prātiśākhyas and the Kātantra in their conventions of affixing -kāra, -varṇa and -varga. He has defined the usage of -kāra and -varga,[389] and the affixation of -varṇa, though undefined, is quite uniform. Thus, the rules in this system look more like rules in the Kātantra, than like Pāṇini's rules.[390]

12.7.5. Hemacandra's grammar must be clearly distinguished from the VPr. The VPr defines savarṇa with scope equal to P.1.1.9, but the rules where the term savarṇa is used do not need such a broad conception. Such is not the case with Hemacandra. Hemacandra needs this broader conception of savarṇa for some of his rules. Hemacandra's rule (1.2.21) says that /i/-vowels etc. are respectively replaced by /y/, /v/, /r/ and /l/, if followed by a non-homogeneous vowel.[391] This rule does not need the broader conception. But the rules given below require this conception.

Hem. (1.3.14) says that an augment /m/ and a word-final /m/, if followed by a consonant, are replaced by a sound homogeneous with the following (para-sva).[392] By this rule /m/-/y/ is changed to /ỹ/-/y/, and /m/-/k/ is changed to /ṅ/-/k/. The second case requires the broader notion of homogeneity. This is quite similar to Pāṇini's procedure.[393] The other rule which needs the broader conception is Hem. (1.3.48): "If a non-nasal stop, /ś/, /ṣ/ or /s/ is preceded by a consonant and followed by a homogeneous sound from this very group, it may be optionally deleted."[394] Thus, in the sequence -/ṇ/-/ḍ/-/ḍh/-, /ḍ/ might be optionally deleted. This requires homogeneity of /ḍ/ and /ḍh/, which can only be obtained by the broader conception. This is also parallel to Pāṇini.[395]

12.7.6. The notion of /ṛ/ and /ḷ/ being homogeneous does not seem to have been accepted by Hemacandra. He always treats them separately and sometimes even writes separate rules.[396] However, this notion seems to have entered his system through later commentators. Hemahaṁsagaṇi, in his Nyāya-saṁgraha, mentions the following maxim: "An operation prescribed with reference to /ṛ/ also applies to /ḷ/."[397] This seems to be based on the supposed homogeneity of /ṛ/ and /ḷ/.

12.7.7. A comparison of Pāṇini's grammar with Hemacandra shows that though the broader conception adopted by Hemacandra is not unnecessary, still his terminological dependence on the Kātantra did not allow him to fully utilize the power of this conception. Thus, compared to Pāṇini, Hemacandra's utilization of sva is more restricted.

12.8. THE ŚABDĀNUŚĀSANA OF MALAYAGIRI

12.8.1. Malayagiri's Śabdānuśāsana is not available to us in its entirety, but a substantial portion of it has been recovered and published recently by Bechardas J. Doshi. Fortunately, this portion is sufficient to give us a complete idea of his conception of homogeneity. Following his Jain predecessors, Malayagiri prefers the term sva for savarṇa. Malayagiri (dvitīya-sandhi, 1) defines sva as based on identity of the points of articulation and internal effort.[398] He considers spirants to be slightly open and avoids any rule such as P.1.1.10.[399] Similarly, he considers /a/ to be open, and hence there is no problem of non-homogeneity of /a/ and /ā/.[400]

12.8.2. However, Malayagiri does not have a rule of savarṇa-grahaṇa like P.1.1.69. Like Hemacandra, Malayagiri is also terminologically dependent on the Kātantra to a great extent. The conventions for the affixation of -kāra, -varṇa and -varga are similar to the Kātantra. He also rules that a consonant marked with /U/ stands for its varga.[401] He does not use the notion of sva in this rule. Malayagiri is also dependent on the Śiva-sūtras of Pāṇini and the modified version of Śākaṭāyana. He defines short and long /a/, /i/ and /u/ to be /a-Ṇ/; short and long /i/, /u/, /ṛ/ and /ḷ/ to be /i-K/; /e/ and /o/ as /e-Ṅ/; and /e/, /o/, /ai/ and /au/ as /e-C/.[402] This definition of /i-K/ is based on Pāṇini's Śiva-sūtras, and not on the modified version of Śākaṭāyana, because he has only /ṛ-K/.[403] It could have been based on Jainendra's version, but there is no certainty about that version. However, Malayagiri defines /y/, /v/, /r/ and /l/ by the term /ya-Ñ/.[404] This is clearly based on Śākaṭāyana's version, where we have /ha/-/ya/-/va/-/ra/-/la/-/Ñ/, which is different from Pāṇini.[405]

12.8.3. With this mixed terminology, Malayagiri still needs the broader conception of sva. Though some of his rules could certainly use the restricted conception of the Kātantra, other rules require the broader notion. For instance, the rule (tṛtīya-sandhi, 2) says: "/i-K/ sounds are replaced by [the corresponding] /ya-Ñ/ sounds, if followed by a non-homogeneous vowel."[406] This rule does not need the broader conception of savarṇa. Similarly, the rule (tṛtīya-sandhi, 5) says: "A simple vowel, if followed by a homogeneous vowel, is replaced by a long vowel, along with the following."[407] This also does not need the broader conception.

But there are other rules, which need the broader conception. These rules require homogeneity of /g/ and /ṅ/, /ḍ/ and /ṇ/, /t/ and /n/ etc., which can only be obtained in the broader conception of sva.[408] Malayagiri draws an important distinction. He uses the term sarūpa for total identity.[409] This is different from sva. In general, Malayagiri's treatment of sva is very similar to Hemacandra.

12.9. THE MAGDHABODHA-VYĀKARAṆA

12.9.1. The Magdhabodha-vyākaraṇa of Bopadeva shortens the term savarṇa by rṇa, by retaining the last syllable of the older term. This is similar to his usage of the terms sva, rgha etc. for hrasva and dīrgha. The term pluta is reduced to plu.[410] Not only is this shortform different from other systems, this conception itself is quite different from other conceptions.

12.9.2. Bopadeva defines rṇa as: (Mugdh. 6): "Similar (sama) stops (ñapa) and simple vowels (/a-K/) are rṇa with each other [within the groups]; and /ṛ/ and /ḷ/ [/ṛ-K/, though dissimilar] are also [rṇa with each other]."[411] Bopadeva explains similarity (sāmya) in terms of identity of the points of articulation.[412] This is quite a different conception, and reflects Bopadeva's independent thinking. The condition of identity of the points of articulation applies separately to stops and simple vowels, and hence there is no need of a rule like P.1.1.10. As an exception to this identity of points of articulation, homogeneity of /ṛ/ and /ḷ/ is specifically given. The definition is very clear and does not leave any doubt about Bopadeva's intentions.

12.9.3. With this definition, Bopadeva gives us his rule of rṇa-grahaṇa: (Mugdh). 7): "The sounds capa (i.e. /c/, /ṭ/, /t/, /k/ and /p/), if marked with /U/, and the sound /a-K/ (i.e. /a/, /i/, /u/, /ṛ/ and /ḷ/), if without any marker, stand for their homogeneous sounds."[413] Thus, /cU/, /ṭU/, etc. stand for the respective vargas, and short simple vowels stand for the respective long and extra-long varieties, if they are not marked with /T/ etc. The sound /ṛ/ also stands for /ḷ/. This is the total extent of rṇa-grahaṇa, which is smaller compared to Pāṇini's homogeneous-representation, where diphthongs and semi-vowels also stand for their homogeneous sounds.

12.9.4. Bopadeva has extensively used the procedure of

rṇa-grahaṇa, but the term rṇa occurs only once more. The rule (Mugdh. 22) says: "When [a vowel] is followed by a rṇa 'homogeneous' sound, both are replaced by a long variety."[414] This is the only rule where the term rṇa is used.

The fact that the Kātantra uses the term savarṇa only with simple vowels, and that, on other occasions, it has successfully used the notion of sasthāna,[415] seems to have influenced Bopadeva's thinking. At the same time, he must have realized the benefits of the Pāṇinian procedure of homogeneous-representation over the Kātantra and others, in reducing the expression of the rules. Thus, Bopadeva adopted a reduced version of P.1.1.9 and P.1.1.69. In this conception of homogeneity, Bopadeva stands alone.

12.10. THE SĀRASVATA-VYĀKARAṆA

12.10.1. The Sārasvata-vyākaraṇa of Anubhūti-svarūpācārya seems to have been constructed by combining features of Pāṇini and the Kātantra. It uses terms like samāna and nāmin, which come from the Kātantra, but it has its own modified version of the Śiva-sūtras, which is used to formulate shortforms. There is no general featural definition of savarṇa, but short, long and extra-long varieties of simple vowels are considered to be savarṇa.[416] Except for the inclusion of extra-long vowels, this seems to be parallel to the Kātantra notion of savarṇa. The Vṛtti explains conventions for affixation of -kāra, -varṇa and /-t/, which are similar to the Kātantra.[417] The Sārasvata defines the terms /kU/, /cU/ etc. for the respective vargas.[418] The notion of savarṇa is used mostly with vowels.[419]

12.10.2. Though the term savarṇa is not defined with respect to consonants, one rule uses it in such a context. Sārasvata (990) says: "If a jhas sound [i.e. non-nasal stops, /ś/, /ṣ/ and /s/] is followed by a savarṇa sound from the same group, and is preceded by a has sound [i.e. a consonant], then it is deleted."[420] This requires the expanded notion of savarṇa, which does not exist in the Kāntantra. The Vṛtti quotes a statement: "The members of a varga are savarṇas among themselves."[421] This brings in the Pāṇinian notion of savarṇa, by the back door. Looking at the total implementation of the term, we can say that the scope of the concept of savarṇa in the Sārasvata is the same as in the Mugdhbodha. But the latter has given a definition of [sava]rṇa, and has the procedure of rṇa-grahaṇa, which does not exist in the former.

12.10.3. The Sārasvata rules in homogeneity of /ṛ/ and /ḷ/ vowels.[422] This system goes further and also speaks of homogeneity of /r/ and /l/; and quotes the view of the Ālaṁkārikas that /ḍ/ and /l/, /ś/ and /s/, and /b/ and /v/ are also homogeneous.[423] This actually refers to dialectal variation in the Middle Indo-Aryan. This device has been frequently used in Sanskrit poetry.

12.11. SOME MINOR SYSTEMS

12.11.1. The Sarasvatī-kaṇṭhābharaṇa of Bhojadeva closely follows Pāṇini, with certain minor differences. Bhoja's definition of savarṇa is identical with P.1.1.9, except that he uses clearer terminology. He uses sthāna for the point of articulation and āsya-prayatna for internal effort.[424] Bhoja also accepts P.1.1.10 (nājjhalau) as his rule 1.1.102.[425] This is the only non-Pāṇinian system that has accepted this rule. However, Bhoja splits Pāṇini's savarṇa-grahaṇa. His rule 1.2.2 (utā savargaḥ) says that a sound marked with /U/ also stands for its varga. Then the rule 1.2.4 (avidhīyamāno'ṇ sasavarṇaḥ) says that an /a-Ṇ/ sound which is not being ruled in stands for itself and its homogeneous sounds. Both of these rules are covered by P.1.1.69. In making use of the notion of varga, Bhoja seems to be combining the Kātantra with Pāṇini.

12.11.2. We shall also briefly look at the Pāli grammars of Moggallāna and Kaccāyana, since Burnell thinks that they show influence from the lost school of the Aindra grammar.[426] The Moggallāna grammar starts with the list of 33 sounds, and says that the first ten of them are vowels (sara), i.e. /a/, /ā/, /i/, /ī/, /u/, /ū/, /e/, /ai/, /o/ and /au/.[427] Then it says that among them two by two are termed savaṇṇa (= savarṇa) with each other.[428] This only refers to the simple vowels. This fits well with the Kātantra type of system. The sounds /ṛ/ and /ḷ/ do not appear in Pāli. The sounds /ai/ and /au/ also do not appear in Pāli, but are listed with other sounds.

12.11.3. The Kaccāyana grammar clearly declares that the technical terms of the Sanskrit grammatical systems have been adopted.[429] The Kaccāyana grammar uses the term savaṇṇa without defining it. It is used only once in the rule Kacc. (1.2.3).[430] This rule explains a usage like na upeti changing into nopeti. It says that when /a/ of na is deleted before /u/ of upeti, /u/ changes to /o/ which is asavaṇṇa with /u/. Here the term asavaṇṇa seems to have been used in the sense of "different." The commentary Kaccāyana-vaṇṇanā says that short vowels are mutually homogeneous with the respective long vowels, and explains the term savaṇṇa with sarūpa "having identical form."[431] Though this last explanation may not stand with the Sanskrit grammarians, the previous one is within the influence of the Kātantra. Thus, both the grammatical systems show influence of the Kātantra, which may ultimately be traced back to Burnell's Aindra school of grammar.

I shall briefly refer to some of the non-Pāṇinian systems where my information comes from secondary sources. G. B. Palsule (1974, p. 26) discusses technical terms from the Harināmāmṛta-vyākaraṇa of Jīva Gosvāmin. The term for simple vowels in this system is daśāvatāra "ten incarnations, ten simple vowels," i.e. /a/, /ā/, /i/, /ī/, /u/, /ū/, /ṛ/, /ṝ/, /ḷ/ and /ḹ/ [daśa daśāvatārāḥ, 3]. Of these ten simple vowels, the homorganic pairs are homogeneous ekātmaka "with the same self" [teṣām dvau dvau ekātmakau, 4]. Palsule says (ibid.) that the term for asavarṇa in this system is anekātmaka. The Harināmāmṛta uses the term viṣṇu-varga for varga [te māntāḥ pañca pañca viṣṇu-vargāḥ, 19], and uses affixation of -rāma for -kāra of other systems [varṇa-svarūpe rāmaḥ, 37]. The Supadma-vyākaraṇa of Padmanābha defines savarṇa as: vargya-svarau sajātīyau savarṇau (1.1.15) (K. C. Chatterji (1948), p. 285). This seems to make use of the concept of jāti "universal" to define homogeneity. This is rather unique, because we find that these two concepts are kept distinct in other systems. Similarly this system also seems to extend the concept of universal to members of a varga. This is also unique. The Prayoga-ratna-mālā of Puruṣottama defines that two homorganic (sasthāna) simple vowels are homogeneous with each other, and /ṛ/ and /ḷ/ are also homogeneous with each other [sasthānākau savarṇaḥ (?) syāt sāvarṇyam ṛ-ḷ-varṇayoḥ, 1.1.9] (K. C. Chatterji (1948), p. 285). This is very similar to the Mugdhabodha conception of (sava-)rṇa.

CHAPTER XIII

A HISTORICAL OVERVIEW

13.1. Having reached the other end of the line, we can have an overview of the development of the notion of savarṇa and its implementation. Several scholars have compared and contrasted simply the definitions of savarṇa in different systems, without going into the function and implementation of this concept in those respective systems.[432] Such comparisons, though indeed very useful, do not give us the real relationships between these systems. For instance, the VPr definition of savarṇa is identical with Pāṇini's definition in its scope, but it is absolutely unnecessary to justify the usage of that term in that text. The definitions of the Jainendra, Śākaṭāyana, Hema-śabdānuśāsana etc. are identical with Pāṇini's definition, but the Jainendra follows Pāṇini's implementation, Śākaṭāyana follows Kātyāyana's suggestion of universal-mention, while Hemacandra retains a strong influence of the Kātantra. Thus, the definitions alone are not quite sufficient to give us the real historical relationships.

13.2. The term savarṇa is a very old term. It appears in the Ṛgveda (10.17.2) and the Atharvaveda (18.2.33), where Sāyaṇa explains it by sadṛśa "similar" and samāna-rūpa "having similar appearance." The term sāvarṇya also appears in the Ṛgveda (10.63.9), but here it stands for Manu, the son of Savarṇā. The earlier usage is, however, noteworthy. Though it has nothing to do with varṇa "sound," and is rather connected with varṇa "color," its general meaning of similarity must have contributed to the later grammatical notion.

In the early Vedic, we have more mythological and philosophical speculation on the speech-phenomenon, but in the Brāhmaṇa texts we start getting a glimpse of the ancient grammatical activity. The Aitareya-Brāhmaṇa knows the distinction between -varṇa and -kāra, ghoṣa and ūṣman.[433] The Gopatha-Brāhmaṇa mentions a whole range of grammatical terminology, which we later find utilized by the known grammatical texts.[434] The Taittirīya-Upaniṣad quotes subject headings of an ancient Śikṣā.[435] Weber has collected a large number of grammatical terms from the Vedic Kalpa-sūtras.[436] These were self-expressive terms and, according to Burnell, they formed the technical terminology of the Aindra School of Grammar, whose continued existence is seen in the Prātiśākhyas, Kātantra and some of the later systems.[437] Pāṇini brought in more mathematical expressions, which were meaningful only according to the technical conventions of the system, and were mainly aimed at brevity in the expression of rules. He redefined some of the older terms and gave them a more comprehensive meaning.

13.3. The word varṇa primarily means color, but was used to stand for sounds in later days. It is important to see how the word standing for color could have been transfered to stand for sounds. This has already created a long controversy. In Goldstücker's Pāṇini, we find the first full scale discussion of this problem. Before Goldstücker, Weber argued that varṇa stands for "coloring," or specializing of the sound. [Compare: rakta "colored" = "nasalized," Indische Studien, Vol. IV, Berlin, 1858, p. 109]. Max Müller followed Weber. Then came Goldstücker who argued that varṇa refers to written letters, "arising naturally from its primitive sense 'colour'" [Goldstücker (1860), pp. 38-9]. Goldstücker used this argument to substantiate his view that Pāṇini knew the script. Batakrishna Ghosa gives an explanation which makes more sense:

> This meaning of the word varṇa should have been developed first in the Brāhmaṇas of the Sāmaveda in which we constantly come across locutions like rathantara-varṇā ṛk "verse which gets the colour of Rathantara Sāman in chant." In these passages the word varṇa is visibly changing its meaning from "colour" to "sound" of melody. Thus, gradually,

> the "sound of melody" became "sound in general." ["Aspects of Pre-Pāṇinian Sanskrit Grammar," B. C. Law Comm. Volume, p. 338; quoted by Chatterji (1948), p. 279.]

K. C. Chatterji himself, however, seems to favor the view that written letters "were covered with a coating of paint" [(1948), p. 279], and hence the word for color came to be used for sounds or letters.

Batakrishna Ghosa's explanation paves the way for a rather more consistent development. However, from very early days we come across association of types of Vedic hymns with different colors in the primary sense of the word "color." In the seventeenth chapter of the RPr, we find a detailed discussion of color distinctions of different types of Vedic hymns. The RPr lists seven different colors [17.8, p. 77]. It says that the fourfold Vedic Chandas is of kapila "brown" color [17.10, p. 78]. However, the RPr does not seem to associate individual sounds with different colors. This is seen in the Yājñavalkya-śikṣā. It says that vowels are white, stops are black, semi-vowels are brown, spirants are redish, yamas are blue, anusvāra is yellow, visarga is white, nāsikya is green, nasal sounds are dark blue, while raṅga is of a mixed color [Śikṣā-saṃgraha, pp. 13-14]. The Yājñavalkya-śikṣā goes further and says that nouns are white, verbs are red, upasargas are brown while the nipātas are black [ibid, p. 14]. Different systems of Yoga and Tantra had different color-classifications of sounds, which had meditational and mystical significance. [For a brief informative account and bibliographical references, see: Yoga, by Ernest Wood, a Pelican Original, first published in 1959, revised reprint of 1971, pp. 153-4.]

As far as the non-mystical aspects are concerned, it seems more probable that the word varṇa "color" came to be used for sounds, by the secondary meaning of "color" standing for musical quality, and later for vocalic quality. It stands not only for a sound, but also for a comprehensive sound quality, mostly the vowel quality. In this extended meaning, it stood for "real sound" which is not affected by quantity, nasality and accent. This notion of a common-substance or real sound is an impressionistic notion. Thus, /a/, /ā/ and /ā3/ have the same sound-substance, and hence they belong to the same varṇa, whose minimal expression is naturally found in the short, non-nasal variety. But /k/ and /kh/ were not thought to have the same real sound-substance, and hence they belonged to different varṇas, and thus the notion of varga "class of homorganic stops" came up. Thus, the notions of varṇa and varga were the earlier notions. Affixation of -varṇa to short vowels to stand for their long and extra-long varieties is a later development based on this ancient notion of varṇa. It goes back to the days of the Brāhmaṇa texts. This stage is perhaps reflected in the Sāmaveda-prātiśākhyas of ancient Śākaṭāyana and Audavraji. However, the notion of savarṇa has not yet emerged.

13.4. The early conception of savarṇa is clearly based on this notion of varṇa. Thus, savarṇa meant "belonging to the same varṇa," having the same real sound-substance. This was perhaps aided by the ancient usage of the word savarṇa "having similar appearance." Thus, /a/ was savarṇa with /ā/, since they had the same real sound-substance. But /k/ and /kh/ were not regarded to be savarṇas, since they were not thought to belong to the same varṇa. There, the conception of varga "class of homorganic stops" and the conception of savargīya "belonging to the same varga" filled the gap. Thus, both the concepts, namely savarṇa and savargīya, function side by side in the Prātiśākhyas [Sec. 10.3.4]. K. C. Chatterji (1948, p. 285) says that "originally 'savarṇa' appears to have been formed after 'samānākṣara' and was, therefore, restricted to the simple vowels." This is difficult to justify. The term savarṇa also appears in the context of consonants in the Prātiśākhyas, and hence it is more appropriate to relate it to a basic conception of varṇa.

The basic notion of savarṇa as founded on the notion of varṇa, was in a way vague. We find that the Prātiśākhyas and the Kātantra adjust this background notion of savarṇa to their specific needs. Thus, as far as vowels are concerned, the RPr and APr restricted the notion of savarṇa to short and long /a/, /i/, /u/ and /ṛ/. The TPr omitted /ṛ/, while the Kātantra also added /ḷ/. This difference from system to system shows the degree of adjustment. Some of the Prātiśākhyas did use the term savarṇa in the context of consonants, but here it was used in the sense of identity of the varṇa. Thus /y/ and /ỹ/ are savarṇas with each other, while /k/ or /ś/ is savarṇa only with itself.

13.5. Pāṇini thought in more sophisticated terms. He did not care if his terms were not self-explanatory, but his main purpose was to achieve more generalization and more compact expression for his rules. He re-examined the categories of varṇa and varga, and tried to cover both of these notions in a single generalization. Through this attempt came the expanded notion of savarṇa. Pāṇini defined his expanded notion of savarṇa in clear featural terms: identity of points of articulation and internal effort. He also gave specific solutions to problems such as unwanted non-homogeneity of /a/ and /ā/, and unwanted homogeneity of certain vowels with spirants. It is possible that this expanded notion of savarṇa existed in pre-Pāṇinian times. Such a notion is seen in the Āpiśali-śikṣā-sūtras, and if these can be proved to belong to the pre-Pāṇinian teacher Āpiśali, that would help us push this notion into pre-Pāṇinian antiquity. Pāṇini not only gave an expanded definition of savarṇa, he also gave the procedure of homogeneous-representation, which is more compact than the older conventions of affixation of -kāra, -varṇa and -varga.

13.6. Then came Kātyāyana, the Vārttikakāra. According to the tradition recorded in the Kathā-sarit-sāgara, he belonged to the Aindra School of Grammar.[438] That he belonged to a non-Pāṇinian tradition can be clearly seen from his terminology, which is identical with that of the Prātiśākhyas and the Kātantra. Kātyāyana had also come under a heavy philosophical influence of the early schools of the Mīmāṁsā system, i.e. the schools of Vyāḍi and Vājapyāyana. Vyāḍi held the doctrine of vyakti-vāda or dravya-vāda "Individualism," while Vājapyāyana held the opposite doctrine of ākṛti-vāda "Universalism." Kātyāyana extensively refers to the linguistic and ontological theories of these two thinkers. Probably under the influence of Vājapyāyana's theory of universals, Kātyāyana returned to the old conception of varṇa with a new philosophical interpretation. Instead of saying that /a/, /ā/ and /ā3/ belong to the same varṇa, Kātyāyana said that they share the same universal /a/-ness, which is naturally expressed by any instance of it. Similarly, /y/ and /ỹ/ are covered by the same universal. However, the universal of /k/ cannot cover /kh/ etc. Thus, the limitations of the conception of a universal are the same as those of the conception of varṇa. Both are equally impressionistic or a priori. Kātyāyana never gave an explicit definition of a sound-universal. With this conception, he attempted to partially replace the procedure of homogeneous-representation. It was not necessary for vowels and semi-vowels, but it was still necessary for stops. Thus, in a way, Kātyāyana returned to the old distinction of varṇa and varga.

13.7. These were the three major directions in the development of the notion of savarṇa and its implementation. Each of the later schools of grammar chose one of these for its model, and some chose to combine them in varying degrees. Thus, Candragomin accepted Kātyāyana's suggestion of universal-mention for vowels, and adopted the notion of varga for stops. Thus, he tried to get rid of the notion of savarṇa. Śākaṭāyana also followed Kātyāyana's universal-mention, but he also defined savarṇa, like Pāṇini, and reserved homogeneous-representation for stops. The grammars of Devanandin and Bhoja are very closely related to Pāṇini's scheme. Hemacandra and Malayagiri defined savarṇa like Pāṇini, but in its implementation they worked out a synthesis of Pāṇini and the Kātantra system. The Sārasvata mostly followed the Kātantra, except in a few cases where it uses the term savarṇa in the Pāṇinian sense. The Mugdhabodha gave an independent definition of savarṇa, but this definition reflects a synthesis of Pāṇini and the Kātantra. The Pāli grammars followed the Kātantra in their usage of the term savaṇṇa. The VPr probably came under the influence of the Pāṇinian system, in its definition of savarṇa, but its implementation is not different from the other Prātiśākhyas. This complex historical development and relationships can be seen in the following diagram:

Historical Development of

Savarṇa

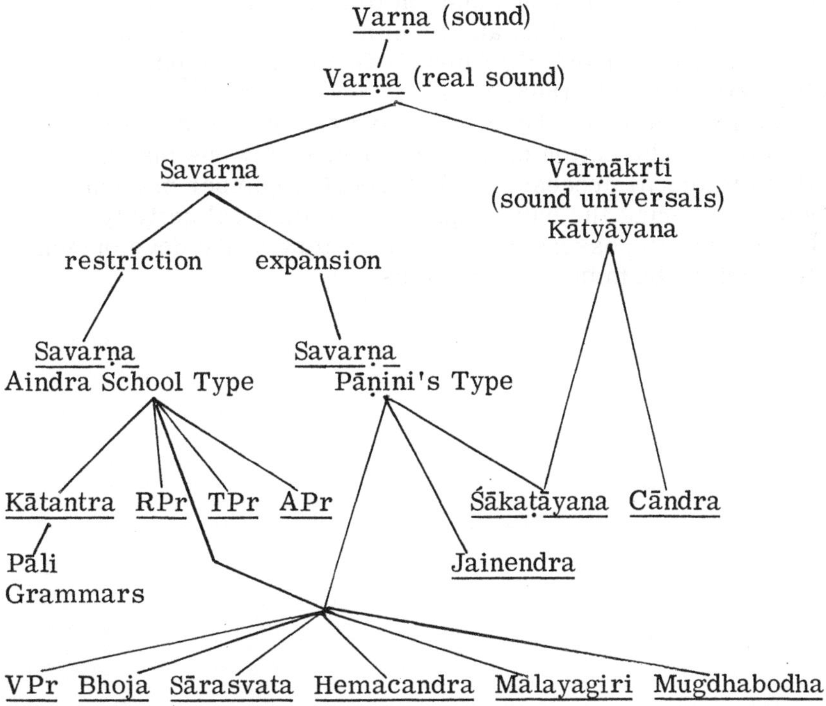

13.8. Thus, the historical development of this conception and its implementation represents a continuous process of rethinking, reformulation and re-examination at each stage. It shows the continued vitality of grammatical reasoning in the traditions of Indian grammar. Kielhorn rightly observed: "It was indeed difficult for later grammarians to add to the store of knowledge which had been collected by Pāṇini, Kātyāyana and Patañjali; nevertheless there has been no lack of scholars who have endeavoured to improve on the arrangement of the Aṣṭādhyāyī, and who, each in his way, have done useful work." ["On the Jainendra-Vyākaraṇa," Indian Antiquary, Vol. 10, March 1881, p. 76.] The linguistic and methodological significance of the post-Pāṇinian grammars was also pointed out by Kielhorn: "Their aim was not to adapt the rules of those that went before them to the changed conditions of the language, but mainly, each after his own fashion to rearrange those rules, and to alter their wording and terminology." ["A Brief Account of Hemachandra's Sanskrit Grammar," Wiener Zeitschrift, Vol. 2, 1888, p. 18.] No system ever lived in a total vacuum, and hence each system is a product of its history. The notion of homogeneity is only one instance of this historical process. Only through a number of such studies, covering the entire span of grammatical activity, will we come to possess a complete history of the development of the Indian Grammatical Theories.

APPENDIX A

THE SCOPE OF SAVARṆA-GRAHAṆA

[In this appendix, I shall present the arguments, which I have already discussed in my article "The Scope of Homogeneous-Representation in Pāṇini," which is due to appear in the Silver Jubilee Volume of the Annals of Oriental Research, University of Madras. I addressed myself to this issue after the main body of this book was already completed. However, this is a very crucial question and hence this appendix has been added.]

1. In his Śiva-sūtras, Pāṇini uses the marker /Ṇ/ twice, i.e. in [1] a-i-u-Ṇ1 and in [6] l(a)-Ṇ2. By P.1.1.71 (ādir antyena sahetā), an initial sound given along with a marker stands for itself and for the intervening sounds, excluding the marker sounds. The first six Śiva-sūtras are as follows:

[1] a-i-u-Ṇ1
[2] ṛ-ḷ-K
[3] e-o-Ṅ
[4] ai-au-C
[5] h(a)-y(a)-v(a)-r(a)-Ṭ
[6] l(a)-Ṇ2

There are about forty shortforms made by using the Śiva-sūtras, and very rarely there is any confusion as to what sounds are included in those shortforms. But the shortforms /a-Ṇ/ and /i-Ṇ/ which are used by Pāṇini very frequently do present problems, because the marker /Ṇ/ is given twice in the Śiva-sūtras. Theoretically, /a-Ṇ/ and /i-Ṇ/ could have two meanings each, depending whether /Ṇ/ belongs to a-i-u-Ṇ1 or to l(a)-Ṇ2.

2. Vyāḍi presents this problem in his Paribhāṣā-sūcana and says that Pāṇini deliberately used the marker /Ṇ/ twice and that a confusion should not obstruct us, and we should rely on the tradition of interpretation for the specific significance of a shortform. Unfortunately, Vyāḍi only presents the problem and refers us to interpretative tradition, but does not state the conclusions in the case of /a-Ṇ/ and /i-Ṇ/ [Paribhāṣā-sūcana, p. 26-7]. The specific attempt to define the scope of /a-Ṇ/ and /i-Ṇ/ is seen for the first time in the versified vārttikas quoted by Patañjali. The authorship of these vārttikas is not yet clearly known, but they certainly seem to be pre-Patañjali. The Śloka-vārttika says:

> Without any doubt [/a-Ṇ/ is formed with the first /Ṇ/] because the following [sounds] do not appear [in the examples of rules with /a-Ṇ/], [except] in P.1.1.69, [where] /a-Ṇ/ [is formed with the second /Ṇ/], because [/ṛ/ is] followed by the marker /T/ [in the rule] P.7.4.7 (ur ṛt). The shortform /i-Ṇ/ is [always] with the second /Ṇ/, since elsewhere /i/ and /u/ are [given separately, and not by the shortform /i-Ṇ/].[439]

Patañjali says that by using the marker /Ṇ/ twice, Pāṇini indicates the maxim that one should not consider a rule to be inoperative because of doubt, but one should understand the specific meaning from the interpretation of the learned.[440] Patañjali clearly says that except in P.1.1.69, the shortform /a-Ṇ/ is always with the first /Ṇ/, and that the shortform /i-Ṇ/ is always with the second /Ṇ/.[441] Thus, according to the tradition, the procedure of homogeneous-representation (savarṇa-grahaṇa) applies to vowels and semi-vowels as they are given in the Śiva-sūtras, and to sounds marked with /U/. Thus the sounds /y/, /v/ and /l/ also stand for /ỹ/, /ṽ/ and /l̃/, and /ṛ/ stands for /ṝ/ and /ṝ3/. Homogeneous-representation goes beyond a-i-u-Ṇ. This also seems to be the view of Kātyāyana.[442] The later Pāṇinian tradition follows the verdict of Patañjali.

3. Kunhan Raja has pointed out several problems in the traditional view about the scope of /a-Ṇ/ in P.1.1.69.

The first problem concerns the diphthongs:

> There are the sounds /e/ and /ai/ which have the same place of articulation and the same effort in production. There is a similar relation between /o/ and /au/. Therefore /e/ and /ai/ become mutually concordant and /o/ and /au/ also become mutually concordant in the same way. If the combination /a-Ṇ/ in this sūtra (P. 1. 1. 69) has the second /Ṇ/ as its final mute, the combination will include the diphthongs and consequently, when Pāṇini uses the sound /e/ and /o/, it includes also the sounds /ai/ or /au/, just as the sound /a/ means both the short /a/ and the long /ā/. This is not acceptable. This leads us to the assumption of another rule that as an exception, there is no concordance between /e/ and /ai/ or between /o/ and /au/. Such an exception is taken to be implied by the fact that while he does not include the long forms of the simple vowels, he gives all the four diphthongs separately. But all such difficulties can be avoided if even in this sūtra /aṇ/ is taken as combined with the first /ṇ/ as mute as in the other sūtras. [443]

This objection assumes that according to Pāṇini /e/ and /o/ are homogeneous with /ai/ and /au/, and then there might be the problem of /e/ and /o/ standing for /ai/ and /au/, and vice versa.

4. Kunhan Raja tries to point out that /ṛ/ need not stand for /ṝ/. The rule he considers is P. 6. 1. 101 (akaḥ savarṇe dīrghaḥ). This rule says that if an /a-K/ sound is followed by a homogeneous sound, both are replaced by a homogeneous long sound. Kunhan Raja comments:

> ...the short /ṛ/ can never be followed by a long /ṝ/; there is also no possibility of a long /ṝ/ sound being followed by a short /ṛ/ sound, in the way in which a short /a/ can follow a long /ā/. ...An example like hotṛ-ṝkāraḥ is only an artificially manipulated one. [444]

He also considers the rule P. 8. 4. 58 (anusvārasya yayi parasavarṇaḥ) which says that /ṁ/, if followed by a /y(a)-Y/ sound [i.e. semi-vowels and stops] changes into a sound homogeneous with the following. Raja says:

> All that is said in the sūtra is that the anusvāra becomes a savarṇa of the following sound, retaining its nasal character.[445]

Kunhan Raja holds that this rule requires /y/, /v/ and /l/ to be homogeneous with /ỹ/, /ṽ/ and /l̃/, but not to stand for them.

5. With these arguments, Kunhan Raja concludes as follows:

> That Pāṇini used the same sound /ṇ/ twice is unhappy. But we can say that of the two combinations possible with this mute one with the first letter /a/ is with the first mute /ṇ/ and one with the second letter /i/ is with the second /ṇ/. But to say that even here, there is an exception, not specifically mentioned by Pāṇini, is a position which I feel very difficult to accept....In this context, the question is not whether a semi-vowel has a savarṇa or not; the point is whether when Pāṇini gives the semi-vowels, he includes the nasalised form of the semi-vowels also in it....What is meant is simply this that when Pāṇini gives the short /ṛ/ sound or the semi-vowels, they do not include the savarṇas also.[446]

Kunhan Raja has rightly separated the two questions: Does a given sound have any homogeneous sounds? Can a given sound stand for its homogeneous sounds? However, his general conclusion needs to be critically examined.

6. Raja says that /e/ and /ai/ are homogeneous, since their "place of articulation is throat-cum-palat and effort is vivṛta (open)."[447] Similarly, /o/ and /au/ are homogeneous, since their "place of articulation is throat-cum-lip and effort is vivṛta (open)."[448] Here K. Raja is clearly following the phonetic description as given by such late texts as the

Siddhānta-kaumudī of Bhaṭṭoji Dīkṣita.[449]

Historically speaking, we do not know exactly what kind of phonetic classifications were there in Pāṇini's mind when he gave his rules. We have to rely on secondary sources. The dates of the different versions of the Pāṇinīya-śikṣā are not very clear, and they seem to be relatively of a late date. There are some subtle indications in Pāṇini's rules which suggest that he treated /e/ and /o/ quite differently from /ai/ and /au/. P.8.2.106 (plutāv aica idutau) says that when /ai/ and /au/ become pluta "extra-long," it is the /i/ and /u/ in these sounds that becomes extra-long, and not the /a/ element. This clearly shows that, for Pāṇini, the sounds /ai/ and /au/ had distinctly two components. By contrast we may infer that the sounds /e/ and /o/ did not have such distinct elements. [Ref.: Bare (1975), pp. 185-93.]

Looking at the vārttikas of Kātyāyana, we find that he clearly distinguishes /e/ and /o/ from /ai/ and /au/. The varttika 4 on P.1.1.48 says that /i/ and /e/ are sasthāna "having the same point of articulation," and the same is true of /u/ and /o/.[450] On the other hand, the vārttika 5 on P.1.1.48 says that in /ai/ and /au/, the latter elements, i.e. /i/ and /u/, are longer segments, compared to the initial /a/.[451] Thus, Kātyāyana seems to hold that /e/ is palatal, /o/ is labial, /ai/ is throatal-palatal and /au/ is throatal-labial. Kātyāyana also says that the diphthongs are more open as compared to simple vowels.[452]

Patañjali says that the element /a/ in /e/ and /o/ is quite indistinct, while /ai/ and /au/ contain a vivṛta-tara "more open" /a/ vowel. He further says that /e/ and /au/ cannot be savarṇa "homogeneous," because they are not tulya-sthāna "with the same point(s) of articulation." The sounds /e/, /o/, /ai/ and /au/ are all sandhy-akṣaras "diphthongs" but, in contrast to /e/ and /o/, the sounds /ai/ and /au/ are described by Patañjali as being samāhāra-varṇas "composite sounds," where there is a mātrā "mora" of /a/, and the other mora is of /i/ and /u/ respectively.[453] This slightly differs from Kātyāyana's point of view concerning proportions of these elements.

This shows that at the early stage of the Pāṇinian tradition, the sounds /e/ and /o/ were looked upon as having one point of articulation, while /ai/ and /au/ were the real composite sounds with double points of articulation. All diphthongs are held to be more open than the simple vowels. This picture has been confirmed by a perusal of the Prātiśākhyas.[454] The Pāṇinīya-śikṣā, in different versions, represents views of a later period, and cannot be taken as representing the views of Pāṇini.[455] Thus, there is no reason to believe that Pāṇini held /e/ and /o/ to be homogeneous with /ai/ and /au/.

7. The second argument of Kunhan Raja is that /ṛ/ in Pāṇini's rules need not stand for /ṝ/. In twenty-five rules, Pāṇini gives short /ṛ/ with the marker /T/, while /ṝ/ is given with the marker /T/ in several rules. The short /ṛ/ is given also without /T/ in several rules.[456] The presence and absence of the marker /T/ is closely connected with the application of homogeneous-representation. The marker /T/ with /ṛ/ or /ṝ/ is not really a conclusive proof that /a-Ṇ/ in P.1.1.69 includes /ṛ/, since the marker /T/ is also used with non-/a-Ṇ/ sounds like /ā/ and /ī/ in a prescriptive function (vidhāyaka-taparakaraṇa), as opposed to its restrictive function (niyāmaka-taparakaraṇa) in the case of /a-Ṇ/ sounds. Wihtout /T/, a non-/a-Ṇ/ sound stands just for itself, while with it, it can cover homogeneous varities of the same quantity.[457]

However, there are cases of /ṛ/ without /T/, where representation of /ṝ/ is absolutely necessary. P.1.2.12 (uś ca), where /uḥ/ is genitive singular of /ṛ/, applies to verb-roots ending in /ṛ/ and /ṝ/ both, giving formations such as kṛṣīṣṭa [kṛ - sīyUṬ - sUṬ - ta] and stīrṣīṣṭa [stṝ - sīyUṬ - sUṬ - ta] . As the Kāśikā-vṛtti explains:

> The marker /T/ is attached to [the substitute /ṛ/ in P.7.4.7 (ur ṛt)] , so that even in the place of a long substituendum [/ṝ/] , the short [/ṛ/] alone would be effected as the substitute. For example: acīkṛtat.[458]

P.3.2.171 (ād-ṛ-gama-hana-janaḥ kikinau liṭ ca) applies to roots ending in /ṛ/ and /ṝ/, and yields formations like cakri [kṛ-Ki/KiN] and tituri [tṝ-Ki/KiN].[459] P.1.1.51 (ur aṇ ra-paraḥ) says that the substitutes of /ṛ/ in the form of /a/-vowels, /i/-vowels and /u/-vowels are followed immediately by /r/. This needs to apply not only to the substitutes of short /ṛ/, but also to the substitutes of the long /ṝ/ [e.g. P.7.1.100 (ṝta id dhātoḥ), P.3.3.57 (ṝd-or ap) etc.]. These examples conclusively prove that /ṛ/ in Pāṇini needs to stand for /ṝ/ also, and hence the scope of /a-Ṇ/ in P.1.1.69 could not have been limited to a-i-u-Ṇ.

8. Thus, there is no doubt that the shortform /a-Ṇ/ extends up to the second /Ṇ/, in P.1.1.69. The question whether /y/, /v/ and /l/ need to stand for /ỹ/, /ṽ/ and /l̃/ is, as we shall see, a far more complex question, and needs much deeper attention than was given by Kunhan Raja. There are the following considerations:

Prima-Facie Argument [A]. If /y/, /v/ and /l/ do not represent /ỹ/, /ṽ/ and /l̃/, then these nasal semi-vowels will not be designated as /h(a)-L/. P.1.1.7 (halo'nantarāḥ saṁyogaḥ) says that two /h(a)-L/ sounds without a gap are called saṁyoga "cluster." Thus, the sequences like /ỹy/, /ṽv/ and /l̃l/ will not be legally clusters. This could create several problems. For this reason, we might say that /y/, /v/ and /l/ must stand for /ỹ/, /ṽ/ and /l̃/ also.

This argument is not really valid. The nasal /ỹ/, /ṽ/ and /l̃/ in cases like saỹyantā are obtained by P.8.4.58 (anusvārasya yayi para-savarṇaḥ) from /ṁ/, which is itself obtained from /m/ by P.8.3.23 (mo'nusvāraḥ). P.8.4.59 (vā padāntasya) makes P.8.4.58 optional, if /ṁ/ is at the end of a pada "finished word." The question is as follows. Is /ỹ/ derived by P.8.4.58 to be treated as siddha "effected" for P.1.1.7 (halo'nantarāḥ saṁyogaḥ), which defines two or more immediate /ha-L/ sounds as a saṁyoga "cluster?" By P.8.2.1 (pūrvatrāsiddham), rules in the Tripādī, last three quarters of the Aṣṭādhyāyī, are to be treated as if asiddha "not effected," for the rest of the grammar. Even within these last three quarters, a rule is to be considered to be *asiddha* "not effected" with respect to all the preceding rules.

In the present case, we have to go into still more details. On P. 8. 2. 1, Patañjali says that the *saṁjñā-sūtras* [designation-rules] and the *paribhāṣā-sūtras* [maxims of interpretation] apply wherever their conditions of application are found. These rules operate even with respect to the *asiddha*-section. [*naiṣa doṣaḥ/ yady apīdaṁ tatrāsiddhaṁ, tat tv iha siddham/ katham/ kārya-kālaṁ saṁjñā-paribhāṣaṁ, yatra kāryaṁ tatropasthitaṁ draṣṭavyam*, *MB*, Vol. III, p. 354-5; *kārya-kāla-pakṣe tu tripādyām apy upasthitir iti viśeṣaḥ*, *Paribhāṣenduśekhara*, ed. by K. V. Abhyankar, Pt. I, Poona, 1962, p. 2.] This might lead us to think that /ỹ/ derived by P. 8. 4. 58 is *siddha* "effected" for the *saṁjñā*-rule P. 1. 1. 7. However, I think the situation is different. Patañajli's discussion indicates that if a *saṁjñā* "technical term" is found in a *Tripādī*-rule, then the respective rule defining that technical term has to apply with respect to that *Tripādī*-rule. In such a case, whatever rules are *siddha* "effected" with respect to that particular *Tripādī*-rule are also to be treated *siddha* with respect to that *saṁjñā*-rule. [The case of the term *pragṛhya* is discussed by Nāgeśa, see: *Paribhāṣenduśekhara*, pp. 3-4.] No rule after P. 8. 4. 58 uses the term *saṁyoga* or any other term dependent on the term *saṁyoga*. Therefore, P. 8. 4. 58 cannot be *siddha* "effected" for P. 1. 1. 7 in any way. Hence, in the place of the sequences /ỹy/, /ṽv/ and /l̃l/, P. 1. 1. 7 finds /my/, /mv/ and /ml/, which are eligible to be termed *saṁyoga*. This is the original picture in the system of Pāṇini. Thus, /ỹ/, /ṽ/ and /l̃/ need not be covered by /y/, /v/ and /l/ in /ha-L/ in P. 1. 1. 7.

The Pāṇinian system has to work this way. For instance, in a case like *supīḥṣu*, the sequence /ḥṣ/ cannot become a *saṁyoga* "cluster," if /ḥ/ derived by P. 8. 2. 66 (*sasajuṣo ruḥ*) and P. 8. 3. 15 (*khar-avasanayor visarjanīyaḥ*) is *siddha* for P. 1. 1. 7 (*halo'nantarāḥ saṁyogaḥ*). The sound /ḥ/ is not a /ha-L/ sound in the original system of Pāṇini. Actually, /ḥ/ is *asiddha* with respect to P. 1. 1. 7, and hence the rule P. 1. 1. 7 finds /s/ in the place of /ḥ/, consequently making /sṣ/ a real *saṁyoga*. The same has to be the case for sequences of an *anusvāra* and a consonant. The *anusvāra* effected by a rule like P. 8. 2. 23 (*mo'nusvāraḥ*) has to be *asiddha* for P. 1. 1. 7, so that there can be a *saṁyoga* in terms of the original /m/ or /n/ and the following consonant. Only with such a procedure can we explain why Pāṇini did not feel it necessary to include the *ayogavāhas* in the *Śiva-sūtras*.

However, in one context, Patañjali seems to accept /ỹy/, /ṽv/ and /l̃l/ to be *saṁyogas*, by saying that /y/, /v/ and /l/ stand for /ỹ/, /ṽ/ and /l̃/, implying thereby that they are /ha-L/ sounds, thus making /ỹy/ etc. real *saṁyogas*.[460] Considering the above given arguments, we may regard this passage in Patañjali as not reflecting the exact Pāṇinian procedure. As we shall see later on, Patañjali has accepted a *vārttika* of Kātyāyana, which proposes to regard /ỹ/ etc. to be *siddha* "effected" in the context of rules of doubling (*dvirvacana*).

Prima-Facie Argument [*B*]. If /y/, /v/ and /l/ do not stand for their nasal counterparts, then these nasal semi-vowels' will not be included in a *pratyāhāra* "shortform" such as /y(a)-R/. Thus a rule like P. 8. 4. 47 (*anaci ca*, *yaraḥ* from P. 8. 4. 45) will not apply to sequences such as -/ỹy/-. This rule says that a /y(a)-R/ sound preceded by a vowel and not followed by a vowel is optionally doubled. For this reason, we would want to include /ỹ/, /ṽ/ and /l̃/ in /y(a)-R/ through /y/, /v/ and /l/.

This argument is also full of problems. The sound /m/ is changed to /ṁ/ by P. 8. 3. 23 (*mo'nusvāraḥ*), while this *anusvāra* is changed to a nasal semi-vowel by P. 8. 4. 58 (*anusvārasya yayi parasavarṇaḥ*). However, the rule for doubling, i. e. P. 8. 4. 47 (*anaci ca*) stands in between these two rules, so that for this rule the nasal semi-vowel is as if non-effected (*asiddha*), while only /ṁ/ is effected (*siddha*). Hence it is not included in /y(a)-R/, and hence cannot be doubled by P. 8. 4. 47. Kātyāyana goes ahead and makes several suggestions. He proposes to include *anusvāra* in the *Śiva-sūtras*, as well as he proposes that for the sake of doubling *para-savarṇa* "substitute homogeneous with the following" should be regarded as siddha "effected."[461] This creates several possibilities. Either an anusvāra could be doubled, or a nasal /ỹ/ etc. could be doubled by regarding it to be a /y(a)-R/ sound. However, we are not sure if these provisos are intended by Pāṇini.

Prima-Facie Argument [C]. By P.8.4.57 (ano'pragṛhya-syānunāsiko vā) a word-final /a/-vowel, /i/-vowel or /u/-vowel is optionally nasalized, if the word is not a pragṛhya. Thus, we may optionally have nadī or nadī̃ Suppose that nadī̃ is followed by atra, would the nasal /ī̃/ change into a nasal /ỹ/ by P.6.1.77 (iko yaṇ aci)? In such a case, we may want /y(a)-Ṇ/ to include the nasal semi-vowels also.

This is also a dubious argument. The nasal final vowels are obtained by P 8.4.57, which belongs to the last three quarters. Therefore, for P.6.1.77, the nasal /ī̃/ is still considered to be non-effected (asiddha), and hence we cannot get nasal /ỹ/ any way.

9. The evidence considered so far for inclusion of semi-vowels in /a-Ṇ/ in P.1.1.69 is quite inconclusive. At this stage, we should refer to Patañjali who has raised this exact question, and it is of historical importance to see how he struggles to find a purpose for this inclusion. What follows is a translation of the relevant passages from Patañjali's Mahābhāṣya:

[A] Question:
For what purpose the semi-vowels have been included in /a-Ṇ/ [in P.1.1.69 (aṇ-udit savarṇasya cāpratyayaḥ)] ?

[B] Explanation of the Purpose:
In [the examples] saỹyantā, saṽvatsaraḥ, yal̃lokam and tal̃lokam, the [substitutes] homogeneous with the following [i.e. /ỹ/, /ṽ/ and /l̃/, effected by P.8.4.58 (anusvārasya yayi parasavarṇaḥ)] are regarded as being non-effected (asiddha) [for P.8.4.47 (anaci ca) and hence] only the anusvāra [i.e. /ṁ/]

is doubled [by P. 8. 4. 47]. Thus, [in the expressions sammyantā, sammvatsaraḥ, yammlokam and tammlokam], after the second [/m̐/] has been [substituted] by a sound homogeneous with the following [i.e. after having obtained samỹyantā, samṽvatsaraḥ, yamḹlokam and tamḹlokam by P. 8. 4. 58], those [/ỹ/, /ṽ/ and /l̃/] should be represented by [/y/, /v/ and /l/ in] /y(a)-Y/ [in P. 8. 4. 58]. This would finally allow application of P. 8. 4. 58 to the first [/m̐/, yielding saỹỹantā, saṽṽvatsaraḥ, tal̃l̃okam and yal̃l̃okam]."

[C] Objection:
That is not the purpose. [Kātyāyana] will say later [on P. 8. 2. 6]: 'In effecting doubling, a substitute homogeneous with the following (para-savarṇa) should be considered effected (siddha).' Since [such a substitute] is said to be effected, it would remain so [and will not be considered to be /m̐/].

[D] Reiteration of the Purpose:
In that case, when a substitute homogeneous with the following (para-savarṇa) is effected [i.e. /ỹ/, /ṽ/ and /l̃/, by P. 8. 4. 58], that should be represented by [/y/, /v/ and /l/ in] /y(a)-R/ [in P. 8. 4. 47 (anaci ca, yaraḥ from P. 8. 4. 45], so that [by P. 8. 4. 47] there could be doubling [of /ỹ/, /ṽ/ and /l̃/].

[E] Rejection of the Purpose:
Doubling [of /ỹ/, /ṽ/ and /l̃/] may not take place [by P. 8. 4. 47 (anaci ca)].

[F] Reiteration of the Purpose:
[We need doubling of /ỹ/, /ṽ/ and /l̃/ by P. 8. 4. 47], since there is a difference [in the resulting forms]. If there is doubling, the form [saỹỹantā] would have three /y/-s. If there is no doubling, then the form [saỹyantā] would have two /y/-s.

[G] Rejection of the Purpose:
[Even if there is doubling], there is no difference

[in the forms]. Even if there is doubling, the form [finally] contains only two /y/-s. How could this be? By P. 8. 4. 64 (halo yamāṁ yami lopaḥ) one of the /y/-s will be deleted. [The rule says: A /y(a)-M/ sound preceded by a consonant and followed by a corresponding /y(a)-M/sound is (optionally?) deleted.]

[H] Reiteration of the Purpose:
Still there is a difference. After doubling, the form might be with two /y/-s [if the deletion rule P. 8. 4. 64 applies], and it might be with three /y/-s [if P. 8. 4. 64 does not apply]. If doubling does not take place, then the form will have only two /y/-s. How could such a difference not be there? [There will be no difference in the form] if the deletion rule [P. 8. 4. 64] is obligatory. However, it is optional.

[I] Rejection of the Purpose:
Let [the rules] be in such a way that there is no difference [in forms].

[J] Reiteration of the Purpose:
Option must continue [in P. 8. 4. 65 (jharo jhari savarṇe) from P. 8. 4. 62 (jhayo ho'nyatarasyām)], since by P. 8. 4. 49 (śaro'ci), Pāṇini prohibits doubling. [P. 8. 4. 65 means: a /jh(a)-R/ sound preceded by a consonant and followed by a homogeneous /jh(a)-R/ sound is (optionally?) deleted. P. 8. 4. 49 means: If followed by an /a-C/ sound (i.e. a vowel), a /ś(a)-R/ (i.e. /ś/, /ṣ/ and /s/) is not doubled.] How is this indication [justified]? [It is justified] because, if the deletion rule [i.e. P. 8. 4. 65 (jharo jhari savarṇe) were obligatory, there would be no purpose in negation [of doubling by P. 8. 4. 49 (śaro'ci)] ....If there is doubling, then the [obligatory] deletion by P. 8. 4. 65 would take place. The teacher realizes that the deletion is optional, and hence prescribes negation of doubling [in specific cases, by P. 8. 4. 49]. [Note: The implication is that if option continues from P. 8. 4. 62 to P. 8. 4. 65, it obviously continues through P. 8. 4. 64 (halo yamāṁ yami lopaḥ).

Once this rule is optional, to derive a form such as sayyyantā with three /y/-s, we need /y/, /v/ and /l/ to stand for /ỹ/, /ṽ/ and /l̃/ in P. 8. 4. 58 (anusvārasya yayi parasavarṇaḥ). Thus, this argument establishes the purpose.]

[K] Rejection of the Purpose:
This is not a [justifiable] indication....Therefore, even if the deletion rule [i.e. P. 8. 4. 65] is obligatory still the rule for negation [of doubling, i.e. P. 8. 4. 49] must be given. [Note: We need not go into the arguments in this section. The argument consequently means that P. 8. 4. 64 (halo yamāṁ yami lopaḥ) must be obligatory, and ultimately would mean that /y/, /v/ and /l/ need not stand for /ỹ/, /ṽ/ and /l̃/. This is the objector's view.]

[L] Patañjali's Conclusions:
Thus, it is extremely unclear in Pāṇini's [system] to the teachers, whether option continues or not.[462]

This is a statement of frustration on the part of Patañjali, a clear indication that there was probably no direct teacher-student tradition linking Patañjali with Pāṇini. However, Patañjali accepts elsewhere that P. 8. 4. 64 (halo yamāṁ yami lopaḥ) is optional.[463] That would indicate that Patañjali accepts forms such as sayyyantā with triple clusters, which require that /y/, /v/ and /l/ should stand for /ỹ/, /ṽ/ and /l̃/. The whole discussion shows that Patañjali was at great pains in justifying inclusion of semi-vowels in homogeneous-representation, and finally he himself was not sure of the conclusions.

10. Looking at the whole argument we may sum it up as follows. There are three axioms:

(1) P. 8. 4. 64 (halo yamāṁ yami lopaḥ) is optional.
(2) An anusvāra can be duplicated by P. 8. 4. 47 (anaci ca). This depends on inclusion of the anusvāra in the Śiva-sūtras. This has been proposed by Kātyāyana and seems to have been accepted by Patañjali.[464]

(3) The parasavarṇa "substitute homogeneous with the following" effected by P.8.4.58 needs to be considered as effected (siddha) for P.8.4.47.[465]

Of these three axioms, we need either (1) and (2) or (1) and (3) to justify inclusion of semi-vowels in the rule P.1.1.69. It is impossible to establish with any certainty historical validity of any of the three axioms stated above. Patañjali himself has declared the uncertainty of the first, while the other two are suggestions of Kātyāyana.

11. Perhaps, Pāṇini's intention in the formulation of P.1.1.69 was for achieving a very wide morphophonemic generalization, of which different parts may have varying degrees of utility in his grammar.[466] It is possible that he constructed these meta-rules before conceiving the specific operation rules. Thus, certain elements in his meta-rules may have later remained unutilized. Traditionally, the only practical purpose is the doubling of nasal semi-vowels. It depends on P.8.4.64 being optional. Kaiyaṭa says that though the argument for indication (jñāpaka) has fallen through, still the tradition of the Pāṇinian teachers accepts P.8.4.64 to be optional.[467] Hari Dīkṣita in his Bṛhacchabdaratna says that the usage of /a-Ṇ/ in P.1.1.69 itself is an indication that P.8.4.64 is optional. If P.8.4.64 is not optional, then the purpose of /a-Ṇ/ beyond the limit of /a-C/ cannot be justified.[468] Nāgeśa refutes this argument.[469] However, Hari Dīkṣita's argument alone can explain to some extent why Patañjali eventually considered P.8.4.64 to be optional.

12. There is no doubt that Kātyāyana, who presupposes that parasavarṇa "substitute homogeneous with the following" be considered effected (siddha) in the context of doubling, intends such a doubling and accepts clusters like /ỹỹy/, /ṽṽv/ and /l̃l̃l/.[470] Patañjali and the later tradition accepts this notion. What is historically not certain is if Pāṇini himself accepted this. Pāṇini's rules as they stand do not allow such doubling. For the doubling rule P.8.4.47 (anaci ca), /ỹ/, /ṽ/ and /l̃/ effected by P.8.4.58 are non-effected (asiddha), while /ṁ/ effected by P.8.3.23 is effected (siddha). However, an anusvāra is not included in the Śiva-sūtras.

It is not a /y(a)-R/ sound and hence cannot be doubled. Thus, ultimately there is no doubling of nasal semi-vowels.

It is quite probable that Pāṇini himself never intended doubling of anusvāra and nasal semi-vowels. Thus, this may never have been the purpose for inclusion of semi-vowels in the rule P.1.1.69. If we look at the Prātiśākhyas, we find support for the view that there is no possibliity of clusters like /ỹỹy/, /ṽṽv/ and /l̃l̃l/. The Prātiśākhyas state very clearly that a consonant followed by a homogeneous consonant is not doubled.[471] There seems to be consensus of the Prātiśākhyas on this point. Under such circumstances, without any positive proof, it is hard to accept that Pāṇini allowed such doubling. It is not clear why Kātyāyana developed such a notion. It may be that this was his deductive attempt to find a practical purpose for inclusion of semi-vowels in P.1.1.69. Ultimately, we can only state that Pāṇini most certainly included semi-vowels in /a-Ṇ/ in P.1.1.69, but for what practical purpose, we do not know.[472]

NOTES

1. Kielhorn (1876a), p. 52, and also S. D. Joshi (1968), Intr. p. iv. We find a stong traditional assertion of this opinion in Maitreyarakṣita's *Tantrapradīpa*: *na hi bhāṣyakāra-matam anādṛtya sūtrakārasya kaścanābhiprāyo varṇayituṁ yujyate/ sūtrakāra-vārttikakārābhyāṁ tasyaiva prāmāṇya-darśanāt/ ...uttarottarato bhāṣyakārasyaiva prāmāṇyam*, quoted by S. C. Chakravarti, Introduction to *Dhātupradīpa*, pp. 2-3.

2. Belvalkar (1915), p. 35.

3. For an example, see: Deshpande (1972), p. 233.

4. Thieme (1935a), p. x.

5. This traditional view is in fact quite a late notion, and most of the modern scholars now believe in Pāṇini's authorship of these *sūtras*. The most recent and comprehensive study is: Cardona (1969).

6. For the discussions on this point by Kātyāyana and Patañjali, see: *MB*, Vol. I, Sec. I, p. 59 ff.

7. For a misinterpretation of this notion, see: "These *sūtras* must be understood in such a way that the last consonant of each of them is the notational symbol for the preceding group: /n/ is the symbol of the short vowels, /k/ is the notational symbol of the sonatic liquids etc." Zgusta (1969), p. 405. This is obviously wrong.

8. Thieme (1935a), p. 101.

9. Burnell (1875), p. 22.

10. *savarṇa-saṁjñāyām bhainna-deśeṣv atiprasaṅgaḥ prayatna-sāmānyāt*, *Vārttika 2* on P.1.1.9, *MB*, Vol. I, Sec. I, p. 153.

11. *siddhaṁ tv āsye tulya-deśa-prayatnaṁ savarṇam*, *Vārttika 2* on P.1.1.9, ibid.

12. taddhitāntam āsyam/ āsye bhavaṁ āsyam, "śarīrāvayavād yat"/ kim punar āsye bhavam? sthānaṁ karaṇaṁ ca/ MB, Vol. I, Sec. I, p. 154.

13. VPr (i. 43) samāna-sthāna-karaṇāsya-prayatnaḥ savarṇaḥ. Uvaṭa's commentary says: ko'sāv āsya-prayatno nāma, samvṛtatā vivṛtatā ca aspṛṣṭatā spṛṣṭatā ca īṣat-spṛṣṭatā ardha-spṛṣṭatā cety āsya-prayatnaḥ, VPr (W), pp. 118-9. The Varṇa-ratna-pradīpikā-śikṣā of Amareśa and the Yājñavalkya-śikṣā also speak of these six types of internal efforts (āsya-prayatna), see: Śikṣā-saṁgraha, pp. 120 and 132.

14. Breloer (1929), p. 116.

15. Thieme (1935a), p. 94. For a counter argument, see: Cardona (1965), p. 227.

16. Thieme (1935c), p. 22.

17. ibid.

18. See: "Varṇa ist anderseits auch nicht ein einzelner 'gesprochener Laut', noch auch ein 'Phonem', sondern bezeichnet eine Abstraktion, die keine linguistische Wirklichkeit hat: varṇa 'Farbe, Gattung' benennt speziell cine 'Lautgattung'. Z. B. avarṇa ist 'die Gattung der /a/-Laute (d.h. /a/, /ā/ und /ā3/)', z. B. /k/, /kh/, /g/, /gh/ und /ṅ/ sind savarṇa 'von gleicher Gattung', weil sie alle am Velum artikuliert werden." Thieme (1957c), p. 666.

19. bhedādhiṣṭhānā hi savarṇa-saṁjñā, yadi yatra sarvaṁ samānaṁ tatra syāt, savarṇa-saṁjñā-vacanam anarthakaṁ syāt/ MB, Vol. I, Sec. I, p. 156.

20. prayatna-viśeṣaṇam āsyopādānam/ santi hi āsyād bāhyāḥ prayatnāḥ, te hāpitā bhavanti/ teṣu satsv asatsv api savarṇa-saṁjñā siddhā bhavati/ ibid, 1. 153.

21. nāsikāyā āsyāntargatatve'pi mukha-nāsiketi sūtre nāsikātiriktāvayavaka-mukhasyaiva grahaṇena tat-sāhacaryād atrāpy āsya-padena tādṛśasyaiva grahaṇam bodhyam/ MB-P-U, Vol. I, Sec. I, p. 154.

22. aṇudit savarṇasya iti śāstraṁ sataḥ savarṇasyāṇā

grahaṇam bhavati ity etāvanmātram bodhayati, na tv aprasiddhaṁ savarṇaṁ kalpayati/, Ratnaprakāśa on MB, MPV, pp. 170-1.

23. See: ākṛti-grahaṇāt siddham, Vārttika 13 on the Śiva-sūtra 1, and also: avarṇākṛtir upadiṣṭā sarvam avarṇa-kūlaṁ grahīṣyati, tathevarṇākṛtis tathovarṇākṛtiḥ/ MB, Vol. I, Sec. I, p. 70.

24. See: evañ ca kṛtvā dharma-śāstram pravṛttam 'brāhmaṇo na hantavyaḥ,' 'surā na peye'ti, brāhmaṇa-mātraṁ ca na hanyate, surā-mātraṁ ca na pīyate/ yadi dravyam padārthaḥ syād, ekam brāhmaṇam ahatvā, ekāṁ ca surām apītvā anyatra kāma-cāraḥ syāt/ MB, Vol. I, Sec. II, p. 92.

25. See the Vārttikas: 1) hal-grahaṇeṣu ca, Vt 15 on the Śiva-sūtra 1, MB, Vol. I, Sec. I, p. 71, and 2) tadvac ca hal-grahaṇeṣu, Vt on P.1.1.69, MB, Vol. I, Sec. I, p. 375. On this Vt, Bhartṛhari comments: hal-grahaṇeṣu ca/ tatra grahaṇaka-śāstrasyāvyāpāraḥ, MB-D, p. 57. This statement of Bhartṛhari that P.1.1.69 does not apply to consonants needs some modification. P.1.1.69 does apply to /y/, /v/ and /l/, which are included in the shortform /a-Ṇ/. Only then these sounds can stand for /ỹ/, /ṽ/ and /l̃/. If P.1.1.69 were meant to apply only to vowels, Pāṇini could have used the shortform /a-C/ instead of /a-Ṇ/.

26. savarṇe'ṇ-grahaṇam aparibhāṣyam ākṛti-grahaṇāt, Vt on P.1.1.69, MB, Vol. I, Sec. I, p. 373.

27. Cardona (1968), p. 448.

28. See: "The Śiva-sūtras at the beginning of Pāṇini's grammar are sophisticated presentation of Sanskrit sounds, but not a complete list, because, e.g. /a/ stands not only for /a/, but also for /á/, /à/, /ā/, /ā́/, /ā̀/, /ā3/ etc., i.e. /a/ denotes the genus of /a/ sounds." Scharfe (1971), p. 7.

29. See: "It (i.e. /a/) stands for all its varieties 18 in number, Pat. avarṇākṛtir upadiṣṭā sarvam avarṇa-kulam grahīṣyati." Ghatage (1972), p. 158. Also see: "But there are some sounds lacking (in the Śiva-sūtras),

which cannot have been unknown to Pāṇini, first of all the long vowels /ā/, /ī/, /ū/,.... Of course, the long vowels were known to the great grammarian: as a matter of fact they already appear in 1.1.1. vṛddhir ādaic, or at least one of them, the long /ā/. And the introduction to the Mahābhāṣya tells us, that the long vowels are always, unless expressly otherwise stated, implied when mentioning short ones." Sköld (1926), p. 9. He also says: "Now, why do the long vowels not appear in the Śiva-sūtras? Already the Indian commentators explained this fact by stating, that in Pāṇini's work short vowels usually stand for the long ones also. And this opinion seems to have been unanimously accepted by Western scholars." Ibid., p. 21. These scholars seem to blur the distinction between the two procedures of savarṇa-grahaṇa and ākṛti-grahaṇa.

30. Biardeau (1964), p. 372.

31. aṇ-grahaṇaṁ kurvataḥ sūtra-kṛto nāyam pakṣo'bhipretaḥ, SKB, p. 36.

32. na tāvad vārttikaṁ dṛṣṭvā sūtra-kṛtaḥ pravṛttiḥ, SKB, p. 39.

33. atra...savarṇa-grahaṇaṁ, jāti-nirdeśo vā, LSS, pp. 104-5, and also: sūtra-matenāha-savarṇeti, bhāṣya-matenāha-jātīti, Cidasthimālā on LSS, p. 122.

34. tat-sūtre jāti-pakṣasyābhāvāc ca, Cidasthimālā on LSS, p. 104.

35. See the note: 23.

36. ākṛti-grahaṇāt tu siddham/ pratyāhāre'nuvṛtti-nirdeśe ca jātir eva codyate na vyaktiḥ/ vyakty-upādānaṁ tu yathā nālikera-dvīpa-nivāsina idam upadiśyate-ayam gaur eṣa tvayā na padā spraṣṭavya iti/ sa tam bālaṁ kṛṣṇaṁ kṛśaṁ copadiṣṭo vṛddhaṁ śabalaṁ sthūlam api na spṛśati/ MB-D, p. 57. Annambhaṭṭa tries to give some formal explanation of the perception of a universal like atva "/a/-ness" which is common to /a/, /ā/ and /ā3/: kevala-kaṇṭhyatve sati svaratvam atva-jāter vyañjakaṁ, tac ca dīrgha-plutayor api samānam/, Uddyotana on MB-P, MPV, p. 115.

37. aṣṭa-kṛtvo go-śabda uccarita iti vadanti/ nāṣṭau go-śabdā iti/ ...na hi te sadṛśa iti pratīyanti, kin tarhi sa evāyam iti/ ...naiṣa vinaṣṭaḥ yata enam punar upalabhāmahe/ "[The people] say that the word go 'cow' is uttered eight times, but they do not [say that] eight go-words [were uttered]. They do not think that [the second utterance] is similar [to the first], but [they understand the second] to be the same [as the first]. The [first sound] has not been destroyed, since we find the same sound [manifested] again." Śābara-bhāṣya on MS, Vol. I, Part I, p. 87-9. Also: saṁyoga-vibhāgā nairantaryeṇa kriyamāṇāḥ śabdam abhivyañjanto nāda-śabda-vācyāḥ/ tena nādasyaiṣā vṛddhir na śabdasya, "The conjunctions and disjunctions [of the air] which are continuously produced are called nādas 'physical sounds' which manifest the [real] sound. Therefore, this kind of prolonging etc. belongs to the physical sound and not to the real sound." Śābara-bhāṣya on MS, Vol. I, Part I, p. 84.

38. utpanno ga-kāro naṣṭo ga-kāra iti pratītyā varṇānām anityatvāt 'so'yam gakāra' iti pratyabhijñāyāḥ seyam dīpa-jvāletivat sājātyāvalambanatvāt, "The sounds are non-eternal, since there are cognitions that the sound /g/ is produced and that it has been destroyed. Therefore, the recognition of the type 'this is that /g/-sound' rests on [two sounds] belonging to the same universal. This is similar to the cognition 'this is the same flame of the lamp.'" Dīpikā on TS, p. 54, also: KM, p. 851.

39. katvādikaṁ tu dhvani-niṣṭhaṁ, dhvani-viśeṣa-vyaktayaḥ anantā janyāś ca, MB-P, Vol. I, Sec. I, p. 152.

40. iṣṭa-buddhy-arthaś ca varṇānām upadeśaḥ/ iṣṭān varṇān bhotsyāmahe iti/ na hy anupadiśya varṇān iṣṭā varṇāḥ śakyā vijñātum, MB, Vol. I, Sec. I, p. 60.

41. iṣṭa-buddy-arthaś ceti ced udāttānudātta-svaritā-nunāsika-dīrgha-plutānām apy upadeśaḥ, Vt, MB, Vol. I, Sec. I, p. 60.

42. ākṛty-upadeśāt siddham, Vt, avarṇākṛtir upadiṣṭā sarvam avarṇa-kulaṁ grahīṣyati/ tathevarṇākṛtiḥ/ tathovarṇākṛtiḥ/ MB, Vol. I, Sec. I, p. 60.

43. ākṛty-upadeśāt siddham iti cet saṁvṛtādīnām pratiṣedhaḥ, Vt., MB, Vol. I, Sec. I, p. 60. Patañjali mentions the following faults of the pronounciation of vowels: saṁvṛta "closed pronounciation," kala "pronouncing a sound in a wrong point of articulation," dhmāta "a short vowel appearing long, because of using too much air," eṇīkṛta "an unfinished sound, which leaves doubt about its exact nature," ambūkṛta "that which is heard as if not clearly coming out of the mouth," ardhaka "that which is heard with half of its regular quantity," grasta "unclear or suppressed at the root of the tongue," nirasta "harsh (Kaiyaṭa), fast (Nāgeśa)," pragīta "as if sung," upagīta "affected by the tones of the nearing sounds," kṣviṇṇa "trembling," romaśa "high sounding," avalambita "mixed with another sound," nirhata "too dry," sandaṣṭa "as if prolonged," virkīrṇa "extending into another sound." Patañjali says that consonants have different faults of pronounciation. The above explanations are based on the commentaries of Bhartṛhari, Kaiyaṭa and Nāgeśa [MB-D, p. 43; MB-P and MB-P-U, Vol. I, Sec. I, p. 60].

44. evaṁ tarhi aṣṭādaśadhā bhinnāṁ nivṛtta-kalādikām avarṇasya prattyāpattiṁ vakṣyāmi/ sā tarhi vaktavyā, MB, Vol. I, Sec. I, p. 61. Also: akārasya nidarśanārthatvāt sarva-varṇānāṁ śāstrānte prattyāpattir ity arthaḥ, MB-P, and tathā ca prattyāpatty-āśrayaṇe gauravam iti bhāvaḥ, MB-P-U, Vol. I, Sec. I, p. 61.

45. liṅgārthā tu prattyāpattiḥ, Vt; yady apy etad ucyate, athavaitarhy anekam anubandha-śataṁ noccāryam, it-saṁjñā ca na vaktavyā, lopaś ca na vaktavyaḥ/ yad anubandhaiḥ kriyate tat kalādibhiḥ kariṣyate/ MB, Vol. I, Sec. I, p. 61. This has been elaborated by the commentators by showing how new rules could be formulated by using the faulty varieties of pronounciation. "For example, in order to show that a root is one of those with which occur the endings called ātmanepada, Pāṇini lists (in the appendix called Dhātu-pāṭha) consonant-final roots with a final nasalized anudātta vowel, which by [A 1: upadeśe'j anunāsika it] is an it. Vowel-final roots are listed with a final /ṅ/ which is it by [A 2:

hal antyam P. 1. 3. 3]. Pāṇini then formulates a rule (1. 3. 12) anudātta-ṅita ātmanepadam 'The ātmanepada endings occur after roots marked with anudātta or /ṅ/.' Now for 1.3.12, a new rule would be formulated: kalād ātmanepadam 'After roots pronounced with kala....''' Cardona (1969), p. 10. For the original commentatorial discussions, see: MB-P and MB-P-U, Vol. I, Sec. I, p. 61.

46. siddhyaty evam apāṇinīyaṁ tu bhavati, MB, Vol. I, Sec. I, p. 61.

47. [siddhānta-bhāṣyam] athavā idaṁ tāvad ayaṁ praṣṭavyaḥ: kveme saṁvṛtādayaḥ śrūyerann iti? āgameṣu/ āgamāḥ śuddhāḥ paṭhyante/ vikāreṣu tarhi/ vikārāḥ śuddhāḥ paṭhyante/ pratyayeṣu tarhi/ pratyayāḥ śuddhāḥ paṭhyante/ dhātuṣu tarhi/ dhātavo'pi śuddhāḥ paṭhyante/ prātipadikeṣu tarhi/ prātipadikāny api śuddhāni paṭhyante/ yāni tarhy agrahaṇāni prātipadikāni/ eteṣām api svara-varṇānupūrvī-jñānārtham upadeśaḥ kartavyaḥ/śaśaḥ ṣaṣa iti mā bhūt/ mañcako mañjaka iti mā bhūt/ āgamāś ca vikārāś ca pratyayāḥ saha dhātubhiḥ/ uccāryante tatas teṣu neme prāptāḥ kalādayaḥ/ MB, Vol. I, Sec. I, p. 62. The commentary Ratnaprakāśa on the MB says that this reference to "unlisted nominals" also indirectly refers to unlisted verb-roots and affixes: dhātu-pratyayayor apaṭhitayor upalakṣaṇam idam, Ratnaprakāśa, MPV, p. 121.

48. K. V. Abhyankar (1969), pp. 51-2. Also: "This is not to suggest that Pāṇini's grammar be remolded to list all nominal bases of the language. As Kaiyaṭa says: nominal bases with uṇādi affixes and the nominal bases such as pṛṣodara 'spotted-belly' are recognized as correct because they are used by the instructed. Hence, all are included in the grammar." Cardona (1969), p. 11. However, I think that here Patañjali is trying to demonstrate how the follower of universal-mention is finally cornered. He is faced with listing all the nominals in order to exclude the faulty pronounciations covered by universal-mention. Patañjali's expression upadeśaḥ kartavyaḥ "listing would have to be made" is quite clear. Kātyāyana was probably not aware that his proposal would

lead to such consequences. Patañjali has lead the argument to its inevitable logical conclusion. In a different context, Patañjali clearly says that if one proposes to make a complete teaching of all unlisted and underived nominals, it would involve undesirable prolixity [yāny etāni prātipadikāny agrahaṇāni, teṣām etenābhyupāyenopadeśaś codyate, tad guru bhavati, MB, Vol. I, Sec. I, p. 65. Also: pratipada-pāṭhasyāśakyatvāt, MB-P, and sarvāṇy agrahaṇāni prātipadikāni vivṛtākāra-yuktāni paṭhanīyānīty arthaḥ/ ... tad guru bhavati, tasmād iti/ MB-P-U, Vol. I, Sec. I, p. 65]. Patañjali narrates a story that Bṛhaspati started teaching Indra, by listing all the words, but could not finish his instruction even within a thousand divine years. The sample of such a listing given by Patañjali is gaur aśvaḥ puruṣo hastī śakunir mṛgo brāhmaṇaḥ [MB, Vol. I, Sec. I, pp. 42-3]. This story indicates impossibility of listing all words. However, apparently there were some efforts in such a direction. Patañjali uses the term śabda-pārāyaṇa "a [full] listing of all words," and Bhartṛhari says that this is a conventionally established term and is the name of a work [MB-D, p. 17]. Interestingly enough, the word nāma-pārāyaṇa occurs in the first verse of the Kāśikā-vṛtti [Vol. I, p. 3]. The Nyāsa says that it is a work with which one can go to the end of nominal-stems, while the Pada-mañjari explains this to be a work where the words listed in Pāṇini's gaṇa-pāṭha are explained [KS-N and KS-P, Vol. I, p. 4]. In 1803, Colebrooke hinted at the possible existence of such voluminous texts ["On the Sanskrit and Prakrit Languages," Asiatic Researches 7, 1803; reprinted partially in Staal (1972), p. 42].

49. tasmān na śiṣṭa-prayogam antareṇaitad bhavati kalādi-nivṛttir upapanneti, MB-D, p. 46. Annambhaṭṭa says that the Bhāṣya passage upadeśaḥ kartavyaḥ "teaching of [unlisted nominals] should be made" implies that such a teaching has not been done by Paṇini, and if all such nominals were to be listed, it would be a case of pratipada-pāṭha "a word by word listing" of all usages. That certainly could not be a solution (parihārānupapattiḥ). Therefore, Kaiyaṭa gives another explanation, i.e. one

must rely on the usage of the Śiṣṭas. [nanu upadeśaḥ kartavya ity uktyā sūtrakāreṇānupadiṣṭatvāvagateḥ sarveṣām upadeśāṅgīkāre pratipada-pāṭha-prasaṅgāt parihārānupapattiḥ/ ata āha śiṣṭa-prayuktatveneti/, Uddyotana, MPV, p. 110.

50. yasya punar [varṇaika-deśā varṇa-grahaṇena] gṛhyante, ra ity eva tasya siddham, MB, Vol. I, Sec. I, p. 84.

51. lādeśe ca ṛkāra-grahaṇaṁ kartavyam/ kṛpo ro laḥ/ ṛkārasya ceti vaktavyam/ ihāpi yathā syāt/ kḷptaḥ, kḷptavān iti/ MB, Vol. I, Sec. I p. 84.

52. athavobhayataḥ sphoṭa-mātraṁ nirdiśyate/ ra-śruter la-śrutir bhavati, MB, Vol. I, Sec. I, p. 84.

53. athavā sphoṭa-mātram ity ākṛti-nirdeśo'yam ity uktam bhavati/ ...ākṛty-āśrayaṇasyedam prayojanam, antar-bhūtānantar-bhūtayo rephayoḥ pratipatty-artham, MB-D, p. 76.

54. sphoṭa-mātram iti jāti-sphoṭa ity arthaḥ/ tataś cāntar-bhūtānantarbhūta-repha-lakāra-vyakti-vyaṅgyaṁ sāmānyaṁ sthāny-ādeśa-bhāvenāśrīyate/ MB-P, Vol. I, Sec. I. p. 84. Kaiyaṭa's argument is upheld by the commentary Nārāyaṇīyam: anugata-buddhi-vedyatvāj jāteḥ, antargatatve api 'ra' ity-ādi-rūpa-sad-bhāvāj jāty-abhyupagamaḥ/...'ra' ity-ādy-anubhava-mātreṇa jātiṁ vastu-satīm asatīṁ vā svīkṛtya śabdānuśāsana-pravṛtter nāyam artho yuktyā bādhanīyaḥ/, Nārāyaṇīyam, MPV, p. 171.

55. On this passage, John Brough says: "This can be approximately rendered in modern terminology, 'In both the cases the phoneme is meant, i.e. "an allophone of the /r/-phoneme is replaced by an allophone of the /l/-phoneme."' It is of interest to observe that Patañjali realized that for the phonology of Sanskrit it is convenient to regard /r/ and /ṛ/ as belonging to the same phoneme." Brough (1951), p. 37. Perhaps, Brough is reading too much into Patañjali's statement. Patañjali does not even consider /r/ and /ṛ/ to be homogeneous (savarṇa) [rephoṣmaṇāṁ savarṇā na santi, MB, Vol. I, Sec. I, p. 88]. The consonantal /r/ is considered to be

īṣat-spṛṣṭa "with slight contact," while /r/ is vivṛta "open." Thus, they are not homogeneous with each other. The relationship is rather like part and whole. The phonemic identity is not between /r/ and /ṛ/, but rather between /r/ occurring independently, and /r/ as a part of /ṛ/. This has been clarified by S. D. Joshi (1967), p. 16. Thus, /r/ and /ṛ/ do not belong to the same sphoṭa, but /r/ inside and outside belongs to the same sphoṭa. Whitney thought that /r/ and /l/ were originally phonetically the same with /ṛ/ and /ḷ/. Whitney on TPr, p. 59. He also says: "Some consonants are capable of use as vowels. The consonants most often employed with vocalic quality are /l/, /n/ and /r/. A higher grade of vocalic capacity belongs to /r/ and /l/ than to any other of the sounds reckoned as consonantal, in virtue of the more open position assumed by the mouth organs in their utterance, which gives them a share in the sonorousness and continuability characteristic of the vowels." Whitney (1884), pp. 362-3. In contrast to Whitney's conception, Indian phoneticians considered /ṛ/ and /ḷ/ to be rather composite sounds, with vocalic and consonantal parts.

56. yat tu svatantrāsvatantra-sādhāraṇa-jāti-paratayā etad-bhāṣya-vyākhyānam iti tan na/ tādṛśa-jātau mānābhāvāt, MB-P-U, Vol. I, Sec. I, p. 85. This explanation of Nāgeśa agrees with that of the commentary Ratnaprakāśa on the MB. This commentary says that the Bhāṣya does not indicate the existence of a universal (jāti) common to /r/ inside and /r/ outside. The Bhāṣya refers only to the sound (dhvani-mātra) which is common to /r/ which is the locus of /r/-ness, i.e. independent /r/, and the /r/ sound in /ṛ/. [MPV, pp. 169-170.]

57. Cardona (1969), p. 7. Also: ṛti *ṛ vā, ḷti *ḷ vā ity ubhayatrāpi vidheyaṁ varṇa-dvayaṁ dvi-mātram, ādyasya madhye dvau rephau tayor ekā mātrā, abhito'j-bhakter aparā/ dvitīyasya tu madhye dvau la-kārau, śeṣam prāgvat, SK, p. 7.

58. yathākāro'-ṇtvād dīrgha-plutāv api gṛhṇāti, evam bhaktim api grahīṣyati iti/ ākṛti-grahaṇe vā sarvatrākṛter bhāvāt, MB-D, p. 76.

59. idaṁ varṇa-turīyam anyatrādṛṣṭaṁ kvacit, sāvarṇyam api nāsti/ na hy atra samudāya-prayatnād anyo'vayava-prayatno nāpi sthānam/ na tv eṣa varṇa-bhāgaḥ śaknoti jātim upavyañjayitum/ MB-D, pp. 76-7.

60. tasya bhāgasya sphuṭa-pratibhāsāviṣayatvāt jāty-abhivyakti-hetutvābhāvāc ceti bhāvaḥ, MB-P, Vol. I, Sec. I, p. 85.

61. atvādi-jātīty arthaḥ/ evaṁ ca na kenāpy acā tad-grahaṇam iti bhāvaḥ/ atra jāty-abhivyakti-hetutvābhāve sphuṭa-pratibhāsāviṣayatvaṁ hetuḥ/ MB-P-U, Vol. I, Sec. I, p. 85.

62. edaitor odautoś ca na mithas sāvarṇyam/ ai-au-c iti sūtrārambha-sāmarthyāt/ SK, p. 3.

63. ṛkāralkāroyoḥ savarṇa-vidhiḥ ity asya vārttikakāra-vākyatvāt sūtrakāreṇānāśritatvād atra ḷkāropadeśaḥ kṛtaḥ/ MB-P, Vol. I, Sec. I, p. 72. Also: vastutaḥ sūtra-mate ḷkārasya ṛkāreṇa sāvarṇyābhāvena grahaṇābhāvāt, Jyotsnā on LSS, p. 127. Thieme realizes the unhistoricity of Kātyāyana's statement and calls it "ein Postulat." Thieme (1935b), p. 171.

64. asya hi ḷkārasyālpīyāṁś caiva hi prayoga-viṣayaḥ/ yaś cāpi prayoga-viṣayaḥ so'pi kḷpisthasya/ MB, Vol. I, Sec. I, p. 72.

65. Cardona (1965b), pp. 310-1.

66. Thieme (1935a), p. 112.

67. ṛkāra-ḷkārayoḥ savarṇa-vidhiḥ, Vt, MB, Vol. I, Sec. I, p. 158.

68. Deshpande (1972), p. 230. On this vārttika, Devasthali comments: "This is a vārttika composed by Kātyāyana, who coming about two centuries after Pāṇini sought to remove the deficiencies in P's rules. It is not impossible that some deficiencies might have crept into the Aṣṭādhyāyī in spite of P; but what is also [and even more] likely is that the language which formed the basis of his rules, being a living language, underwent several modifications, thus making P's rules deficient in course of time." Devasthali (1969), p. 7. The general thesis of language

change being the basis of Kātyāyana's vārttikas is advocated by Devasthali elsewhere ["The Aim of the Vārttikas of Kātyāyana," Munshi Felicitation Volume, Bharatiya Vidya Bhavan, Bombay, 1962]. Whatever its independent merits, this thesis cannot be really applied to Kātyāyana's proposed homogeneity of /ṛ/ and /ḷ/. The reason is not historical linguistic change. Devasthali himself says that /ṛ/ and /ḷ/ are said to be homogeneous despite the fact that they have different points of articulations [Devasthali (1969), p. 7]. The only reason Kātyāyana needed this homogeneity is the change in linguistic attitude. Pāṇini looked at the use of /ḷ/ only in the object language, i.e. only in the forms of √kḷp, while Kātyāyana also tried to take care of grammatical expressions with /ḷ/, and imitation expressions etc. [For details, see: above, Sec. 3.12-13.] Siddheshwar Varma (1929, p. 7) believes that there was actually a real linguistic change, i.e. /ṛ/ and /ḷ/ came to be pronounced at the same point of articulation and hence their homogeneity was inevitable. He claims that the later Pāṇinīyas did not realize the contradiction in giving different points of articulation for /ṛ/ and /ḷ/, and also saying that they are homogeneous. Though certain traditions recorded in the Prātiśākhyas and Śikṣās did accept /ṛ/ and /ḷ/ to have the same point of articulation, there is no proof that this was universal and was accepted in the Pāṇinian tradition. Thieme has discussed and refuted Varma's views, Thieme (1935a), P. 108. Interestingly, we find a totally different view in Viśveśvarasūri's VSSN, p. 90. Viśveśvarasūri refers to the view of the RPr that /ṛ/ and /ḷ/ are both jihvā-mūlīyas "produced at the root of the tongue," and says that this naturally leads to their homogeneity. He refers [Ibid, pp. 90-1] to an important indication in Pāṇini's rule: ṛd-upadhāc cākḷpi-cṛteḥ P.3.1.110. This rule refers to roots with /ṛ/ as their pre-final sound, except kḷp and cṛt. This could be interpreted to suggest that Pāṇini did accept homogeneity of /ṛ/ and /ḷ/. However, it may also be argued the kḷp is the normal way of referring to the meta-root kṛp, and hence the rule need not imply homogeneity of /ṛ/ and /ḷ/.

69. yadi tarhi ṛkāra-grahaṇe ḷkāra-grahaṇaṁ sannihitam bhavati, ur aṇ ra-paraḥ, ḷkārasyāpi raparatvam prāpnoti, MB, Vol. I, Sec. I, p. 159.

70. ḷkārasya laparatvaṁ vakṣyāmi/ tac cāvaśyaṁ vaktavyam/ asatyāṁ savarṇa-saṁjñāyāṁ vidhy-artham/ tad eva satyāṁ repha-bādhanārtham bhaviṣyati/ ibid. The statement of Patañjali, namely "I shall prescribe (vakṣyāmi) [the substitute vowel] for /ḷ/ to be followed by /l/," is actually a totally new provision, which is not found in Pāṇini's rules. However, Bhartṛhari takes vakṣyāmi to be the same as vyākhyāsyāmi-"I shall [re-]interpret." Then Bhartṛhari introduces the notion of the shortform /rA/, formulated by declaring the /a/ in laṆ to be nasalized and hence being an it "marker." Thus, from /r/ in hayavaraṬ to /A/ in lAṆ, we get /r/ and /l/ in the shortform /rA/. [ḷkārasya laparatvaṁ vakṣyāmi vyākhyāsyāmīty arthaḥ/ raṭ laṇ iti lakāre yo'kāraḥ asau anunāsikaḥ pratijñāsyate/ ataḥ svenānyenetaraḥ it iti rephaḥ ādiḥ tan-madhyasya saṁjñā bhaviṣyati/ ur aṇ raparaḥ iti rephas tan-madhyaṁ lakāram pratyāyayati/ evam api ubhayoḥ ra-lau kasmān na bhavataḥ/ MB-D, p. 149.] This interpretation is followed by the later tradition up to Bhaṭṭoji Dīkṣita. Nāgeśa, however, criticizes this shortform, for being unhistorical. He points out that Pāṇini independently uses /r/ and /l/ in rules like P. 7.2.2 (ato lrāntasya). He also notes that if /a/ in laṆ were a meta-element, Pāṇini would have used the shortform /yA/ for yaṆ [LSS, pp. 24-6]. A. M. Ghatage has missed the point in his explanation: "A nasalized form (of /a/) is used by P as an it in Śiva-sūtra 6, taking advantage of the fact that Skt. uses no nasal vowels as distinctive." Ghatage (1972), p. 158. For the right historical view, see: K. M. K. Sharma (1968), p. 29. Also: Thieme (1935b), p. 200.

71. yadā ca ṛkāra-ḷkārayoḥ savarṇa-vidhir ākṛti-grahaṇāc ca grahaṇaka-śāstram pratyākhyāyate tadā saty api śruti-bhede ekākṛtitvam eva yathā hrasva-dīrghayor iti/ MB-D, p. 64.

72. vārttika-mate savarṇe'ṇ-grahaṇam aparibhāṣyam ākṛti-grahaṇād iti siddhāntād ṛkāre ḷkāra-sādhāraṇa-jāti-viraheṇākṛti-grahaṇāsambhavāt/ SKB, p. 39.

73. tasmād aṇ-grahaṇam pratyācakṣāṇasya tat-sthāne ṛgrahaṇam karttavyaṁ/ SKB, p. 40.

74. ārabdhe'pi vārttike ṛkāra-ḷkārayoḥ sāvarṇyasyānityatāṁ jñāpayituṁ karttavya eva ḷkāropadeśaḥ/ tena kḹ3pta-śikha ity atra guror anṛta iti plutaḥ siddhyati/ anyathā anṛta iti niṣedhaḥ syāt/ ṛkāreṇa ḷkāra-grahaṇāt/ SKB, p. 39.

75. ṛ-ḷ-varṇayoḥ sāvarṇyam ity anena samāna-jātitvasya evātideśena...na doṣaḥ/ LSS, p. 129. Also: sāvarṇya-vacanena samāna-jāty-atideśam eva vakṣyati, Cidasthimālā on LSS, p. 127.

76. samāno varṇo jātir ity arthaḥ/ varṇāśramācāravān ity ādau varṇa-padena jāter vyavahārāt iti bhāvaḥ, Sadāśivabhaṭṭīya on LSS, p. 129.

77. lakāra-rephayoś ca samāna-śrutitā kavi-sampradāye prasiddheti ṛtva-jātir ḷkāre'py asty eveti tatrāpi na doṣaḥ/ BSS, Vol. I, p. 66.

78. a-i-u-ṇ iti eṣu jāti-paro nirdeśaḥ/ ...tatra yady api hrasva-dīrgha-pluta-sādhāraṇī jātir asti tathāpi tasyā atra na nirdeśaḥ/ aṇ-udit-sūtre aṇ-grahaṇāt/ kin tu tad-vyāpyā hrasva-mātra-vṛttir api sā svīkriyate, vyavahāra-balāt/ tasyā atra nirdeśaḥ/ (ata evāsya cvau ity ādau aṇ-udit-sūtra-pravṛttiḥ)/ ata eva 'dīrghāṇām anantvena savarṇāgrāhakatvam' iti siddhāntaḥ saṅgacchate/ na caivam api dīrghādīnām actvaṁ na syāt/ iṣṭāpatteḥ/ aṇ-udit-sūtra-pravṛttyā, lakṣaṇayā vājādi-padais tad-upasthitiḥ śāstre ity agre nirūpayiṣyāmaḥ/ ...yad vā vyāpaka-jāti-nirdeśa evātra/ aṇ-udit-sūtra-prayojanaṁ tu vakṣyate/ BSS, Vol. I, pp. 2-3; also SKB, p. 37.

79. Actually, /a/ and /h/ do not have the same internal effort, according to the Pāṇinian tradition. The short /a/ is saṁvṛta "closed," while /h/ is vivṛta "open." In order to have homogeneity of closed /a/ with open /ā/, Pāṇini considers /a/ also to be open, within the system. The final rule of his system, P.8.4.68 (a a), reinstates

closed /a/ for open /a/ in the object language. There were other traditions, which considered short /a/ to be open even in the object language. For instance: Ṛktantra-vyākaraṇa (3.8) says: vivṛta-taram akāraikāraukāraṇām. The same view is adopted by Abhayanandin in his Jainendra-mahāvṛtti [see: Sec. 12.4.1] and by Hemacandra in his Bṛhad-vṛtti [see: Sec. 12.7.3]. For views of the Prātiśākhyas, see. n. 261. Also Rāmajñā Pāṇḍeya (1965), p. 160, says that the Gauḍas pronounce open short /a/. K. C. Chattopadhyaya (1974) argues that Pāṇini himself considered /a/ as an open sound. The later Pāṇinīyas, however, had a closed short /a/ under the influence of ancient Dravidian and they designed the final rule of the Aṣṭādhyāyī, P.8.4.68 (a a), to explain away the problem. I have dealt with Chattopadhyaya's argument in my article "Phonetics of Short /a/ in Sanskrit," which is due to appear in the Indo-Iranian Journal.

80. jāti-pakṣe doṣa eva na, itva-śatvādi-jāter bhedāt, Cidasthimālā on LSS, P. 122, and also Sadāśiva-bhaṭṭīyam on LSS, p. 122. Bhaṭṭoji is also aware of this implication: vārttika-mate tu hakārākārayor eka-jāty-anākrāntatvād eva nātiprasaṅgaḥ, SKB, p. 123.

81. V. N. Misra (1966), p. 105, gives a very confusing account of this rule. This view is discussed in Sec. 5.9.

82. udid-grahaṇaṁ karttavyam eva/ nahi vargyāṇām ekākṛti-yogo'sti, MB-P, Vol. I, Sec. I, p. 375. Also the commentaries on LSS, p. 129 and 130.

83. atredam bodhyam/ vyaktiḥ padārtho guṇāḥ bhedakāḥ ity abhimānenātra sūtre'ṇ-grahaṇam iti, LSS, p. 132.

84. upātto'pi viśeṣaḥ nāntarīyakatvāj jāti-prādhānya-vivakṣāyāṁ na vivakṣyata ity arthaḥ/ MPB, Vol. I, Sec. I, p. 60.

85. atra (jāti) pakṣe a-i-u-ṇ-sūtra-śeṣokta-bhāṣya-rītyā tapara-sūtrasya jāti-grahaṇa-prāpta-savarṇa-grahaṇa-niyāmakatvavad apratyaya ity asya yoga-vibhāgena tat-prāpta-savarṇa-grahaṇa-niṣedhakatvāt tyadādīnām aḥ ity ādau vidheye na doṣaḥ/ LSS, pp. 129-30. Also: jāti-

pakṣe'py anayaiva paribhāṣayā savarṇa-grahaṇaṁ vāraṇīyam, LSS, p. 125.

86. For various interpretations of P. 1. 1. 70, see: Sec. 8.5-6. Also: Deshpande (1972), pp. 213, 249-51.

87. tadvac ca tapara-karaṇam, Vt on the Śiva-sūtra 1, MB, Vol. I, Sec. I, p. 71. Also: Deshpande (1972), p. 213, fn. 19, and p. 231.

88. evaṁ ca kṛtvā taparāḥ kriyante/ ākṛti-grahaṇenāti-prasaktam iti kṛtvā/ MB, Vol, I, Sec. I, p. 71.

89. tulya-nyāyāj jāti-grahaṇa-prayuktātiprasaṅga-nivāraṇāya taparatvavat vidheye tyadādīnām aḥ ity ādau tad-vāraṇāya apratyaya iti etad iti bodhitam, MB-P-U, Vol. I, Sec. I, p. 71, and p. 376.

90. Deshpande (1972), p. 211, Fn. 15; and Cardona (1965a) p. 227.

91. See: Sec. 8.5-6.

92. aṣṭana ā vibhaktāv ity atra yatnādhikyād dīrgha-vyakti-samavetaṁ sāmānyaṁ gṛhyate, MB-P, Vol. I, Sec. I, p. 374. Also: atra tu ākāra-grahaṇe jāti-nirdeśād akāra-grahaṇam prāpnoti/ tat tu na prāpnoti, prayatna-bhedāt/ yathā pūrva-vayā brāhmaṇaḥ pratyuttheyaḥ/ plutasya tu prāpnoti/ tatrāpi parihāraḥ/ plutaś ca viṣaye smṛtaḥ iti/ MB-D, p. 57.

93. kecit tu dīrgha-ṣaḍ-bheda-vṛtty-ātva-jāter eva atva-vyāpyāyās tatra nirdeśa iti vadanti/ MB-P-U, Vol. I, Sec. I, p. 374.

94. Deshpande (1972), pp. 210-5, 238-42.

95. ibid, p. 239.

96. i ceti hrasvaḥ supaṭhaḥ, SK, p. 272.

97. See: n. 94.

98. SK, p. 2. Traditionally, the term ūṣman is applied to /ś/, /ṣ/, /s/ and /h/, in the Pāṇinian tradition. Sometimes Patañjali uses this term with reference to aspirate stops, but in the present context, the term stands only for /ś/, /ṣ/, /s/ and /h/ [yady api varga-dvitīya-

caturthayor api sthāne'ntaratama-sūtra-bhāṣyād ūṣmatvam, tathāpi 'vivṛtam ūṣmaṇām' ity atraita eva gṛhyante/ LSS, p. 117]. The TPr (i.9) says: pare ṣaḍ ūṣmāṇaḥ "The latter six sounds are ūṣmans," and Whitney comments on this as follows: "Namely, the three sibilants, /ś/, /ṣ/, and /s/, the jihvāmūlīya, χ, the upadhmānīya, ϕ, and the aspiration, /h/. As regards the sounds to which the name ūṣman 'flatus,' shall be given, the phonetic treatises are at great variance. The Vāj. Pr. (viii.22) limits the class to sibilants and /h/; the Ath. Pr. (see note to i.31) apparently adds the guttural and labial spirants and the more indistinct visarjanīya; the Rik Pr. (i.2), those and the anusvāra." Whitney on the TPr, p. 14.

99. vivṛtaṁ svaroṣmaṇām, Ṛktantra-vyākaraṇa 3.7; tatrābhyantaraḥ (21), saṁvṛtatvaṁ vivṛtatvaṁ spṛṣṭatvam īṣat-spṛṣṭatvaṁ ca (22), Cāndra-varṇa-sūtras, Śikṣā-sūtrāṇi, p. 25; (ūṣmaṇāṁ) karaṇa-madhyaṁ tu vivṛtam, TPr (ii.45); svarānusvāroṣmaṇām aspṛṣṭaṁ sthitam, RPr, Trayodaśa-paṭala 3; ūṣmaṇāṁ ca svarāṇāṁ ca vivṛtaṁ karaṇaṁ smṛtam, verse 29, Die Pāṇinīya-śiksā, p. 355; vivṛtaṁ ca svaroṣmaṇām, Māṇḍūkī-śikṣā, Śikṣā-saṁgraha, p. 469.

100. śaṣasahānāṁ yathā-kramam ikāra-ṛkāra-ḷkārākārāḥ sūtra-mate yady api tulyāsya-prayatnās tathāpi na savarṇāḥ/ nājjhalāv iti tan-niṣedhāt/ SKB, p. 118.

101. atra hi sūtre 'ac' iti ikāro gṛhyamāṇaḥ savarṇaṁ gṛhṇāti iti śakārasyāpi grahaṇam asti/ svātmani kriyā-virodhād asminn eva sūtre idam eva na vyāpriyata iti savarṇatva-niṣedha ikāra-śakārayoḥ nāsti/ ...asti ca pūrveṇa savarṇatvam ikāra-śakarayor iti bhāvaḥ/ MB-P, Vol. I, Sec. I, p. 160; also LSS, p. 122.

102. This problem does not arise with other vowels like /i/ or /u/. The sound /a/ is an /a-Ṇ/ sound and represents its homogeneous sounds. The sounds /ś/, /ṣ/ and /s/ could be perhaps represented by /i/, /ṛ/ and /ḷ/, but cannot represent them, since they are not /a-Ṇ/ sounds. Bhaṭṭoji mentions various problems which this would create. He says: tathā ca pūrva-pakṣa-vārttikam-ajjhaloḥ pratiṣedhe śakāra-pratiṣedho'jjhaltvāt iti/ atra śakāra-grahaṇaṁ śarām upalakṣaṇam/ kiñ ca avarṇasyā-

ṣṭādaśadhā bhinnasya parasparaṁ sāvarṇyaṁ na syāt/ tataś ca 'daṇḍāgram' ity ādau dīrgho na syāt/ tathā hi hakāreṇa grahaṇāt akāro hal, akṣu pāṭhāc ca ac/ SKB, p. 121.

103. ajjhaloḥ pratiṣedhe śakāra-pratiṣedho'jjhaltvāt, Vt. on P.1.1.10, MB, Vol. I, Sec. I, p. 160.

104. ac caiva hi śakāro hal ca/ kathaṁ tāvad actvam/ ikāraḥ savarṇa-grahaṇena śakāram api gṛhṇātīty evam actvam/ halṣu copadeśād dhaltvam/ BM, Vol. I, Sec. I, p. 160.

105. tatra savarṇa-lope doṣaḥ, Vt. on P.1.1.10, paraśśatāni karyāṇi/ jharo jhari savarṇe iti lopo na prāpnoti/ MB, Vol. I, Sec. I, p. 160.

106. siddham anactvāt, Vt. on P.1.1.10, MB, Vol. I, Sec. I, p. 160.

107. Apparently, Patañjali himself is not quite sure of the interpretation of this vārttika. He gives another alternative explanation of the sequence: siddham anactvāt, vākyāparisamāpter vā. In this second interpretation, he says: siddham etat/ katham/ anctvāt/ katham anactvam/ vākyāparisamāpter vā/ MB, Vol. I, Sec. I, p. 162. In this interpretation, both the vārttikas together form one solution, but as Patañjali himself notes, the word vā "or" becomes purposeless [asmin pakṣe vā ity etad asamarthitam bhavati, MB, Vol. I, Sec. I, p. 162].

108. siddham etat/ katham/ anactvāt/ katham anactvam/ 'spṛṣṭaṁ sparśanāṁ karaṇam'/ 'īṣat-spṛṣṭam antaḥ-sthānām'/ 'vivṛtam ūṣmaṇām,' īṣad ity anuvartate/ 'svarāṇāṁ ca' vivṛtam, īṣad iti nivṛttam/ MB, Vol. I, Sec. I, p. 160.

109. sūtra-pratyākhyāna-sādhāraṇam uktam/ prayatna-bhedād ajjhaloḥ savarṇa-saṁjñāyāḥ prāptir eva nāstīty arthaḥ/ MB-P, Vol. I, Sec. I, p. 161.

110. vastutas tūkta-rītyā (prayatna-bhedena) sūtram eva nārambhaṇīyam ity arthaḥ/ SKB, p. 121.

111. "AP 1.31 reads ūṣmaṇām vivṛtam ca, in which ca refers to īṣat of 1.30, hence the spirants are classed as īṣad-vivṛta." Cardona (1965a), p. 226. This interpretation

of the APr 1.31 clearly follows Patañjali. This, however, may not necessarily be the meaning of the original rule. See: Sec. 4.7.

112. *bhāṣyakārās tu 'nājjhalau' ity asya pratyākhyānāvasare ūṣmaṇāṁ svarāṇāṁ ceṣad-vivṛtatvaṁ vivṛtatvaṁ ceti vailakṣaṇyaṁ vakṣyanti*/ *SKB*, p. 117. Also: *sapta-prayatnā iti bhāṣya-rītyā*..., *Sadāśivabhaṭṭīya* on *LSS*, p. 92. *bhāṣyakāra-mate tu prayatna-bheda eveti vakṣyate*/ *SKB*, p. 118.

113. *bhāṣya-mate tu santu sapta-prayatnāḥ*, *LSS*, p. 103.

114. *svarāṇām ūṣmaṇāṁ caiva vivṛtaṁ karaṇaṁ smṛtam/ tebhyo'pi vivṛtāv eṅau tābhyām aicau tathaiva ca*/ *iti śikṣā-vākyāt vivṛtatara-vivṛtatamayoḥ pratītyā nājjhalāv iti sūtra-bhāṣyād ūṣmaṇām īṣad-vivṛtatvasya ca pratītyā*..., *LSS*, p. 103. The verse quoted by Nāgeśa is No. 29 in the Yajus Recension of the *Pāṇinīya-śikṣā* [See: *Die Pāṇinīya-śikṣā*, p. 355].

115. *tathā ca śikṣā-vivṛta-karaṇāḥ svarāḥ, tebhya e o vivṛtatarau, tābhyām ai au, tābhyām apy ākāraḥ, saṁvṛto'kāraḥ*/, *KS-P* and *KS-N*, Vol. I, p. 22. Also: *Śikṣā-sūtrāṇi*, pp. 3-4, 12, 25.

116. *avarṇasya tarhi aicoś ca savarṇa-saṁjñā prāpnoti*/ [*na*], *vivṛtatarāvarṇāv etau*/ *MB*, Vol. I, Sec. I, p. 155; also: *santu sapta-prayatnāḥ*/ *māstu ca nājjhalāv iti sūtram*/ *ata eva 'tulyāsye'ti sūtre bhāṣye avarṇasyaicāṁ ca sāvarṇyam āśaṅkya vivṛtataratvenaiva parihṛtam*/ *BSS*, Vol. I, p. 48.

117. *tadā* (*bhāṣya-mate*) *santu sapta-prayatnāḥ*/ *evaṁ ca edaitor odautoś ca na sāvarṇya-prasaktiḥ prayatna-bhedād ity alam*/ *BSS*, p. 48. Also: *MB-P-U*, Vol. I, Sec. I, p. 161.

118. *śaṣasahānāṁ yathā-kramam ikāra-ṛkāra-ḷkārākārāḥ sūtrakāra-mate tulyāsya-prayatnāḥ*/ *SKB*, p. 118.

119. *na ca 'nājjhalāv' iti nirdeśena bhāṣyokta-prayatna-bhedasya sūtrakārābhipretatvaṁ kalpyate iti vācyam*/ *BSR*, p. 12.

120. nājjhalāv iti sūtreṇa vivṛtatva-vyāpyānām eṣāṁ savarṇa-samjñānupayuktatva-bodhanam ity āśayāt/, LSS, p. 103. The commentary Viṣamapadavivṛti on LSS (p. 102) believes that P.1.1.10 is necessary even after accepting Patañjali's proposal of prayatna-bheda. It points out that the special variety /*ḷ/ is īṣat-spṛṣṭa "with slight contact" like the consonant /l/, and both have the same point of articulation, i.e. danta "teeth." For this reason, they would be mutually homogeneous. To avoid this, we have to take recourse to P.1.1.10. That /*ḷ/ is īṣat-spṛṣṭa is quite clear. It is also clear that this special variety /*ḷ/ is not homogeneous with /ḷ/ which is vivṛta "open." See: "...die beiden Laute [/*ṛ/ und /*ḷ/] nicht 'ac' heissen, wenn sie nicht ausdrücklich durch Hinzufügung einer Angabe so genannt werden. Sie sind also weder in den ŚS. [Śiva-sūtra] aufgeführt, noch den dort aufgeführten Lauten /ṛ/ und /ḷ/ 'gleichlautig.'" Thieme (1935b), p. 181. The view expressed by Viṣamapadavivṛti involves some element of anachronism. The sounds /*ṛ/ and /*ḷ/ are not mentioned by Pāṇini, but are introduced by Kātyāyana in his vārttikas ṛti *ṛ vā and ḷti *ḷ vā on P.6.1.101 (akaḥ savarṇe dīrghaḥ). It is quite possible that these sounds themselves are of a later date in Sanskrit usage. Again the commentatore are not sure if these sounds are vocalic. We could say that /*ḷ/ [i.e. əllə] is less vocalic than /ḷ/ [i.e. ələ] and is more vocalic than /l/.

121. bhāṣya-mate tu santu sapta-prayatnāḥ/ evaṁ caidaitoś ca na sāvarṇya-prasaktiḥ, prayatna-bhedād iti bodhyam/ nājjhalāv iti sūtram api prayatna-bheda-prāpta-sāvarṇyā-bhāvānuvādakaṁ sat tasyaiva bodhakam/ ata eva bhāṣye tan na vaktavyam iti noktam/ LSS, p. 103. Also: atra pakṣe nājjhalāv iti sūtram pratyākhyātam iti bhramaṁ nirācaṣṭe/ Cidasthimālā on LSS, p. 103. Madhukar Phatak (1972, pp. 146-7) says that even Pāṇini knew the subdivisions of vivṛta into īṣad-vivṛta etc., but he did not accept them in the context of the notion of homogeneity. Jagadīśa Citrācārya [Śikṣā-śāstram, p. 12] ascribes a fivefold division of internal efforts to Pāṇini including īṣad-vivṛta. These suggestions are groundless.

122. yadi tu sūtra-vṛttyādiṣu śraddhā-jāḍyam apahāya prayatna-bhedād evaitad-vyāvarttya-sāvarṇyānāṁ na sāvarṇyam ity ucyate, tadā santu sapta-prayatnāḥ, māstu ca nājjhalāv iti sūtram/ BSS. Vol. I, p. 48.

123. Kielhorn (1876b), p. 193.

124. Śikṣā-sūtrāṇi, pp. 3-4. Limaye (1974, pp. 57-8) refers to this passage in the Āpiśali-śikṣā, and says that Patañjali probably quotes from this Śikṣā. In support of his view, he quotes a passage from Vṛṣabhadeva's commentary on the Vākya-padīya which ascribes the above passage in Patañjali to a Śikṣākāra. B. A. van Nooten (1973, p. 409) thinks that Patañjali quotes from the Āpiśaliśikṣā, rather than the Śikṣā quoting Patañjali. However, I think that the Āpiśaliśikṣā in its present form is post-Patañjali. If he knew this text as we know it, he would have directly quoted this Śikṣā to show that spirants are īṣad-vivṛta "slightly open," instead of quoting the SCA and reinterpreting it. For more details on the chronology of the Āpiśaliśikṣā, see my article now in preparation for the Journal of the Oriental Institute, Baroda, "The Date of the Āpiśali-śikṣā-sūtras."

125. Thieme (1935a), p. 87, Fn. 2.

126. APr, p. 360. Also see: n. 111.

127. Die Pāṇinīya Śikṣā, pp. 355-6.

128. Ibid, p. 355.

129. īṣad-vivṛta-karaṇā ūṣmāṇaḥ/vivṛta-karaṇā vā/ Śikṣā-sūtrāṇi, p. 12.

130. īṣad-vivṛta-karaṇā ūṣmāṇaḥ/ Śikṣā-sūtrani, p. 3.

131. R. Pandeya (1965), p. 202.

132. VPr (W), pp. 118-9: ardha-spṛṣṭatāsya-prayatnā ūṣmāṇo'nusvāraś ca.

133. ūṣmāṇo'rdha-spṛśaḥ/ Yājñavalkya-śikṣā, Śikṣā-saṁgraha, p. 32.

134. ardha-spṛṣṭāś ca vijñeyā ūṣmāṇo varṇa-vedibhiḥ/, Varṇa-ratna-pradīpikā-śikṣā, Śikṣā-saṁgraha, p. 120.

135. S. C. Vasu (1891), Vol. I, pp. 62-3.

136. Ibid.

137. Ibid., p. 13.

138. See: Sec. 7.2.2.

139. S. D. Joshi (1969), p. 23. His footnote 127 on p. 23 says: "The principle of grahaṇa means that all vowels included in the pratyāhāra /aṆ/ stand for themselves and their corresponding homo-organic varieties also." This needs to be enlarged, since semi-vowels also represent their homogeneous varieties by P.1.1.69. Similarly, P.1.1.69 also says that sounds marked with /U/ stand for their homogeneous sounds.

140. Ibid., fn. 128.

141. Ibid., fn. 130. On the maxim grahaṇān-grahaṇe grahaṇābhāvaḥ, which is quoted by Kaiyaṭa, S. D. Joshi says: "The quotation is probably from the lost part of Bhartṛhari's Mahābhāṣya-dīpikā." It is actually found in MB-D, p. 174 (Swaminathan's edn.). Also see n. 161.

142. evaṁ ca hal iti sūtre lakārasya it-saṁjñāyāṁ satyām 'ādir antyena sahetā' iti hal-saṁjñā-siddhau 'hal antyam' iti sūtra-pravṛttiḥ; 'hal antyam' iti sūtreṇa hal-sūtre lakārasya it-saṁjñāyām 'ādir antyena sahetā' iti hal-saṁjñā-siddhiḥ/ ity evaṁ 'hal antyam,' 'ādir antyena' ity anayoḥ paraspara-sāpekṣatvena anyonyāśrayatvād abodhaḥ/ Bālamanoramā on SK (M), Vol. I, p. 5.

143. eka-śeṣa-nirdeśād vā, Vārttika 5 on P.1.1.3, MB, Vol. I, Sec. II, p. 130.

144. hal ca hal ca hal, hal-antyam it saṁjñam bhavati/ MB, Vol. I, Sec. II, p. 130.

145. hasya l hal/ hal ity ekaḥ ṣaṣṭhī-tatpuruṣaḥ/ dvitīyaḥ pratyāhāraḥ/ MB-P, Vol. I, Sec. II, p. 130.

146. tasmād vākya-dvayam apy anta-pada-ghaṭitam/ dvandvānte śrūyamāṇasyaiva pratyekaṁ sambandhāt/ tayoś ca tantreṇoccāraṇam bhāṣye iti hal-sūtrāntyam antyaṁ ca hal it ity eva bhāṣyārthaḥ/ ekaśeṣa-śabdena ca bhāṣye tantraṁ lakṣyate/ MB-P-U, Vol. I, Sec. I, p. 130.

147. hal antyam/ hal iti sūtre'ntyam it syāt/ ādir antyena sahetā/ antyenetā sahita ādir madhyagānāṁ svasya ca saṁjnā syāt/ / iti hal-saṁjñāyām/ hal-antyam/ upadeśe'ntyaṁ hal it syāt/, SK, p. 1.

148. yathā ac ca gheḥ ity ādau guṇa-darśanena ghi-śabdasyāpi ghi-saṁjñā-bodhyatvam/ LSR, p. 21.

149. nanv evaṁ 'tulyāsya-prayatnaṁ savarṇaṁ,' 'nājjhalāv' ity adāv 'akaḥ savarṇe dīrghaḥ' iti dīrgho'pi na pravartteteti cet, na, savarṇa-saṁjñādy-uttara-kāle pravarttamānasya dīrgha-śāstrasya daṇḍāḍhakādāv iva ihāpy apratibaddha-pravṛttikatvāt, uddeśyatāvacchedaka-rūpākrāntatvāviśeṣāt/...anyathā vyākaraṇa-śāstra-pariśīlana-vikalānāṁ kvāpi śābda-bodho na syāt/ tathā vaiyākaraṇānām api vyākaraṇa-sūtra-ghaṭaka-śabdeṣu vyākaraṇād eva sādhutva-bodhe tad-uttara-kāle ca vākyārthāvagatau ātmāśrayānyonyāśraya-cakrakāṇāṁ durvāratvāt iti dik/ SKB, p. 122.

150. yat tu varṇopadeśa-kāle'jādi-saṁjñānām aniṣpādāt. sandhir neti/ tan na/ varṇopadeśa it-saṁjñāyām ac-pratyāhāre ca jñāte, 'upendra' ity ādau taṭastha ivoddeśyatāvacchedakāvacchinne varṇopadeśādāv api pravṛtter āpādayituṁ śakyatvāt/ vākyāparisamāpti-nyāyasya tu nāyaṁ viṣayaḥ/ vākyārthāpratibandhakatvāt/ ...ata eva 'sarūpāṇām,' 'nājjhalāv' ity ādāv ekaśeṣa-dīrghādi siddhyati/ spaṣṭā ceyaṁ rītir 'bhute' iti sūtre tṛtīye bhāṣya-kaiyaṭayoḥ/ tatra hi 'bhūte ity adhikārā-śrayā niṣṭhā, bhūta-kriyā-viṣaya-niṣṭhā-vidhānāśrayo bhūtādhikāra' ity anyonyāśrayam āśaṅkya, 'bhūta-śabdo hi nityaḥ, śāstraṁ cānvākhyāna-mātram' ity āśritya samāhitam/ BSS, Vol. I, pp. 3-4. Patañjali discusses this question in detail. The affixes Kta and KtavatU, called niṣṭhā, are prescribed under the section bhūte "to signify past tense" [P.3.2.84]. Now the word bhūta itself is derived by applying the affix Kta to the root bhū. This involves an apparent interdependence. Unless we derive the word bhūta, there cannot be a prescription of the affix Kta, and unless this affix is prescribed, we cannot have the word bhūta. This is solved by saying that the word bhūta is actually nitya "eternal, existing in the usage," and the science of grammar only explains

the existing words. Also see: MB-P-U, Vol. I, Sec. I, p. 63.

151. Misra (1966), p. 105.

152. vākyāparisamāpter vā, Vārttika 4 on P. 1. 1. 10, MB, Vol. I, Sec. I, p. 161.

153. varṇānām upadeśas tāvat/ upadeśottara-kālet-saṁjñā/ it-saṁjñottara-kāla 'ādir antyena sahetā' iti pratyāhāraḥ/ pratyāhārottara-kālā savarṇa-saṁjñā/ savarṇa-saṁjñottara-kālam 'aṇudit savarṇasya cāpratyaya' iti savarṇa-grahaṇam/ etena sarveṇa samuditena vākyena anyatra savarṇānāṁ grahaṇam bhavati/ MB, Vol. I, Sec. I, p. 161.

154. anumānaṁ dvividhaṁ svārtham parārthaṁ ca/...yat tu svayaṁ dhūmād agnim anumāya para-pratipatty-artham pañcāvayavaṁ vākyam prayuṅkte, tat parārthānumānam/ yathā parvato vahnimān dhūmavattvāt/ yo yo dhūmavān sa vahnimān yathā mahānasaḥ/ tathā cāyam/ tasmāt tathā iti/ TS, p. 37.

155. tataḥ 'ādir antyena sahetā' iti pratyāhāra-siddhiḥ/ tato 'nājjhalāv' ity etad-vākyārtha-bodhaḥ/ tato'pavāda-viṣaya-parihāreṇa savarṇa-saṁjñā-niścaye sati grahaṇaka-śāstra-pravṛttiḥ/ na tv etat-sūtra-niṣpatti-samaye/ SKB, p. 121.

156. niṣedha-paryālocanaṁ vinā notsargasya vākyārtho lakṣye pravṛttiś ca/ 'kṅiti ce' ti sūtre niṣedha-sūtrāṇām paribhāṣātvāṅgīkāreṇaikavākyatāyā eva yuktatvāt/ nājjhalāv iti sūtrāt pūrvam ikārādiṣu saṁjñā-pravṛtti-samaye ajjhalor api pravṛttatvena bhuktavantam prati mā bhuṅkthāḥ iti vākyasyeva niṣedha-vākyasya vaiyarthyāpatteḥ/ BSS. Vol. I, p. 68.

157. tathā caitat-paryālocanottaraṁ savarṇa-padārtha-jñāne jāte'ṇudit ity asya vākyārtha-bodhaḥ/ vākyārtha-bodhe padārtha-jñānasya kāraṇatvāt/...vākyasya aparisamāptatvaṁ ca savarṇa-pada-vācya-nirṇayaṁ vinā savarṇa-grahaṇa-bodhanāsāmarthyam iti bodhyam/ BSS, Vol. I, p. 68.

158. itaḥ pūrvaṁ grahaṇaka-śāstram eva na niṣpannam iti kathaṁ na paryālocayeḥ/ SKB, p. 122; also: PM, p. 53.

159. a-i-u-ṇ, nājjhalāv ity ādau dīrghādīnāṁ na grahaṇam, tat-praṇayana-kāle tad-arthasyaiva ajñānena hrasvābhiprāyeṇaiva prayuktatvāt/ BSR, p. 13.

160. Thieme (1935b), p. 206.

161. iha tu nāsti grahaṇam 'aṇudit savarṇasya cāpratyaya' iti/ kiṁ kāraṇam? asmin grahaṇe apariniṣpannatvāt saṁjñā-saṁjñi-sambandhasya, grahaṇāṇ-grahaṇe grahaṇābhāvaḥ, grahaṇaka-śāstrasya anabhinirvṛttatvāt, grahaṇāntarasya cābhāvāt, svātmani ca kriyā-virodhāt/ tatra hi aṇ-grahaṇe grahaṇaka-śāstram anabhinirvṛttam, kriyamāṇatvāt saṁjñā-saṁjñi-sambandhasyà/ grahaṇāntaraṁ ca nāsti/ svātmani ca kriyā viruddhyate/ yathā ghaṭo nātmānaṁ śaknoti spraṣṭum/ MB-D, pp. 174-5 (Swaminathan's edn.).

162. īṣad ity asyānanuvṛttiṁ samāna-prayatnatāṁ ca svīkṛtya sūtrārambha-pakṣe'py āha-vākyāparisamāpter veti/ SKB, p. 121.

163. ākārasya tapara-karaṇaṁ savarṇārtham, bhedakatvāt svarasya, Vārttikas 13-4 on P.1.1.1, MB, Vol. I, Sec. I, p. 113.

164. abhedakā guṇā ity eva nyāyyam/ kuta etat/ yad ayam asthi-dadhi-sakthy-akṣṇām anaṅ udātta ity udātta-grahaṇaṁ karoti/ yadi bhedakā guṇāḥ syuḥ, udāttam evoccārayet/ MB, Vol. I, Sec. I, p. 113.

165. asandehārthas tarhi takāraḥ/ MB, Vol. I, Sec. I, p. 114.

166. aṇ savarṇasyeti svarānunāsikya-kāla-bhedāt, Vārttika 1 on P.1.1.69, MB, Vol. I, Sec. I, p.

167. taduktaṁ vārttika-kāreṇa-ākārādīnāṁ tapara-karaṇaṁ savarṇārtham, bhedakatvāt svarasya iti/ aṇ savarṇasyeti svarānunāsikya-kāla-bhedād iti uktavato bhedakatvam evābhipretam/ sūtrakārasya ca savarṇe'ṇ-grahaṇāt... bhedakatvam apy astīty anumīyate/, MB-D, p. 155.

168. atredam bodhyam/ vyaktiḥ padārtho guṇāḥ bhedakā ity abhimānenātra sūtre'ṇ-grahaṇam iti/ LSS, p. 132.

169. aṇudit-sūtre'ṇ-grahaṇād anityeyam iti dhyeyam/ Paribhāṣā-vṛtti by Nīlakaṇṭha Dīkṣita, PBS, p. 312.

170. abhedakā udāttādaya iti siddhāntasya ca te savarṇa-saṁjñā-bhedakatvena na vivakṣitā ity arthaḥ/ BSS, Vol. I, p. 47.

171. See: n. 19.

172. tatrānuvṛtti-nirdeśe savarṇāgrahaṇam anaṇtvāt, Vārttika, MB, Vol. I, Sec. I, p. 66.

173. ekatvād akārasya siddham, Vārttika, MB, Vol. I, Sec. I, p. 66.

174. ākṛti-grahaṇāt siddham, Vārttika, MB, Vol. I, Sec. I, p. 70.

175. rūpa-sāmānyād vā, Vārttika, MB, Vol. I, Sec. I, p. 71.

176. nanu ca savarṇa-grahaṇenātiprasaktam iti kṛtvā taparāḥ kriyeran/ ... pratyākhyāyate tat-'savarṇe'ṇ-grahaṇam aparibhāṣyam, ākṛti-grahaṇāt' iti/ MB, Vol. I, Sec. I, p. 71.

177. eko'yam akāro yaś cākṣara-samāmnāye, yaś cānuvṛttau, yaś ca dhātv-ādi-sthaḥ/ MB, Vol. I, Sec. I, p. 66.

178. ekaivākāra-vyaktir udāttādi-pratibhāsas tu vyañjaka-dhvani-kṛtaḥ/ MB-P, Vol. I, Sec. I, p. 66.

179. yadi punar ime varṇāḥ-ādityavat syuḥ, Vt. --tad yathādityaḥ anekādhikaraṇastho yugapad deśa-pṛthaktveṣu upalabhyate/ MB, Vol. I, Sec. I, p. 66. punar apy ekatva-nityatve sādhayati/ MB-P-U, Vol. I, Sec. I, p. 70. Compare: ādityavad yaugapadyam, MS 1.1.15, and yat tv eka-deśasya sato nānā-deśeṣu yugapad darśanam anupapannam iti/ ādityam paśya devānām-priya/ ekaḥ sann aneka-deśāvasthita iva lakṣyate/ Śabara on MS, Vol. I, Pt. I, p. 80. Also: Biardeau (1964), p. 178 ff.

180. Viśveśvarasūri clearly says: tasmād aṣṭādaśaivākāra-vyaktayo nityāḥ, VSSN, p. 83. He has a detailed discussion of the Nyāya and Mīmāṁsā views on this point [ibid. pp. 77 ff.].

181. kāryatve nityatāyāṁ vā kecid ekatva-vādinaḥ/ kāryatve nityatāyāṁ vā kecin nānātva-vādinaḥ// VP, I. 70, P. 7. The commentary Ratnaprakāśa on the MB says that those who consider that there is only one sound individual must

accept sounds to be eternal, and those who consider that there are many sound individuals must accept that sounds are non-eternal. Those who accept that there are many sound individuals and yet accept that sounds are eternal have not properly understood the meaning of the Bhāṣya. [eka-vyakti-vādinām mate hi varṇānāṁ nityatāvaśyābhyupeyā/ aneka-vyakti-vādi-mate tv anityataiveti/ ...evaṁ cāneka-vyaktikatva-pakṣe'pi varṇānāṁ nityatvaṁ ye'ṅgīkurvanti te tv atratya-bhāṣya-sva-rasānabhijñā bhrāntā eveti spaṣṭam eva sudhiyām/ Ratnaprakāśa, MPV, p. 132.]

182. vyakti-pakṣe grahaṇaka-śāstrārambhāt/ MB-P, Vol. I, Sec. I, p. 63; also: vyaktiḥ padārtho guṇā bhedakāḥ ity abhimānenātra sūtre'ṇ-grahaṇam/ LSS, p. 132.

183. ekā avarṇa-vyaktir iti pakṣe tu yady api siddhyati/ MB-P-U, Vol. I, Sec. I, p. 373.

184. ānya-bhāvyaṁ tu kāla-śabda-vyavāyāt and yugapac ca deśa-pṛthaktva-darśanāt, Vārttikas, MB, Vol. I, Sec. I, p. 69.

185. ānya-bhāvyaṁ tv akārasya kāla-śabda-vyavāyāt/ ... kāla-vyavāyāt-daṇḍa agram/ śabda-vyavāyāt-daṇḍaḥ/ na caikasyātmano vyavāyena bhavitavyam/ bhavati cet, bhavaty ānya-bhāvyam akārasya/...yugapac ca deśa-pṛthaktva-darśānān manyāmahe-ānya-bhāvyam akārasyeti/ yad ayaṁ yugapac ca deśa-pṛthaktveṣūpalabhyate/ aśvaḥ, arkaḥ, arthaḥ iti/ na hy eko devadatto yugapat srughne ca bhavati madhurāyāṁ ca/ MB, Vol. I, Sec. I, p. 68.

186. tad yathā tān eva śāṭakān ācchādayāmaḥ, ye mathurāyāṁ, tān eva śālīn bhuñjmahe, ye magadheṣu tad evedam bhavataḥ kārṣāpaṇaṁ yan mathurāyāṁ gṛhītam, anyasmiṁś cānyasmiṁś ca rūpa-sāmānyāt tad evedam iti bhavati/ evam ihāpi rūpa-sāmānyāt siddham/ MB, Vol. I, Sec. I, p. 71. Referring to this passage, the commentary Ratnaprakāśa says that similarity (sādṛśya) in this context has to be accepted in a specific sense: there should be difference of two individuals with identity of all properties. [tatra sādṛśyaṁ sarva-dharma-sāmye sati vyakti-bheda-prayuktaṁ grāhyam, Ratnaprakāśa, MPV, p. 121.]

187. rūpa-sāmānyād vā/ katham ayam parihāraḥ/ tatra kecid varṇayanti/ yady apy ākṛtir naiva syād evam api na doṣaḥ/ yathā kārṣāpaṇādiṣv asatyāṁ jātau bhavatas tāvan mathurāyāṁ kārṣāpaṇam asty atha cārtha-vastv eva/ MB-D, p. 58.

188. siddhaṁ tv avasthitā varṇā vaktuś cirācira-vacanād vṛttayo viśiṣyante, Vārttika on P.1.1.70.

189. See: n. 166.

190. See: n. 188.

191. hrasva-dīrgha-plutās tu svata eva bhinnā bhinnair dhvanibhir abhivyajyanta iti teṣāṁ kāla-bhedaḥ/ MB-P, Vol. I, Sec. I, p. 378. Nāgeśa totally reinterprets Kaiyaṭa: kaiyaṭe hrasva-dīrgha-plutās tu svata eva bhinnā ity asya vyañjaka-bhedenāropita-bhedā eva bhinnair dhvanibhir vyajyanta ity arthaḥ/ MB-P-U, Vol., Vol. I, Sec. I, p. 379. This is not true to Kaiyaṭa's intention.

192. varṇāntaratvam evāhuḥ kecid dīrgha-plutādiṣu, Kumārila's Śloka-vārttika, Sphoṭa-vāda section, verse 45.

193. svabhāva-bhedān nityatve hrasva-dīrgha-plutādiṣu/ prākṛtasya dhvaneḥ kālaḥ śabdasyety upacaryate// śabdasyordhvam abhivyakter vṛtti-bhedaṁ tu vaikṛtāḥ/ dhvanayas samupohante śabdātmā tair na bhidyate// VP, I.76-77. See: "Whereas length in terms of the time required for utterance (duration or quantity) is a phonological parameter according to some modern linguists, the parameter of temporal length is not applied by the Pāṇinians in determining the varṇas. In other words, the former may hold that the difference between /u/, /ū/ and /ū̄/ ...is phonemic in Sanskrit, for a variation in meaning results when one is substituted for the other in some minimal pairs; for example, pura 'city' and pūra 'flood.' But a Pāṇinian does not hold that /u/, /ū/ and /ū̄/ are three distinct varṇas of the Sanskrit language; he reduces all these forms to a sort of common-factor form in his list of the varṇas and sees two different realizations of one varṇa in pura and pūra. Thus, he attributes the difference in temporal length to

the sound-substance rather than to the entity which the sound-substance manifests." Aklujkar (1970), p. 10. This needs to be modified slightly. Pāṇini and Kātyāyana considered length etc. to be distinctive features [see: Sec. 6.5-8 and Sec. 6.12 above]. The Pāṇinīya-śikṣā [verse 3] says: triṣaṣṭiś catuḥṣaṣṭir vā varṇāś śambhumate matāḥ "In the view of Śiva, there are sixty-three or sixty-four varṇas 'sounds.'" Here, we have to count short and long vowels as separate varṇas. Even in the Prātiśākhyas, we find short and long vowels listed separately. At the same time, there exists a higher-level notion of varṇa "sound-class," which is seen in the affixation of -varṇa to short vowels to include long varieties. However, this class-notion is not contradictory to short and long vowels being phonemically distinct. The higher notion of varṇa, or the notions of savarṇa-grahaṇa or Kātyāyana's varṇākṛti are all supra-phonemic notions. They are rather convenient ways of grouping sounds which are phonemically distinct from each other. These notions are in the background of Bhartṛhari's notion of sphoṭa, which also stands on a supra-phonemic level. Bhartṛhari himself considered features of length etc. to be phonemically distinctive, though they were not distinctive at the supra-phonemic level of sphoṭa [see: Sec. 6.13].

194. Deshpande (1972), pp. 226-7.

195. Ibid., p. 233.

196. Ibid., p. 239.

197. Thieme (1958), p. 33.

198. Ibid.

199. agṛhīta-savarṇānām eva nājjhalāv iti niṣedha iti sthitam/ SKB, p. 123. Viśveśvarasūri [VSSN, p. 242] refers to a difference of opinion between Kaiyaṭa and Bhaṭṭoji Dīkṣita. Kaiyaṭa says that P.1.1.10 is needed to avoid undesired homogeneity between /a/ and /h/, and /i/ and /ś/. Bhaṭṭoji adds to this /ṛ/ and /ṣ/, and /ḷ/ and /s/. These two cases are not mentioned by Kaiyaṭa. Viśveśvarasūri says the Kaiyaṭa accepted the RPr view

that /ṛ/ and /ḷ/ are both jihvāmūlīya "produced at the root of the tongue," and hence they cannot be homogeneous with /ṣ/ and /s/, which are cerebral and dental respectively. Viśveśvarasūri believes that the same view was shared by Pāṇini and Kātyāyana. He also points out [VSSN, p. 244] that if P.1.1.69 were to apply to P.1.1.10, different varieties of /a/ will not be homogeneous with each other.

200. evam īkāro'py atrekāreṇa na gṛhyata iti īkāra-śakārayoḥ savarṇatvam asti/ MB-P, Vol. I, Sec. I, p. 161.

201. yad etad 'akaḥ savarṇe dīrgha' iti pratyāhāra-grahaṇaṁ, tatrekāra īkāraṁ gṛhṇāti, śakāraṁ na gṛhṇāti/ MB, Vol. I, Sec. I, p. 161.

202. atra ca na īkaro gṛhīto nāpi śakāra iti ikāra-śakārayoḥ pratiṣiddhā savarṇa-saṁjñā, īkāra-śakārayos tulyatvāt sāvarṇyam, iti kumārī śete iti sāvarṇya-kāryam ekādeśaḥ prāpnoti/ aj-adhikārān nivartate/ MB-D, p. 153.

203. MB-P, Vol. I, Sec. I, p. 161; KS, Vol. Iv, p. 571; SKB, p. 123; Rūpāvatāra, Pt. I, p. 11; Prakriyā-Kaumudī, Pt. I, pp. 67-8; SK, p. 7.

204. yadā tūṣmaṇām īṣad-vivṛtatvam āśritya 'nājjhalāv' iti sūtram pratyākhyāyate, tadeha 'aci' iti nānuvartanīyam/ PM, p. 173. Also: BSS, Vol. I, p. 205.

205. katham punar idam pratyudāharaṇam upapadyate, yāvatā 'aṇudit savarṇasya cāpratyayaḥ' ity atra hakāreṇa ākāro gṛhyata iti/ asti hy ākārasya hakāreṇa saha savarṇatvaṁ, tulya-sthāna-prayatnatvāt/ sthānam asti hy anayos tulyam iti 'akuhavisarjanīyāḥ kaṇṭhyāḥ' iti/ prayatno'pi tulyaḥ-'vivṛtaṁ karaṇam ūṣmaṇāṁ svarāṇāṁ ca' iti/ tasmāt saty apīṅkor iti prāpnoty eva mūrdhanyaḥ, 'nājjhalāv' iti savarṇa-saṁjñā-[a] -pratiṣedhād iti cet, naiṣa doṣaḥ/ yad ayaṁ 'vayasyāsu mūrdhno matup' ity atrākārād uttarasya sakārasya mūrdhanyam akṛtvā nirdeśaṁ karoti, tato'vasīyate hakāro gṛhyamāṇo nākāraṁ grāhayati; anyathā 'vayasyāsu' iti nirdeśaṁ na kuryāt/ KS-N, Vol. 6, p. 544.

206. yathā...īkāra-śakārayoḥ sāvarṇyam apratiṣiddhaṁ, tathā ākāra-hakārayor api/ tataḥ kim? hakāreṇākārasya grahaṇāt ṣatva-prasaṅgaḥ? naiṣa doṣaḥ, hakāro vivṛtaḥ, ākāro vivṛtataraḥ/ ...evaṁ ca kṛtvā 'iṣṭakāsu,' 'vayasyāsu' ity ādayo nirdeśā upapadyante/ KS-P, Vol. 6, p. 544.

207. evaṁ sthite 'mālāsu' ity ādau ṣatvaṁ na syāt/ hakāreṇākāra-grahaṇe sati 'gaurīṣu' ity ādivat iṇaḥ paratvānapāyāt/ kiñ ca 'viśvapābhiḥ' ity atra 'ho ḍhaḥ' iti ḍhatvaṁ syāt/ 'vāg āśīḥ' ity atra 'jhayo ho'nyatarasyām' iti ākārasya ghakāraḥ syāt/ 'gāsīdhvam' ity atra 'iṇaḥ ṣīdhvam' iti mūrdhanyādeśaḥ syāt/ 'dāsīṣṭa' ity ādau 'dāder dhātor ghaḥ' iti ghatvam syāt/ 'rāma āyāti' ity ādau 'haśi ca' ity utvaṁ syāt/ 'devā āyānti' ity ādau 'hali sarveṣām' iti nityo yalopaḥ syāt/ 'cākhāyitā' ity ādau 'yasya halaḥ' iti yalopaḥ syāt/ 'śyenāyitā' ity ādau 'kyasya vibhāṣā' iti lopas syāt/ 'niccāyya' ity atra 'halo yamāṁ yami lopaḥ' iti yalopaś ca syāt iti bahūpaplava-prasaṅgaḥ/ SKB, p. 123.

208. yiyā3so ity ādau 'guror anṛtaḥ' iti plutād ākārāt parasya sanaḥ ṣatvam/ SKB, pp. 123-4. Also: PM, p. 53.

209. atrocyate-ākāro na hakārasya savarṇaḥ 'tato'py ākāraḥ' ity a-i-u-ṇ-sūtrodāhṛta-śikṣā-rītyā bhinna-prayatnatvāt/ 'savarṇe'ṇ-grahaṇam aparibhāṣyam ākṛti-grahaṇāt' iti vārttika-mate tu hakārākārayor eka-jāty-anākrāntatvād eva nātiprasaṅgaḥ/ yad vā ākāra-sahitaḥ ac āc, sa ca hal ca ājjhalāv iti sūtre ākara-praśleṣo vyākhyeyaḥ/ tenākārasyācāṁ ca halbhiḥ saha sāvarṇyaṁ niṣidhyate/ ākāra-praśleṣe liṅgaṁ tu 'kāla-samaya-velāsu tumun' ity ādi-nirdeśāḥ/ atra pakṣe āś ca ā3ś ceti dvandvena savarṇa-dīrgheṇa ca 'nājjhalāv' iti sūtre dīrghāt paraḥ pluto'pi nirdiṣṭa iti vyākhyeyam/ tena 'yiyā3so' ity ādau 'guror anṛtaḥ' iti plutād ākārāt parasya sanaḥ ṣatvaṁ nety avadheyam/ bhāṣya-mate tūṣmaṇām īṣad-vivṛtā-bhyupagamena sāvarṇya-prasaktir eva nāstīti sūtra-pratyākhyānāt sakalam anāvilam/ SKB, pp. 123-4; also PM, p. 153.

210. ākāra-praśleṣe liṅgaṁ tu 'kāla-samaya-velāsu tumun' ity ādi-nirdeśāḥ/ SKB, pp. 123-4; also PM, p. 52.

This device of inserting a sound in the rule to yield a new interpretation is not unfamiliar in the Pāṇinian tradition. Kielhorn comments: "A long or even a short vowel often results from the coalition of two or more vowels. How this simple fact may be turned to account in grammatical discussions, may be seen from the following examples. In Vol. I. p. 501, Kātyāyana states that the single vowel /ā/ (ḍā), which by P.II.4.85 is substituted in the Periphrastic Future for the ordinary personal terminations ti and ta, takes place of the whole original termination (and not merely, according to P.I.1.52, of their final letters), because /ā/ may be regarded as a combination of the two vowels /ā/-/ā/; and that for this reason Pāṇini is justified in not attaching the Anubandha /ś/ to the substitute ḍā (compare P.I.1.55). According to Patañjali, Pāṇini might similarly have omitted the Anubandha /ś/ of the term aś in P.II.4.32 (Vol. I, p. 481), and of the term aś in P.VII.1.27 (Vol. III, p. 251), because even (short) /a/ may be regarded as a combination of /a/-/a/. According to Patañjali, again, loka- in P.II.3.69 may be regarded as the result of the combination /la/-/u/-/uka/-, and no additional rule is required to teach that words like cikīrṣu, which are formed with /u/, are not construed with the genitive case (Vol. I, p. 469)." Kielhorn (1887), p. 248. Kielhorn also rightly expresses his doubts about the validity of such interpretations [Kielhorn (1887), p. 245].

211. ukta-nirdeśād eva sāvarṇyābhāvasya kalpane tu ānumānika-vacana-kalpanāpātaḥ/ pada-vibhāga-mātra-tātparya-kalpane tu na kiñcid gauravam/ BSR, p. 52. Also: LSR, pp. 52-3. Nārāyaṇabhaṭṭa in his Prakriyā-sarvasva accepts that Pāṇini's usages are sufficient to avoid homogeneity of /ā/ and /h/, and there is no need to reinterpret P.1.1.10. [nājjhalau ity atra dīrgha-haloḥ sāvarṇyāniṣedhāt ākārasya hakāreṇa savarṇa-grahāt iṇtvena 'somapāsu' 'ramāsu' ity ādau ṣatvaṁ prāptaṁ 'vayasyāsu mūrdhno matup' iti nirdeśān na syāt/ Prakriyā-sarvasva, Pt. IV, p. 150: also: S. Venkata Subromonia (1972), p. 102.] This is similar to Jinendrabuddhi's view. See: n. 205.

212. rephosmaṇāṁ savarṇā na santi/ MB, Vol. I, Sec. I, p. 88. Limaye (1974, p. 46) considers this to be a quotation from the Āpiśali-śikṣā. He considers several lines from the MB as being quotations from this text [ibid., pp. 56-8].

213. Abhyankar (1969), p. 100.

214. vṛttau bhāṣye tathā dhātu-nāma-pārāyaṇādiṣu/ viprakīrṇasya tantrasya kriyate sāra-saṁgrahaḥ// KS, Vol. I, p. 3.

215. "...the compilers of the Kāśikā have diligently used that grammar (i.e. Cāndra-vyākaraṇa), although they never mention it." Kielhorn, "The Chandra-Vyākaraṇa and the Kāśikā-vṛitti," The Indian Antiquary, June, 1886, p. 184.

216. Quoted in Kielhorn (1891), p. 107.

217. S. C. Vasu (1891), Vol. I, p. 13.

218. Renou (1966), Vol. I, p. 5.

219. Böhtlingk (1887), p. 3.

220. On the history of the interpretation of halantyam (P.1.3.3), see: Thieme (1957a), pp. 51-3.

221. [A]: P.1.2.45 (arthavad adhātur apratyayaḥ prātipadikam), P.8.3.41 (idudupadhasya cāpratyayasya).
[B]: 1) apratyaya iti cet tib-ekādeśe, Vt. 13 on P.1.2.45.
2) ciṇo luki ta-grahaṇānarthakyaṁ saṁghātasyāpratyayatvāt, Vt. 1 on P.6.4.104.
3) lumati pratyaya-grahaṇam apratyaya-saṁjñāpratiṣedhārtham, Vt. 1 on P.1.1.61.
4) yathāgṛhītasyādeśa-vacanād apratyayasthe siddham, Vt. 4 on P.6.1.13.
5) mamaka-narakayor upasaṁkhyānam apratyayasthatvāt, Vt. 4 on P.7.3.44.

222. Deshpande (1972), 1p. 237-8 and 242-3.

223. KS, Vol. 1, p. 244. As an example, KS cites the affixes /u/ and /a/ taught by P.3.2.168 and P.3.3.102. But in other places, it again seems to accept the

Maxim [1], see: KS, Vol. 5, p. 631.

224. Renou (1966), Vol. I, p. 21.

225. Deshpande 91972), pp. 224-5 and 242-3.

226. Pāṇini's rules do not allow a substitute sound to be given with both the markers, i.e. /Ś/ and /T/. The marker /Ś/ with a substitute shows that the unit with /Ś/ replaces the whole substituendum and not just the final sound [i.e. P.1.1.55 (anekāl-śit sarvasya)]. This obviously means that with reference to substitutes marked with /Ś/, the rule P.1.1.50 (sthāne'ntaratamaḥ) does not apply and the substitute as given will be effected. Therefore, Patañjali's argument concerning P.2.3.3 (idama iś) is a weak argument.

227. Deshpande (1972), pp. 237-8, 242-4.

228. Ibid., pp. 208-210.

229. 1) P.8.4.66 (ur at), all /ṛ/ > short /a/.
2) P.7.4.95 (at smṛ-dṝ...), /ṝ/ (in dṝ) > short /a/.
3) P.1.2.17 (sthā-ghvor ic ca), /ā/ > short /i/.
4) P.6.4.34 (śāsa id aṅ-haloḥ), /ā/ > short /i/.
5) P.1.2.50 (id goṇyāḥ), /ī/ > short /i/.
6) P.6.4.114 (id daridrasya), /ā/ > short /i/.
7) P.7.1.100 (ṝta id dhātoḥ), /ṝ/ > short /i/.
8) P.7.4.40 (dyati-syati-mā-sthām it ti kiti), /ā/ > short /i/.
9) P.7.4.7 (ur ṛt), all /ṛ/ > short /ṛ/.

230. Deshpande (1972), pp. 236-7.

231. aṣṭan-janādi-pathi-mathy-ātveṣv āntaratamyād anunāsika-prasaṅgaḥ, Vt. 1 on P.7.2.84.

232. Kaiyaṭa has the following comment on this vārttika: anaṇtvād eva bhāvyamano'ṇ savarṇān na gṛhṇātīti parihāro noktaḥ, MB-P, Vol. III, p. 158. "[Kātyāyana does accept the Maxim (1), but] the solution that an introduced /a-Ṇ/ sound does not represent its homogeneous sounds is not offered, simply because [the substitute /ā/ is] a non-/a-Ṇ/ sound." Kaiyaṭa's assumption has no base.

234. Patañjali on P.6.1.185 says: "The procedure of the teacher indicates that an introduced /u/ does represent its homogeneous sounds, since Pāṇini attaches /T/ to /u/ in P.6.1.131 (*diva ut*)." [*ācārya-pravṛttir jñāpayati bhavaty ukāreṇa bhāvyamānena savarṇānāṁ grahaṇam iti yad ayaṁ diva ut iti ukāraṁ taparaṁ karoti*/ *MB*, Vol. II, p. 801.] Nāgeśa [*MB-P-U*, Vol. II, p. 801] offers P.6.1.111 (*ṛta ut*) as an indication for the same maxim.

235. Deshpande (1972), pp. 237-8, 242-3.

236. For instance, if the Maxim [2] is accepted, it will also apply to /u/ affixes which are introduced, and then they would also represent their homogeneous varieties. Thus, it would be necessary to make a separate statement to exclude them.

237. *Paribhāṣā-sūcana*, *PBS*, p. 15.

238. Ibid., p. 16.

239. *PBS*, Intr. pp. 12-3.

240. *dravyābhidhānaṁ vyāḍiḥ*, *Vt.* on P.2.1.1.

241. See: Sec. 8.8 and n. 132. For more arguments, see: Deshpande (1972), p. 226, Fn. 37.

242. S. D. Joshi (1969), Intr. p. 10.

243. *Paribhāṣā-sūcana*, *PBS*, p. 25. K. V. Abhyankar, the editor, quotes another reading in the footnotes: *aṇudit savarṇam eva gṛhṇāti na varṇa-mātram*. This is not supported by the auto-commentary [see: n. 244], and also its sense makes it redundent.

244. *udit varṇo gṛhyamāṇaḥ sva-vargam eva gṛhṇāti na savarṇa-mātram*/ *kathaṁ jñāyate*/ *yad ayaṁ 'na vibhaktau tusmāḥ'* (P.1.3.4) *ity atra tu-grahaṇād eva siddhe sakārasya grahaṇaṁ karoti*/ *kim etasyā jñāpane prayojanam*/ *'coḥ kuḥ'* (P.8.2.30) *ity atra cu-grahaṇena śakārasyāgrahaṇāt kutvaṁ na bhavati*, *tena viḍ iti siddhaṁ bhavati*/ Ibid., p. 26.

245. The rule *APr* I.33 is given by Whitney as *eke spṛṣṭam* and interpreted to mean that, according to some, vowels

are with contact. In that case, the spirants may as well be with contact. However, the true reading of this rule is eke aspṛṣṭam "According to some, the vowels are without contact." [For details, see: Madhav Deshpande, "New Material on the Kautsa-vyākaraṇa," appearing in the Journal of the Oriental Institute, Baroda.] The TPr, in a way, classifies stops, semi-vowels and spirants together as involving sparśana (ii.33) "contact," as opposed to vowels which have upasaṁhāra (ii.31) "approximation." But later we find in TPr (ii.45) that the middle of the articulator is vivṛta "open" in the case of spirants. This distinguishes spirants from other consonants.

246. Bṛhat-paribhāṣā-vṛtti, PBS, p. 179.

247. udid varṇaḥ 'aṇudit savarṇasya' (P.1.1.69) iti sthāna-prayatnābhyāṁ viśiṣṭam eva savarṇaṁ gṛhṇāti na savarṇa-mātram/ tena 'coḥ kuḥ' (P.8.2.30) iti ku-grahaṇe hakārasya grahaṇaṁ na bhavati/ jñāpakaṁ cātra 'na vibhaktau tu-smāḥ/ (P.1.2.4) ity atra tu-grahaṇaṁ kṛtvā sakāra-grahaṇam iti/ ayaṁ ca nyāya-siddha evārthaḥ sukha-pratipatty-arthaṁ jñāpakenoktaḥ/ Ibid., p. 179.

248. udit savarṇaṁ gṛhṇāti na savarṇa-mātram/ (17)/ mātra-śabdaḥ sākalye/ udid varṇaḥ 'aṇudit savarṇasya' (P.1.1.69) iti sūtreṇa sthāna-prayatnābhyāṁ viśiṣṭam eva savarṇaṁ gṛhṇāti, na tu sthānaika-tulyaṁ savarṇa-mātram/ 'na vibhaktau' (P.1.3.4) ity atra vargāt pṛthak sakāra-grahaṇāl liṅgāt/ 'tulyāsya-prayatnam' (P.1.1.9) iti sthāna-prayatna-viśiṣṭasyaiva savarṇa-saṁjñābhidhānād vā/ tena 'coḥ kuḥ' (P.8.2.30) ity adau na hakārādi-vidhiḥ/ Paribhāṣā-bhāskara by Haribhāskara Agnihotrin, PBS, p. 329.

249. udit savarṇaṁ gṛhṇāti (131)/ na savarṇa-mātram/ sthāna-mātra-tulyaṁ savarṇaṁ gṛhṇātīty arthaḥ/ viśiṣṭasyaiva savarṇa-saṁjñā-vidhānād bhāṣye'darśanāc ceyam prakṣiptā/ ...atha prakṣiptā nirmūlāś ca pradarśyante/ Paribhāṣā-vṛtti of Nīlakaṇṭha Dīkṣita, PBS, p. 315.

250. Burnell (1875), p. 47, extensively quotes from Martin Haug. Also: Kielhorn (1876b), p. 142.

251. Burnell (1875), pp. 47, 50.

252. Kielhorn (1876b), pp. 142-4.

253. Ibid. Franz Kielhorn in his "Indragomin and other Grammarians" [Indian Antiquary, Vol. 15, June 1886, pp. 181-3] discusses Burnell's views on the Aindra School of Grammar. He says: "I have indeed been long aware of the fact that a grammar composed by Indra must have existed, because I knew that that grammar had been used by Hemachandra. But as the fuller name of the author of that work is Indragomin, just as Chandra's fuller name is Chandragomin, I feel no inclination to make it older than Pāṇini." (p. 181) "I would urge my fellow students to cease speaking of an Aindra grammar, or of the Aindra School of grammarians, terms for which, so far as I know, there is no justification, and which are only apt to mislead." (p. 183) Despite Kielhorn's warning, there are enough references to the Aindra grammar that existed before Pāṇini to justify acceptance of such a possibility. It is also possible that Indragomin's grammar was different from this ancient Aindra grammar, just as the pre-Pāṇinian Śākaṭāyana is different from the post-Pāṇinian Jain Śākaṭāyana.

254. "That this science is warranted as much by general reasons as by the explicit reference made to it in the TU 1.2 must not be confounded with the well known treatises going by the name of Śikṣā need hardly be repeated. They are all of them, young elaborations of the definitions laid down in the Prātiśākhyas." Thieme (1935a), pp. 85-6. [The abbreviation TU stands for Taittirīya-Upaniṣad.]

255. Cardona (1965a) presents a brief discussion of the notion of savarṇa in the Prātiśākhyas.

256. hrasvādeśe hrasva-dīrghau savarṇau, RPr, 1st Paṭala, verse 13, p. 7.

257. The sound /ḷ/ would be excluded because there is no long /ḹ/. Though the RPr does not say it explicitly, this can be inferred. The sound /ḷ/ occurs only in the forms of

the root klp, where also it is considered as a transformation of /ṛ/ [madhye sa tasyaiva lakāra-bhāve dhātau svaraḥ kalpayatāv ṛkāraḥ, RPr, 13th Paṭala, verse 14, p. 56]. It never occurs either at the beginning or at the end of a word [padādy-antayor na ḷkāraḥ svareṣu, RPr, Upodghāta, verse 9, p. 3]. Thus, there is no chance of obtaining long /ḹ/.

258. pañca te pañca vargāḥ, RPr, 1st Paṭala, verse 2, p. 5.

259. savarṇa-pūrvasya para-dhruvasya..., RPr, 6th Paṭala, verse 12, p. 31.

260. samānākṣare sasthāne dīrgham ekam ubhe svaram, RPr, 2nd Paṭala, verse 6, p. 9.

261. svarānusvāroṣmaṇām aspṛṣṭaṁ sthitam, RPr, 13th Paṭala, verse 3, p. 55. Also see: "The Rk. Prāt. also fails to note any difference of quality between the long and short values of this vowel (i.e. /a/). But it is very doubtful whether we are to regard the silence of these two treatises upon the point in question as any evidence that they are of notably earlier date than the others, as Weber seems inclined to do: their peculiarity is much more likely to be due to a local or a scholastic difference of pronounciation, or they may have simply disregarded as of little account, the discordance of quality between /a/ and /ā/." Whitney on APr, p. 32. Max Walleser (1927) has considered these alternatives and he concludes as follows: "Mir scheint nun nur die an zweiter Stelle gegebene Erklärung angängig zu sein, nämlich die Annahme, dass der Unterschied in der Aussprache schon in der ältesten Zeit bestanden habe, aber erst nach der Zeit der Ṛk. und Taitt. Pr. bemerkt worden ist, und Zwar aus vier Gründen: ...," p. 195. I tend to agree with his general conclusion [see my "Phonetics of Short /A/ is Sanskrit," appearing in the Indo-Iranian Journal], but his "vier Gründe" are not very convincing. He seems to believe that no sound-changes are heard of or have been observed within the "Literaturschicht der Prātiśākhyen," and that the Vedic speech being a dominating "Kultsprach," any organic sound-changes were generally unlikely. The arguments adduced by

him to prove that the short /a/ was a closed sound are based on the fact that the Sanskrit /ă/ represents Indo-European /a/, /e/ and /o/. They are interesting, but not conclusive.

262. dve dve savarṇe hrasva-dīrghe, TPr (i.3), p. 11.

263. teṣu samānākṣareṣu dve dve hrasve, dve dve dīrghe, hrasva-dīrghe, dīrgha-hrasve vākṣare parasparaṁ savarṇa-saṁjñe bhavataḥ, Tribhāṣya-ratna, TPr, p. 11.

264. atha navāditaḥ samānākṣarāṇi, TPr (i.2), p. 10. Contrast: aṣṭau samānākṣarāṇy āditaḥ, RPr, 1st Paṭala, verse 1, p. 5, referring to /a/, /ā/, /i/, /ī/, /u/, /ū/, /ṛ/ and /ṝ/.

265. na pluta-pūrvam, TPr (i.4), p. 2.

266. saṁjñāyāḥ prayojanaṁ 'dīrghaṁ samānākṣare savarṇa-pare' (x.2) iti, Tribhāṣya-ratna, TPr, p. 11.

267. Whitney on TPr, p. 11.

268. iyam anvartha-saṁjñā/ savarṇatvaṁ nāma sādṛśyam ucyate/ tasmād akārādīnām ikārādibhir na savarṇa-saṁjñāśaṅkā, bhinna-sthāna-prayātnatvād anayoḥ/ saṁjñāyāḥ prayojanaṁ 'dīrghaṁ samānākṣare savarṇa-pare' (x.2) iti/ Tribhāṣya-ratna, TPr, p. 11.

269. varṇaḥ kārottaro varṇākhyā (i.16), TPr, p. 18. hrasvo varṇottaras trayāṇām (i.20), TPr, p.20. prathamo vargottaro vargākhyā (i.27), TPr, p. 25.

270. Whitney on TPr, p. 21.

271. TPr, p. 383.

272. Tribhāṣya-ratna, TPr, p. 383.

273. Whitney on TPr, p. 385.

274. TPr, p. 307.

275. savarṇa-paraḥ savargīya-paraś ca dvitvaṁ nāpadyate/ savarṇaś ca nāma sārūpyam ucyate/ na tulya-sthāna-karaṇatā-mātram/ savargīyaḥ samāna-varga-sambandhī/ Tribhāṣya-ratna, TPr, p. 308; Whitney on TPr, pp. 307-8; Cardona (1965a), p. 234.

276. TPr, pp. 148-9; Cardona (1965a), p. 233.

277. The commentary Vaidikābharaṇa on the TPr (i. 2) says that the term samānākṣara "simple vowels" actually applies to all vowels except the diphthongs. The commentator refers to the RPr where we have eight samānākṣaras, i.e. short and long /a/, /i/, /u/ and /ṛ/. He says that the designations such as these are for the purpose of using them (upayogānuguṇyāt) to formulate rules, and hence for the specific needs of the system in the TPr only nine sounds, i.e. short, long and extra-long /a/, /i/ and /u/ are called samānākṣaras. The term savarṇa is used with reference to these simple vowels in the TPr (i. 3). See: Vaidikābharaṇa, Taittirīya-prātiśākhya, Government Oriental Library Series, Bibliotheca Sanskrita, No. 33, Mysore, 1906, pp. 10-1.

278. APr, p. 148.

279. Ibid., p. 28.

280. Ibid.

281. Whitney on APr, p. 118.

282. APr (iii. 44, 45, 46), pp. 148-9.

283. APr (ii. 31) makārasya sparśe para-sasthānaḥ; Compare: P. 8. 4. 58 (anusvārasya yayi para-savarṇaḥ). APr (iii. 30) sasthāne ca; compare: P. 8. 4. 65 (jharo jhari savarṇe).

284. Thieme (1935a), pp. 85, 95.

285. See: Sec. 4. 7.

286. APr (i. 36) saṁvṛto'kāraḥ, p. 31.

287. Deshpande (1972), p. 230; also: Sec. 4. 9 above.

288. Thieme (1935a), pp. 81-91; his detailed argument is found in Thieme (1937-8), pp. 189-209. Also V. Venkatarama Sarma (1935), pp. 96 ff.

289. VPr, p. 8.

290. VPr (i. 65-84), pp. 10-12.

291. 'ahavisarjanīyāḥ kaṇṭha' (71) iti akārasya mātrikasya dvimātrikasya trimātrikasya kaṇṭha-sthānatā uktā/ tathā 'kaṇṭhyā madhyena' (84) iti samāna-karaṇatā trayāṇām api/ āsya-prayatnas tu bhidyate/ ko'sāv āsya-prayatno nāma/ saṁvṛtatā vivṛtatā ca, aspṛṣṭatā īṣat-spṛṣṭatā spṛṣṭatā ca ardha-spṛṣṭatā ca/ tad yathā saṁvṛtāsya-prayatno'kāro vivṛtāsya-prayatnā itare svarāḥ/ tad yathā aspṛṣṭatāsya-prayatnāḥ svarāḥ, spṛṣṭatāsya-prayatnāḥ sparśāḥ, tathā īṣat-spṛṣṭatāsya-prayatnā antaḥsthāḥ, ardha-spṛṣṭatāsya-prayatnā ūṣmāṇo'-nusvāraś ca/ ayam āsya-prayatnaḥ śikṣā-vidbhir uktaḥ iha gṛhyate/ Uvaṭa on VPr(W), pp. 118-9. Also: Venkatarama Sarma (1935), pp. 169-70. The VPr (i.11) [dve karaṇe] says that there are two karaṇas. The word karaṇa is used by the VPr normally to refer to the articulator [cf. VPr (i.43), (i.75-6), (i.80)]. However, on this rule, Uvaṭa says that there are two karaṇas, i.e. saṁvṛta and vivṛta, which probably refers to open and closed positions of the glottis [cf. RPr (13.1-2), TPr (ii.4-5)]. The commentary of Anantabhaṭṭa gives the same interpretation, but quotes a verse attributed to Kātyāyana, which speaks of four prayatnas: spṛṣṭa "with contact," īṣat-spṛṣṭa "with slight contact," saṁvṛta "closed" and vivṛta "open" [see: Vājasaneyi-Prātiśākhya, with the commentaries of Uvaṭa and Anantabhaṭṭa, Madras University Sanskrit Series, No. 5, Madras, 1934, p. 9]. Here, Anantabhaṭṭa seems to interpret the term karaṇa with the term prayatna. If the vowels and spirants were vivṛta "open," then the VPr would require a rule like P.1.1.10 (nājjhalau) to prohibit homogeneity of vowels with spirants. The very fact that the VPr does not have such a rule is an indication that vowels and spirants had different efforts. Thus Uvaṭa's comments on the VPr (i.72) seem to be quite appropriate. Anantabhaṭṭa, even on the VPr (i.72), sticks to the view that vowels and spirants are both vivṛta "open," without solving the impending question of their homogeneity.

292. savarṇavac ca, VPr (i.72), p. 11. See: ato'kārasya mātrikasya saṁvṛtāsyaprayatnasya itarayoś ca vivṛtāsya-prayatnayor dvimātrika-trimātrikayoḥ

sāvarṇyaṁ tulyaṁ na bhavati, tad-artham idam ārabhyate/ savarṇavac ca kāryam bhavati/ Uvaṭa on VPr(W), pp. 118-9.

293. Thieme (1935a), pp. 89-90.

294. i-c(a)-ś-e-yās tālau, VPr (i.66), p. 10.

295. tālu-sthānā madhyena, VPr (i.79), p. 12.

296. u-v-o-ḥp(a)-pā oṣṭhe, VPr (i.70), p. 11.

297. samāna-sthāna-karaṇā nāsikyauṣṭhyāḥ, VPr (i.81), p. 12.

298. See: n. 116 and 117.

299. Thieme (1935a), p. 93.

300. Ibid., p. 92, Fn. 3. Cardona has criticized Thieme's views regarding Pāṇini's knowledge of sthāna and karaṇa: "The finally accepted analysis of āsya in Bh. ad 1.1.9 is that it is a taddhita derivative with suffix -ya (5.1.6) like dantya. Therefore āsya, analysed as meaning āsye bhavam 'located in the mouth' (Bh. I.61.25), includes a reference to sthāna and, concomitantly, to karaṇa. cf. Bh I.61.25-6 kim punar āsye bhavaṁ, sthānaṁ karaṇaṁ ca....Hence I do not think we can state, with Thieme (Pāṇini and the Veda, 94, n.1), that Pāṇini did not know the doctrine of sthāna and karaṇa." Cardona (1965a), p. 227, fn. 6. Thieme clearly intends 'articulator' or 'active organ' by the term karaṇa in this context.

301. evam api vyapadeśo na prakalpate-'āsye yeṣāṁ tulyo deśa' iti/ vyapadeśivad-bhāvena bhaviṣyati/ siddhyati/ sūtraṁ tarhi bhidyate/ yathā-nyāsam evāstu/ nanu coktaṁ-savarṇa-saṁjñāyām bhinna-deśeṣv ati-prasaṅgaḥ, prayatna-sāmānyāt' iti/ naiṣa doṣaḥ/ na hi laukikam āsyam/ kiṁ tarhi/ taddhitāntam āsyam/ āsye bhavam-āsyam-'śarīrāvayavād yat'/ kim punar āsye bhavam/ sthānaṁ karaṇaṁ ca/, MB, Vol. I, Sec. I, p. 155.

302. karaṇam iti/ spṛṣṭatādi, jihvāyā agropāgra-madhya-mūlāni vā/ MB-P, Vol. I, Sec. I, p. 155. Viśveśvarasūri [VSSN, p. 224] discusses these two interpretations given by Kaiyaṭa, and says that the first, i.e.

karaṇa = spṛṣṭatādi, is vyavahārābhiprāyaṁ na tu tātvikam "according to the conventional use of the term, and not really true." Then he argues that spṛṣṭatā "property of being in contact" etc. stands for different kinds of saṁyogas "conjunctions" and could not be karaṇa "active instrument" in the real sense. They are not "active," but they are "activities" themselves. The second explanation by Kaiyaṭa, i.e. karaṇa = jihvāyā agropāgra-madhya-mūlāni vā, is the proper interpretation, because the tip of the tongue etc. are the "active instruments" (vyāpāravad).

303. yadi tarhi 'sati bhede kiṁcit samānam' iti kṛtvā savarṇa-saṁjñā bhaviṣyati/ śakāra-chakārayoḥ, ṣakāra-ṭhakārayoḥ, sakāra-thakārayoḥ savarṇa-saṁjñā prāpnoti/ eteṣāṁ hi sarvam anyat samānaṁ karaṇa-varjam/ MB, Vol. I, Sec. I, p. 156. Though Viśveśvarasūri considers that the term karaṇa primarily refers to tip of the tongue etc., still on the phrase karaṇa-varjam in the Bhāṣya, he explains karaṇa as internal efforts. [ābhyantara-prayatnas tu śarāṁ vivṛtatvaṁ, chādīnāṁ tu spṛṣṭatvam iti bhedaḥ, VSSN. p. 230.]

304. Thieme (1958), p. 43, fn. 24.

305. Ibid., p. 42.

306. mukha-nāsikā-karaṇo'nunāsikaḥ, VPr (i.75).

307. anusvārasya yayi parasavarṇaḥ (P.8.4.58).

308. antaḥsthām antaḥsthāsv anunāsikām parasasthānām, VPr (iv.9), p. 51.

309. sparśe para-pañcamam, VPr (iv.11), p. 51.

310. siṁ savarṇe dīrghaḥ, VPr, (iv.50), p. 55.

311. anunāsikavaty anunāsikam, VPr (iv.51), p. 56.

312. savarṇe, VPr (iv.110), p. 64.

313. VPr(W), p. 243.

314. ṛkāra-ḷkārayor api savarṇa-dīrghatvam eva bhavati, yady udāharaṇaṁ chandasi labhyate, Uvaṭa on VPr (i.43).

315. ṛhkkau jihvā-mūle, VPr (i. 65); ḷlasitā dante, VPr (i. 69); dantyā jihvāgra-karaṇāḥ, VPr (i. 76); jihvā-mūlīyānusvārā hanu-mūlena, VPr (i. 83), pp. 10-2.

316. svarāś ca ḷkāra-varjam, VPr(i. 87); svarāś ca padāntīyā bhavanti ḷkāraṁ varjayitvā, Uvaṭa on VPr (i. 87); also ḷkāraś cālkāram, VPr (iv. 60); Uvaṭa on this rule says: idaṁ sūtraṁ kecin na paṭhanti, vyarthatvāt.

317. kāreṇa ca, VPr (i. 37); a-vyavahitena vyañjanasya, VPr, (i. 38), p. 7.

318. hrasva-grahaṇe dīrgha-plutau pratīyāt, VPr (i. 63); prathama-grahaṇe vargam, VPr (i. 64), p. 10.

319. rephoṣmaṇāṁ savarṇā na santi/ vargyo vargyeṇa savarṇaḥ/ Śikṣā-sūtrāṇi, p. 15.

320. See: n. 212.

321. īṣad-vivṛta-karaṇā ūṣmāṇaḥ/ vivṛta-karaṇā vā/ Śikṣā-sūtrāṇi, p. 21.

322. Ibid., p. 5.

323. yad yad yasya bhavet sthānaṁ karaṇaṁ vā viśeṣaṇam/ savarṇatvena saṁgrāhya āsya-yatnas tu bhidyate//38// Varṇa-ratna-pradīpika-śikṣā, Śikṣā-saṁgraha, p. 120.

324. dvimātrasyaika-mātrasya saṁvṛtādi-prayatnataḥ/ bhinnasyāpy astu sāvarṇyaṁ tad-artham idam ucyate//, Ibid., pp. 120-1.

325. pratyayasya savarṇatvaṁ (sakāraḥ) yātīti śākaṭāyanaḥ/ avikāraṁ ca śākalyo manyate śaṣaseṣu ca// Ibid., p. 127.

326. Ibid., p. 119.

327. savarṇe (141), savarṇe pare vyañjanaṁ dvir na bhavati/ Prātiśākhya-pradīpa-śikṣā, Śikṣā-saṁgraha, p. 253.

328. Ibid., p. 228.

329. atra ṛkāroccāraṇe viśeṣaḥ/ tathā ca pratijñā-sūtre 'ṛkārasya tu saẏyuktāsaẏyuktasyāviśeṣeṇa sarvvatraivam' / asyārthaḥ/ padānta-madhyeṣu saṁyuktāsaṁyuktasya ṛvarṇasya rekāraḥ syāt/ sarvatra saṁhitāyām pade ca/ yathā kṛṣṇo'sīty atra kreṣṇo'sīty uccāraḥ/ ṛtviyo yataḥ/

atra retviya ity uccāraḥ/ evaṁ 'ṛḷvarṇayor mithaḥ sāvarṇyaṁ vācyam' iti vārttikena ḷkārasyāpi le ity uccāraḥ/ kḷptam ity atra kleptam ity uccāraḥ/ Ibid., p. 296.

330. valhāmasīty atra valehāmasīty uccāro ralayoḥ sāvarṇyāt, Keśavī-śikṣā, Śikṣā-saṁgraha, p. 142. Also: Venkatarama Sarma (1935), p. 441.

331. Kielhorn (1876), p. 197.

332. Though I could not obtain the published edition of the Vyāsa-śikṣā, I was fortunate to obtain a microfilm of a manuscript of this text in the Vaidika Saṁśodhana Maṇḍala, Poona [No. 4564]. In the following notes, I shall augment Lüders with the original Sanskrit quotations from this manuscript.

333. Lüders (1894), p. 5, verse 5 (folio 2): sparśānām pañca pañca syur vargā vargottarasya ca/ tat-prathamādi saṁjñāḥ syuḥ/; verse 10 of Lüders appears to be verse 7 of this Ms.: tulya-rūpaṁ savarṇaṁ syāt (folio 3); verse 13 of Lüders is verse 9 of the Ms.: bhaved akāraḥ kārordhve halām (ākhyā) (folio 4). Perhaps the numbers in Lüders refer to "rules" rather than to verses.

334. Lüders (1894), p. 9. I have not been able to find a parallel verse in my Ms.

335. Ibid. The number 172 of Lüders is verse 116 of the Ms.: ādy-aṣṭasu savarṇordhve dīrgham apluta-pūrvakaḥ (folio 39).

336. Lüders (1894), p. 13. The number 269 of Lüders is verse 183 of the Ms.: antaḥsthodayam aṅgaṁ syāt asavarṇa-parasya ca (folio 55).

337. Lüders (1894), p. 16. However, certain verses found in the Ms. of the Vyāsa-śikṣā indicate a notion similar to Pāṇini's. The verses 78-9 (folio 26) are as follows: nakāro laparas tasya sasthānam anunāsikam/ sparśottaro makāras tu yavalottara eva ca/ anunāsikam eteṣāṁ savarṇam pratipadyate// The usage of the term savarṇa here is quite similar to that in P. 8. 4. 58 (anusvārasya yayi para-savarṇaḥ).

338. āpadyate makāro rephoṣmasu pratyayeṣv anusvāram/ yalaveṣu parasavarṇaṁ, sparśeṣu cottamāpattim// Nāradīya-śikṣā, 2nd Prapāṭhaka, 4th Kaṇḍikā; rephoṣmasu parato makāro'nusvāratvam/...yalaveṣu parasavarṇatā, sparśeṣu parataḥ sparśa-varga-sadṛśottamāpattir makārasya bhavati/ Bhaṭṭa Śobhākara's comm., Nāradīya-śikṣā, p. 60.

339. anantyaś ca bhavet pūrvo'ntyaś ca parato yadi/ tatra madhye yamas tiṣṭhet savarṇaḥ pūrva-varṇayoḥ// 2nd Prapāṭhaka, 2nd Kaṇḍikā, Nāradīya-śikṣā, p. 52.

340. pūrvasya varṇasya savarṇaḥ sadṛśaḥ, Śobhākara's comm., Nāradīya-śikṣā, p. 52.

341. evam ime na lakṣaṇena yuktā, nāpy ākṛtyā, nāpy upadiṣṭāḥ, MB-D, p. 81.

342. rephoṣmaṇāṁ savarṇā na santi/ vargyo vargyena savarṇaḥ/ Āpiśali-śikṣā-sūtras, Śikṣā-sūtrāṇi, p. 5.

343. spṛṣṭa-karaṇāḥ sparśāḥ/ vivṛta-karaṇāḥ svarāḥ ūṣmāṇaś ca/ Ibid., p. 3.

344. saṁvrto'karaḥ, Ibid., p. 4.

345. Burnell (1875), p. 22.

346. Ibid., p. 2.

347. siddho varṇa-samāmnāyaḥ, Kātantra (1.1.1), p. 14. tatra caturdaśādau svarāḥ, Kātantra (1.1.2), p. 14. daśa samānāḥ, Kātantra (1.1.3), p. 14.

348. teṣāṁ dvau dvāv anyonyasya savarṇau, Kātantra (1.1.4), p. 14.

349. Ibid., p. 14.

350. samānaḥ savarṇe dīrghī-bhavati paraś ca lopam, Kātantra (1.2.1), p. 17.

351. ivarṇo yam asavarṇe, na ca paro lopyaḥ, Kātantra (1.2.8); uvarṇo vam, Kātantra (1.2.9); ram ṛvarṇaḥ, Katantra (1.2.10); lam ḷvarṇaḥ, Kātantra (1.2.11), pp. 17-8.

352. abhyāsasyāsavarṇe, Kātantra (3.4.56), p. 70.

353. samānād anyo'savarṇaḥ, Bāla-śikṣā, p. 4.

354. ram ṛvarṇaḥ, Kātantra (1.2.10); lam ḷvarṇaḥ, 1.2.11; ṛvarṇe ar, 1.2.4; ḷvarṇe al, 1.2.5; pp. 17-8.

355. Kātantra-vyākaraṇa [Eggeling's edn.], p. 470. Bhāvasena Traividya in his Kātantra-rūpa-mālā-prakriyā (ed. by Jivaram Shastri, published by Hirachand Nemichand Shreshthi, Bombay, Saṁvat 1952, p. 3) gives ṛkāra-ḷkārau ca as rule 5. His commentary runs as: ṛkāra-ḷkārau ca parasparaṁ savarṇa-saṁjñau bhavataḥ.

356. ṛkāra-ḷkārayoḥ savarṇa-saṁjñā lokopacārāt siddheti bhāvaḥ, Trilocanadāsa's commentary, quoted by Eggeling, ibid., p. 480.

357. yat tu trilocanadāsenoktam ṛkāra-ḷkārayoḥ saṁjñā lokopacārataḥ siddheti tan na/ loke ḷkāre ṛkāra-vyavahārasyādarśanāt/ Laghubhāṣya, p. 14.

358. Kātantra-paribhāṣā-sūtra-vṛtti of Bhāvamiśra, Paribhāṣā-saṁgraha, p. 67.

359. sasthāna-kriyaṁ svam, Jainendra (1.1.2), p. 2.

360. sthānaṁ tālvādi, kriyā spṛṣṭatādikā..., samānā sthāne kriyā yasya, sāmarthyāt sthānam api samānaṁ labhyate/ ...sā caturvidhā...spṛṣṭatā, īṣat-spṛṣṭatā, vivṛtatā, īṣad-vivṛtatā ceti/ Mahāvṛtti on Jainendra-vyākaraṇa, p. 2.

361. anye saṁvṛtam akāram icchanti loke/ śāstra-vyavahāre tu vivṛtam/ etac cāyuktaṁ, loka-śāstrayor uccāraṇam praty aviśeṣāt/ ibid., p. 2. This criticism of Abhayanandin clearly neglects the meta-linguistic purpose of using open /a/ in Pāṇini's grammar.

362. rephoṣmaṇāṁ svā na santi/ vargyaḥ sva-vargyeṇa sva-saṁjño bhavati/ Mahāvṛtti, Jainendra- vyākaraṇa, p. 3.

363. aṇudit svasyātmanā'bhāvyo'taparaḥ, Jainendra (1.1.72), p. 16.

364. yayy anusvārasya parasvam, Jainendra (5.4.132), comp. with anusvārasya yayi parasavarṇaḥ (P.8.4.58). jharo jhari sve, Jainendra (5.4.139) comp. with jharo jhari savarṇe (P.8.4.65). sve'ko dīḥ, Jainendra (4.3.88), comp. with akaḥ savarṇe dīrghaḥ (p.6.1.101). na padānta-dvitva-vare ya-kha-svānusvāra-dī-car-vidhau, Jainendra (1.1.59), comp. with na padānta-dvirvacana-vare-yalopaśvara-savarṇānusvāra-dīrgha-jaś-car-vidhiṣu (P.1.1.58).

365. "The Jainendra grammar, taken as a whole, is a copy of Pāṇini pure and simple, and the sole principle on which it was manufactured appears to be that 'the saving of a half a short vowel affords as much delight as the birth of a son.'" Kielhorn, "On the Jainendra-Vyākaraṇa," Indian Antiquary, Vol. 10, March 1881, p. 76.

366. ranto'ṇ uḥ, Jainendra (1.1.48), uḥ sthāne prasajyamāna eva ranto bhavati/ ...ṛḷkārayoḥ sva-saṁjñoktā/ tena tavalkāraḥ/ ...kathaṁ lantatvam? ranta iti laṇo lakārākāreṇa praśleṣa-nirdeśāt pratyāhāra-grahaṇam/ Mahāvṛtti of Abhayanandin, Jainendra-vyākaraṇa, p. 11. Abhayanindin quotes a Vārttika: ṛkāra-ḷkārayoḥ sva-saṁjñā vaktavyā, ibid., p. 3.

367. jāti-nirdeśaś cāyam, Cāndra-vyākaraṇa, Vol. I, p. 2.

368. utā savargaḥ, Cāndra (1.1.2), Vol. I, p. 10.

369. anusvārasya yayi yam, Cāndra (6.4.151), comp. with anusvarasya yayi para-savarṇaḥ (P.8.4.58). ako'ki dīrghaḥ, Cāndra (5.1.106), comp. with akaḥ savarṇe dīrghaḥ (P.6.1.101). Actually, Bhaṭṭoji Dīkṣita says that the Cāndra rule is better worded than P.6.1.101. [ako'ki dīrgha ity eva suvacam, SK, p. 7.]

370. halo jharāṁ jhari sasthāne lopo vā, Cāndra (6.4.155), comp. with jharo jhari savarṇe (P.8.4.65). There is, however, a rule where Cāndra uses the term savarṇa: dvitve parasavarṇaḥ, Cāndra (6.3.34). The Cāndra-paribhāṣā-sūtras contain the maxim: bhāvyamānot savarṇān gṛhṇāti, Cāndra-vyākaraṇa, Vol. II, p. 397. We should note here that the Vṛtti on Candragomin's rules, which was declared by Liebich to be an

autocommentary (svopajña), has been doubted by scholars for not being a work of Candragomin himself. Thus, this is yet an open question. For a discussion of this point, see: "Ist Candragomin der Verfasser der Cāndra-Vṛtti?," by R. Birwé, Mélanges d'Indianisme à la mémoir de Louis Renou, Publications de l'Institut de Civilisation Indienne, Fascicule 28, Paris, 1968. The same might be said of the Cāndra-paribhāṣā-sūtras.

371. sāmānyāśrayaṇāt dīrgha-plutānunāsikānāṁ grahaṇam, Amoghavṛtti, Śākaṭāyana-vyākaraṇa, p. 1.

372. bhāvyo'g, Śākaṭāyana (1.1.4), p. 2.

373. teyān, Śākaṭāyana (1.1.3), p. 2.

374. svaḥ sthānāsyaikye, Śākaṭāyana (1.1.6), sthānaṁ kaṇṭhādi, āsyam mukhaṁ, tatra bhavam āsyam, spṛṣṭatādi-prayatna-pañcakam, sthānasyoktatvāt, Amoghavṛtti, Śākaṭāyana-vyākaraṇa, p. 3. Comp. with Patañjali's interpretation of āsya in P.1.1.9. [See: Sec. 2.4.]

375. saṁvṛtam akārasyeti, Amoghavṛtti, ibid., p. 3.

376. a a a ity akāra udātto'nudāttaḥ svaritaś cānanunāsiko' nunāsikaś ceti ṣaṭ/ evaṁ dīrgha-plutāv iti dvādaśa varṇa-bhedāḥ parasparasya sve bhavanti/ evam, ivarṇādīnāṁ tv aṣṭādaśa bhedāḥ. Amoghavṛtti, ibid., p. 3.

377. īṣad-vivṛtam ūṣmaṇām, ibid., p. 3.

378. rephoṣmaṇāṁ sve na bhavanti, ibid., p. 3.

379. utā svaḥ, Śākaṭāyana (1.1.2), ibid., p. 2.

380. ukāreṇetā sahopādīyamāno varṇaḥ svasya vargasya saṁjñā bhavaty ātmanā saha, Amoghavṛtti, ibid., p. 2.

381. ṛ ity eva ḷvarṇasya grahaṇam, ibid., p. 1.

382. tathā ca 'ṛty akaḥ' (1.1.75) ityādi ḷkāre'pi siddham bhavati, ibid., p. 1. Also: pp. 15-6, 18.

383. jari jaraḥ sve vā, Śākaṭāyana (1.1.133), ibid., p. 23.

384. Nemichandra Shastri (1963), pp. 92 ff.

385. tulya-sthānāsya-prayatnaḥ svaḥ, Hemacandra (1.1.17).

386. karaṇaṁ tu jihvā-mūla-madhyāgropāgra-rūpaṁ sthānāsya-prayatna-tulyatve sati nātulyam bhavatīti pṛthak noktam, Bṛhad-vṛtti, Hema-śabdānuśāsana, p. 3.

387. īṣad-vivṛtaṁ karaṇam ūṣmaṇām/ vivṛtaṁ karaṇaṁ svarāṇām/ 'ūṣmaṇāṁ ce'ty anye/ ibid., p. 4.

388. akāraḥ saṁvṛta ity anye/ ibid., p. 4/

389. pañcako vargaḥ, Hemacandra (1.1.12), and also: varṇāvyayāt svarūpe kāraḥ, Hemacandra (7.2.156).

390. samānānāṁ tena dīrghaḥ, Hemacandra (1.21.) is closer to Kātantra (1.2.1), TPr (x.2), APr (iii.42) and VPr (iv.50) than to P.6.1.101.

391. ivarṇāder asve yavaralam, Hemacandra (1.2.21). comp. with Kāntantra (1.2.8-11).

392. tau mumau vyañjane svau, Hemacandra (1.3.14).

393. anusvārasya yayi para-savarṇaḥ, P.8.4.58.

394. dhuṭo dhuṭi sve vā, Hemacandra (1.3.48).

395. jharo jhari savarṇe, P.8.4.65.

396. ivarṇāder asve yavaralam, Hemacandra (1.2.21); avarṇasyevarṇādinā edodaral, Hemacandra (1.2.6); ṛty ār upasargasya, Hemacandra (1.2.9) and ḷty āl vā, Hemacandra (1.2.11).

397. ṛkārāpadiṣṭaṁ kāryam ḷkārasyāpi, Maxim 71, Nyāya-saṁgraha, PBS, p. 109.

398. svaḥ sthāna-spṛṣṭatādy-aikye, Malayagiri (2nd sandhi, 1), p. 5.

399. spṛṣṭatā, īṣat-spṛṣṭatā, vivṛtatā, īṣad-vivṛtatā/ ... rephaśaṣasahānāṁ tu sve na santi/ Svopajña-vṛtti, Malayagiri's Śabdānuśāsana, p. 5.

400. Ibid., p. 5.

401. utā sva-vargasya, Malayagiri (2nd sandhi, 14), p. 8.

402. ik etaḥ, Malayagiri (1st sandhi, 6); ṛtaḥ aṇ, (1st sandhi, 8; edādi ec, (1st sandhi, 9); e-o eṅ,

(1st sandhi, 10); Malayagiri's Śabdānuśāsana, p. 3.

403. Śākaṭāyana-vyākaraṇa, p. 1.

404. yaralavā yañ, Malayagiri (1st sandhi, 17), p. 4.

405. Śākaṭāyana-vyākaraṇa, p. 1.

406. ikaḥ asve yañ, Malayagiri (3rd sandhi, 2), p. 10.

407. dīrghaḥ sve saparasvarasya, Malayagiri (3rd sandhi, 5), p. 11.

408. tṛtīyasya svaḥ anunāsikaḥ pañcame, Malayagiri (4th sandhi, 8); pratyaye, Malayagiri (4th sandhi, 9); mnāṁ dhuṭi apadānte, Malayagiri (4th sandhi, 10); p. 17.

409. vyañjanāt yañ-pañcamasya sarūpe vā, Malayagiri (5th sandhi, 4), p. 21.

410. āvat svarghaplu, Mugdhabodha (5), p. 5.

411. ñapo'k samo ṛṇa ṛk ca, Mugdhabodha (6), p. 6.

412. sāmyaṁ tv eka-sthānatvam, Vṛtti, Mugdhabodha-vyākaraṇa, p. 6.

413. capoditākānitā ṛṇaḥ, Mugdhabodha (7), p. 7.

414. saha ṛṇe ṛghaḥ, Mugdhabodha (22), p. 17.

415. Comp. RPr (2nd paṭala, verse 6), APr (ii.31), APr (ii.30), and Cāndra (6.4.155). All these rules use the term sasthāna instead of savarṇa.

416. aiuṛḷ samānāḥ, Sārasvata (1), p. 1; hrasva-dīrgha-pluta-bhedāḥ savarṇāḥ, Sārasvata (2), p. 1.

417. varṇa-grahaṇe savarṇa-grahaṇam/ kāra-grahaṇe kevala-grahaṇam/ tapara-karaṇaṁ tāvanmātrārtham/ Sārasvata-vyākarana, p. 6.

418. ku-cu-ṭu-tu-pu, ibid., p. 4.

419. asavarṇe svare pare pūrvekārokārayor iy-uvau vaktavyau, Sārasvata (771), p. 134; savarṇe dīrghaḥ saha, Sārasvata (52), p. 9.

420. hasāt jhasasya savarṇe jhase lopo vācyaḥ, Sārasvata (990), p. 181.

421. vargyo vargyeṇa savarṇaḥ, qt. in the Vṛtti, Sārasvata-vyākaraṇa, p. 7.

422. ṛḷvarṇayoḥ sāvarṇyaṁ vācyam, Sārasvata (63), pp. 10-1.

423. ṛḷvarṇa-sthānikatvād ralayor api sāvarṇyaṁ vācyam/ ...ralayor ḍalayoś caiva śasayor bavayos tathā/ vadanty eṣāṁ ca sāvarṇyam alaṁkāravido janāḥ/ Sārasvata-vyākaraṇa, pp. 10-1.

424. tulya-sthānāsya-prayatnaḥ savarṇaḥ, Sarasvatī-kaṇṭhābharaṇa (1.1.101), Pt. I, p. 27.

425. nājjhalau, Sarasvatī-kaṇṭhābharaṇa (1.1.102), ibid, p. 28. No other text has a rule parallel to nājjhalau. However, Kṛṣṇadāsa's commentary on the Kautsa-Vyākaraṇa which is identical with the APr [= Śaunakīyā Caturādhyāyikā] interprets the rule naikāraukārayoḥ sthāna-vidhau, APr (i.41), as a rule prohibiting homogeneity of vowels and consonants. This version of the Kautsa-vyākaraṇa, according to Kṛṣṇadāsa's commentary, [Vaidika Saṃśodhana Maṇḍala, Poona, Ms. E4179, folio 9] has a rule: sasthāna-karaṇaṁ savarṇam. This would make two sounds homogeneous with each other if they share the same point of articulation and internal effort. Kṛṣṇadāsa [ibid., folio 5] holds that vowels and spirants are both vivṛta. Thus this creates the same problem that Pāṇini was faced with. Kṛṣṇadāsa interprets naikāraukārayoḥ sthānavidhau as: hrasva-dīrgha-plutānāṁ svarāṇām para-sannikarṣaṇāt a i e ai u o au ebhir vyāñjanānāṁ sandhau sāvarṇyaṁ neti niṣedhaḥ/ nājjhalāv iti pāṇiniḥ/ ibid., folio 5. This is, however, a very doubtful interpretation.

426. Burnell (1875), pp. 60 ff.

427. aādayo titālīsa vaṇṇā, Moggallāna (1.1), p. 1; dasādo sarā, Moggallāna (1.2), p. 1.

428. dve dve savaṇṇā, Moggallāna (1.3), p. 2.

429. para-samaññā payoge, Kaccāyana (1.1.9), p. 12.

430. kva cāsavaṇṇaṁ lutte, Kaccāyana (1.2.3), p. 18.

431. rassa-sarā saka-saka-dīghehi aññamaññaṁ savaṇṇā

nāma sarūpā ti pi vuccanti/ Kaccāna-vaṇṇanā, Kaccāyana-vyākaraṇa, p. 13.

432. Thieme (1935a), pp. 92-3; Nemichandra Shastri (1963), pp. 69-70; Burnell (1875), p. 24.

433. Burnell (1875), p. 27.

434. oṁkāram pṛcchāmaḥ ko dhātuḥ? kiṁ prātipadikam? kiṁ nāmākhyātam? kiṁ liṅgam? kiṁ vacanam? kā vibhaktiḥ? kaḥ pratyayaḥ? kaḥ svaraḥ upasargo nipātaḥ? kiṁ vai vyākaraṇam? ko vikāraḥ? ko vikārī? katimātraḥ? kativarṇaḥ? katy-akṣaraḥ? kati-padaḥ? kaḥ saṁyogaḥ? kiṁ sthānānupradāna-karaṇam? śikṣukāḥ kiṁ uccārayanti? kiṁ chandaḥ? ko varṇaḥ? iti pūrve praśnāḥ, Gopatha-Brāhmaṇa, (i.24).

435. śīkṣāṁ vyākyāsyāmaḥ/ varṇāḥ svaraḥ/ mātrā balam/ sāma santānaḥ/ ity uktaḥ śīkṣādhyāyaḥ/ Taittiriya-Upaniṣad (vii.1.2).

436. Weber, Indische Studien, Vol. iv, p. 75.

437. Burnell (1875), pp. 28 ff.

438. Ibid., pp. 2 ff.

439. asandigdham parābhāvāt savarṇe'ṇ taparaṃ hy ur ṛt, yvor anyatra pareṇeṇ syāt, MB, Vol. I, Sec. I, pp. 97-100.

440. kim punar varṇotsattāv ivāyaṁ ṇakāro dvir anubadhyate? etaj jñāpayaty ācāryaḥ: bhavaty eṣā paribhāṣā-vyākhyānato viśeṣa-pratipattir na hi sandehād alakṣaṇam-iti/ MB, Vol. I, Sec. I, p. 100.

441. aṇuditsavarṇam parihāya pūrveṇāṇ-grahaṇam, pareṇeṇ-grahaṇam iti vyākhyāsyāmaḥ/ MB, Vol. I, Sec. I, p. 100.

442. On P.1.1.1 (vṛddhir ād-aic), Kātyāyana explains the purpose of adding the marker /T/ to /ā/, by saying that /ā/ is a non-/a-Ṇ/ sound and accents etc. are distinctive. Thus, /ā/ would not cover homogeneous varieties differing in accent, unless it is marked with /T/. [ākārasya tapara-karaṇaṁ savarṇārtham bhedakatvāt svarasya, Vārttika on P.1.1.1, MB, Vol. I, Sec. I, p. 113.] He has no such doubts about /ai-C/ sounds

in the same rule. On the other hand, he positively fears that /e-C/ sounds might stand for short /e/ etc., as well as for extra-long varieties. [atapara eca igghrasvādeśe, and ekādeśe dīrgha-grahaṇam, Vārttikas, MB, Vol. I, Sec. I, pp. 78-9.] This clearly indicates that he accepts /a-Ṇ/ in P.1.1.69 to be formed with /Ṇ/ in the Śiva-sūtra: l(a)-Ṇ. Also see: Deshpande (1972), pp. 226, 249-51.

443. Kunhan Raja (1957), p. 70-1.

444. Ibid., p. 71.

445. Ibid., p. 73.

446. Ibid., pp. 73-4.

447. Ibid., p. 80, Fn. 20.

448. Ibid., p. 80, Fn. 19.

449. edaitoḥ kaṇṭha-tālu/ odautoḥ kaṇṭhoṣṭham/ ...vivṛtam uṣmaṇāṁ svarāṇāṁ ca/ SK, p. 2.

450. siddham eṅaḥ sasthānatvāt, Vārttika on P.1.1.48, MB, Vol. I, Sec. I, p. 262.

451. aicoś cottara-bhūyastvāt, Vārttika on P.1.1.48, MB, Vol. I, Sec. I, p. 262.

452. sandhyakṣareṣu vivṛtatvāt, Vārttika, yad atrāvarṇaṁ vivṛtataraṁ tad anyasmād avarṇāt/ ye'pīvarṇovarṇe vivṛtatare te anyābhyām ivarṇovarṇābhayām/ MB, Vol. I, Sec. I, p. 84.

453. praśliṣṭāvarṇāv etau (eṅau), vivṛtatarāvarṇāv etau (aicau)/ etayor eva tarhi mithas savarṇa-saṁjñā prāpnoti/ naitau tuly-sthānau/ MB, Vol. I, Sec. I, p. 155; also: imāv aicau samāhāra-varṇau-mātrāvarṇasya mātrevarṇovarṇayoḥ/ MB, Vol. I, Sec. I, p. 78 and Vol. III, p. 426. Siddheshwar Varma is off the point in describing Patañjali's views: "Here an objector states the opinion, attributed to Śākaṭāyana, that both the elements of the diphthongs /ai/ and /au/ were equal, being one mora each....Patañjali, however, does not accept this opinion; he seems to follow the opinion expressed by the Ṛg-Prāt. and the Pāṇinīya-śikṣā,

that the second element of the diphthongs /ai/ and /au/ was longer." Varma (1929), pp. 180-1. Contrast: bhāṣyakāro vārttikakāram paryanuyuṅkte/ 'aicoś cottara-bhūyastvād' iti vadatā vārttikakāreṇa sama-pravibhāgatvaṁ neṣṭam iti bhāvaḥ, MB-P, Vol. III, p. 427, and sama-pravibhāga-pakṣa eva bhagavato bhāṣyakārasya sammata iti bodhyam, MB-P-U, Vo. III, p. 427, on P.8.2.106.

454. i-c(a)-ś-e-yās talau (i. 66), u-v-o-ḥp(a)-pāḥ oṣṭhe (i. 70), aikāraukārayoḥ kaṇṭhyā pūrvā mātrā, tālvoṣṭhayor uttarā (i. 73), VPr, p. 3; akārārdham aikāraukārayor ādiḥ (ii. 26), ikāro'dhyardhaḥ pūrvasya śeṣaḥ (ii. 28), ukāras tūttarasya (ii. 29), TPr, pp. 65-6; sandhyakṣarāṇi saṁspṛṣṭa-varṇāny eka-varṇavad vṛttiḥ (i. 40), naikāraukārayoḥ sthāna-vidhau (i. 41), APr, pp. 34-5; sandhyāni sandhyakṣarāṇy āhur eke dvisthānataiteṣu tathobhayeṣu/ sandhyeṣv akāro'rdham ikāra uttaraṁ yujor ukāra iti śākaṭāyanaḥ/ mātrā-saṁsargād avare pṛthak-śrutī hrasvānusvāra-vyatiṣaṅgavat pare/ RPr, 13th paṭala, verses 15-6, pp. 56-7; sandhyaṁ dvivarṇam, (3.4.5), Ṛk-tantra, p. 22. The word dvivarṇa here refers to /ai/ and /au/, and clearly refers to their composition in contrast to /e/ and /o/.

455. e ai tu kaṇṭha-tālavyāv o au kaṇṭhoṣṭhajau smṛtau/ ardha-mātrā tu kaṇṭhyā syād ekāraikārayor bhavet/ okāraukārayor mātrā tayor vivṛta-saṁvṛtam/ Pāṇinīya-śikṣā, verses 18-9. These are very unclear lines. Even Weber has different, but much more corrupt lines ["Die Pāṇinīya-śikṣā," Indische Studien, Vol. IV, Berlin, p858, pp. 353-4]. Also: svarāṇām uṣmaṇām caiva vivṛtaṁ karaṇaṁ smṛtam/ tebhyo'pi vivṛtāv eṅau tābhyām aicau tathaiva ca/ Pāṇinīya-śikṣā, verse 21, p. 386. The Pāṇinīya-śikṣā-sūtras have, in this respect, the same thing to say, see: Śikṣā-sūtras, pp. 11, 12, 20-1.

456. Deshpande (1972), pp. 221-2, 225, 236, 238.

457. Ibid., pp. 213-4.

458. tapara-karaṇaṁ dīrghe'pi sthānini hrasva eva yathā syāt-acīkṛtat, KS, Vol. 6, p. 136. Also: Deshpande (1972), pp. 236-7.

459. Deshpande (1972), pp. 236-7, 250-1.

460. Patañjali in his Mahābhāṣya on the Śiva-sūtra l(a)-Ṇ seems to suggest that by P.1.1.69 /y/, /v/ and /l/ stand for /ỹ/, /ṽ/ and /l̃/, and that the sequences /ỹy/ etc. are eligible for the designation saṁyoga "cluster." MB, Vol. I, Sec. I, p. 86. Here he does not bring up the question of /ỹ/, /ṽ/ and /l̃/ being "non-effected" for P.1.1.7 (halo'nantarāḥ saṁyogaḥ), which is quite a legitimate question.

461. dvirvacane parasavarṇatvam, Vārttika on P.8.2.6, dvirvacane parasavarṇatvaṁ siddhaṁ vaktavyam/ saỹyantā, saṽvatsaraḥ, yal̃lokam, tal̃lokam iti parasavarṇasyāsiddhatvāt yara iti dvirvacanaṁ na prāpnoti/ MB, Vol. III, p. 373.

462. [A] atha kimartham antaḥsthānām aṇsūpadeśaḥ kriyate/
[B] iha saỹyantā, saṽvatsaraḥ, yal̃lokam, tal̃lokam iti parasavarṇasyāsiddhatvād anusvārasyaiva dvirvacanam/ tatra parasya parasavarṇe kṛte tasya yay-grahaṇena grahaṇāt pūrvasyāpi parasavarṇo yathā syāt/
[C] naitad asti prayojanam/ vakṣaty etat-dvirvacane parasavarṇatvaṁ siddhaṁ vaktavyam-iti, yavatā siddhatvam ucyate parasavarṇa eva tāvad bhavati/
[D] parasavarṇe tarhi kṛte tasya yar-grahaṇena grahaṇād dvirvacanaṁ yathā syāt/
[E] mā bhūd dvirvacanam/
[F] nanu ca bhedo bhavati-sati dvirvacane triyakāram, asati dvirvacane dviyakāram/
[G] nāsti bhedaḥ, satyapi dvirvacane dviyakāram eva/ katham/ 'halo yamāṁ yami lopaḥ' ity evam ekasya lopena bhavitavyam/
[H] evam api bhedaḥ/ sati dvirvacane kadācid dviyakāram, kadācit triyakāram/ asati dviyakāram eva/ sa eṣa katham bhedo na syāt? yadi nityo lopaḥ syāt/ vibhāṣā ca sa lopaḥ/
[I] yathā'bhedas tathāstu/
[J] anuvartate vibhāṣā śaro'ci yad vārayaty ayaṁ

dvitvam/ (Śloka-vārttika)/ yad ayaṁ 'śaro'ci' iti dvirvacana-pratiṣedhaṁ śāsti, taj jñāpayaty acāryaḥ-anuvartate vibhāṣeti/ kathaṁ kṛtvā jñāpakam? "nitye hi tasya lope pratiṣedhārtho na kaścit syāt" (śloka-vārttika)/ yadi nityo lopaḥ syāt, pratiṣedha-vacanaṁ anarthakam syāt/ astv atra dvirvacanaṁ, "jharo jhari savarṇe" iti lopo bhaviṣyati/ paśyati tv ācāryaḥ-vibhāṣā sa lopaḥ- iti, tato dvirvacana-pratiṣedhaṁ śāsti/

[K] naitad asti jñāpakam/ ...tasmān nitye'pi lope'-vaśyaṁ sa pratiṣedho vaktavyaḥ/

[L] tad etad atyanta-sandigdham ācāryāṇāṁ vartate-vibhāṣā'nuvartate na veti/ MB, Vol. I, Sec. I, pp. 96-7.

463. halo yamāṁ yami lopaḥ ity ekasyātra lopo bhaviṣyati/ vibhāṣā sa lopaḥ/ MB, Vol. I, Sec. I, p. 99.

464. MB, Vol. I, Sec. I, pp. 89-91.

465. KS, Vol. I, p. 52.

466. Bhaṭṭoji Dīkṣita says in his SKB that, since, according to Patañjali, features like nasality are non-distinctive, /y/, /v/ and /l/ would naturally stand for /ỹ/, /ṽ/ and /l̃/, and hence it would be proper to have only /a-C/ in P.1.1.69. However, Pāṇini uses /a-Ṇ/, including semi-vowels, in P.1.1.69, in order to indicate that features like nasality are distinctive and that, without a rule, /y/, /v/ and /l/ cannot stand for /ỹ/, /ṽ/ and /l̃/. yady api guṇānām abhedakatvenaiva sānunāsika-yavalanāṁ dvitva-siddher grahaṇaka-śāstre'j-grahaṇam evocitaṁ na tv aṇ-grahaṇam, tathāpi 'guṇāḥ bhedakāḥ' ity api pakṣaṁ jñāpayitum aṇ-grahaṇam/ SKB, p. 61. For the controversy bhedakā guṇāḥ and abhedakā guṇāḥ, see: Sec. 6.5-6.13, and Deshpande (1972), pp. 226-30.

467. ācāryopadeśa-pāramparyāt tu jñāyate-'anuvartate vibhāṣā' iti/ tasmāt trivyañjana-saṁyoga-śravaṇāya 'aṇudid' iti ṇakāreṇa pratyāhāraḥ kṛto na cakāreṇeti sthitam/ MB-P, Vol. I, Sec. I, p. 97.

468. jñāpakāntaraṁ grāhaka-sūtrasthāṇ-grahaṇam/ tad dhi saỹyantety ādau yādīnāṁ sānunāsikānāṁ dvitvārtham/

lopasya nityatve tu vyartham eva syāt/ BSR, p. 149.

469. aṇ-grahaṇāj jñāpakād ity api kaścit/ tat tu vārttika-kṛtāṇ-grahaṇa-pratyākhyānān noktam/ MB-P-U, Vol. I, Sec. I, p. 97.

470. See: n. 461.

471. savarṇa-savargīya-paraḥ (na dviḥ) (xiv.23), TPr, p. 307; sasthāne ca (iii.30), APr, p. 142; savarṇe (iv.110), VPr, p. 62. These rules would not allow doubling of /ȳ/ in forms like saȳyantā.

472. George Cardona does refer to the commentators' question as to why Pāṇini did not use /a-C/ instead of /a-Ṇ/ in P.1.1.69, and says: "The answer is, of course, that the semi-vowels /y/, etc. given in the śiva-sūtras should denote also their nasal counter-parts /m̐y/ etc." Cardona (1969), p. 35. On p. 21 he discusses the rules involving semi-vowels. In (1965a, pp. 229-30), he discusses how it is necessary to have /y/, /v/ and /l/ homogeneous with /ȳ/, /v̄/ and /l̄/. However, no scholar has so far answered the question as to why /y/, /v/ and /l/ are needed to stand for /ȳ/, /v̄/ and /l̄/.

BIBLIOGRAPHY AND ABBREVIATIONS

PRIMARY SOURCES

APr *Atharvaveda-prātiśākhya* or *Śaunakīyā Caturādhyāyikā*, ed. and tr. with notes by W. D. Whitney, New Haven, 1862.

Bharata-bhāṣyam, by Nānya-bhūpāla, Pt. I., *Adhyāyas* 1-5, *Indirā-kalā-saṁgīta-viśva-vidyālaya-grantha-mālā*, No. 1., Khairagarh, Madhya Pradesh, India, 1961.

Bṛhat-paribhāṣā-vṛtti by Sīradeva, see: *PBS*.

BSR *Bṛhacchabda-ratna* by Hari Dīkṣita, on the *PM*, see: *PM*.

BSS *Bṛhacchabdendu-śekhara* by Nāgeśabhaṭṭa, in three vols., *Sarasvati Bhavana Granthamala*, No. 87, ed. by Sitaram Sastri, Banaras, 1960.

Cāndra-vyākaraṇa, with the *Svopajña-vṛtti*, by Candragomin, two vols, ed. by K. C. Chatterji, Deccan College Publication, Poona, 1953, 1961.

Dhātu-pradīpa, by Maitreyarakṣita, *Savitārāya-smṛti-saṁrakṣaṇa-grantha-mālā*, No. 2., ed. by Srish Chandra Chakravarti, Rajshahi, Bengal, 1919.

Hemacandra-vyākaraṇa-nyāya-saṁgraha by Hemahaṁsagaṇi, see: *PBS*.

Hema-śabdānuśāsana, with the auto-commentary *Bṛhad-vṛtti* (*Svopajña-tattva-prakāśikā*), pt. I, ed. by Candrasāgarasūri, Ujjain, (Vikrama) 2007.

Jainendra-vyākaraṇa by Devanandin, with the *Mahāvṛtti* by Abhayanandin, Bhāratīya Jñānapīṭha, Banaras, 1956.

Kaccāyana-yākaraṇa, critically edited, translated and annotated by L. N. Tiwari and Birbal Sharma, Tara Publications, Banaras, 1962.

Kātantra-paribhāṣā-sūtra-vṛtti by Bhāvamiśra, see: PBS.

Kātantra-vyākaraṇa by Śarvavarman: Das Kātantra, Zur Einführung in die indische einheimische Sprachwissenschaft I, by Bruno Liebich, Heidelberg, 1919. [Page references are given to this edition, unless otherwise indicated.]

Kātantra-vyākaraṇa by Śarvavarman, with the Vṛtti by Durgasiṁha, ed. by J. Eggeling, Bibliotheca Indica, Calcutta, 1874-8.

KM Kārikāvalī-Muktāvalī by Viśvanātha Tarkapañcānana Bhaṭṭācārya, with five commentaries, Sri Balamanorama Series 6, Madras, 1923.

KS Kāśikā-vṛtti by Vāmana and Jayāditya, with the commentaries Nyāsa by Jinendrabuddhi, and Padamañjarī by Haradatta, six vols., Prācya Bharati Series 2, Tara Publications, Banaras, 1965-7.

KS-N Nyāsa by Jinendrabuddhi on KS, see: KS.

KS-P Padamañjarī by Haradatta on KS, see: KS.

Laghubhāṣya, Sarasvatī-kṛta-vyākaraṇa-sūtra-vyākhyānam, by Raghunātha Nāgara, Kṣemarāja Kṛṣṇadāsa (Publ.), Veṅkaṭeśvara Press, Bombay, 1900.

LSR Laghu-śabda-ratna by Nāgeśabhaṭṭa, see: PM.

LSS Laghu-śabdendu-śekhara by Nāgeśabhaṭṭa, with six commentaries, Rajasthan Sanskrit College Series 14, Banaras, 1936.

MB Vyākaraṇa-Mahābhāṣya by Patañjali, with the commentaries Pradīpa by Kaiyaṭa, and Uddyota by Nāgeśabhaṭṭa, three vols., published by Motilal Banarasidass, Delhi, 1967.

MB-D Dīpikā [or Ṭīkā] by Bhartṛhari on MB, ed. by Abhyankar and Limaye, Bhandarkar Oriental Research Institute, Post Graduate and Research Department Series 8, Poona, 1970. The same text is edited under the title Mahābhāṣya-ṭīkā by V. Swaminathan, Pt. I, Hindu-Vishvavidyālayīya-Nepāla-Rājya-Saṁskṛta-Granthamālā, 11, Banaras, 1965. This is occasionally quoted for better readings.

MB-P Pradīpa by Kaiyaṭa on MB, see: MB.

MB-P-U Uddyota by Nāgeśabhaṭṭa on MB-P, see: MB.

Moggalāna-vyākaraṇa, ed. by Bhadanta Ānanda Kausalyāyana, Vishveshvarananda Inst. Publ. 305, Hoshiarpur, 1965.

MPV Mahābhāṣya-Pradīpa-Vyākhyānāni, "Commentaires sur le Mahābhāṣya de Patañjali et le Pradīpa de Kaiyaṭa," Adhyāya 1 Pāda 1 Ahnika 1-4, édition par M. S. Narasimhacharya, Publications de l'Institut Français d'Indologie, No. 51, 1., Pondichéry, 1973.

MS Mīmāṁsā-sūtras by Jaimini, with the Bhāṣya by Śabara, the Tantra-vārttika and Ṭup-ṭīkā by Kumārila, six vols., Ānandāśrama Sanskrit Series 97, Poona, 1929. Third ed. of the pt. I, vol. I, in 1953.

Mugdhabodha-vyākaraṇa by Bopadeva, with commentaries by Durgādāsa Vidyāvāgīśa and Śrīrāma Tarkavāgīśa, ed. and publ. by Jībānanda Vidyāsāgara, Calcutta, 1902.

Nāradīya-śikṣā (sāmavedīyā), with the commentary by Bhaṭṭa Śobhākara, published by Śri Pītāmbara-pīṭha-saṁskṛta-pariṣad, Datia, Madhya Pradesh, 1964.

P Pāṇini-sūtra.

Pāṇinīya-śikṣā (Die Pāṇinīya-śikṣā), Ṛk and Yajus recensions, ed. and tr. into German, by Albrecht Weber, Indische Studien, band IV, Berlin, 1858.

Paribhāṣā-bhāskara, by Haribhāskara Agnihotrin, see: PBS.

Paribhāṣā-sūcana by Vyādi, see: PBS.

Paribhāṣā-vṛtti by Nīlakaṇṭha Dīkṣita, see: PBS.

PBS Paribhāṣā-saṁgraha [A collection of paribhāṣā texts from various systems of Sanskrit grammar], ed. by K. V. Abhyankar, Bhandarkar Oriental Research Institute, Post Graduate and Research Department Series, Poona, 1968.

PM Prauḍha-manoramā by Bhaṭṭoji Dīkṣita, with the commentaries Bṛhacchabda-ratna by Hari Dīkṣita and Laghu-śabda-ratna by Nāgeśabhaṭṭa, up to the Avyayībhāva section, Nepal Rajya Hindu

Viśvavidyālaya Series 3, Banaras, 1964.

Prakriyā-kaumudī, by Rāmacandra, with Prasāda commentary by Viṭṭhala, ed. by K. P. Trivedi, Bombay Sanskrit and Prakrit Series, LXXVIII (Pt. I), LXXXII (Pt. II), 1925 and 1931.

Prakriyā-sarvasva, by Nārāyaṇabhaṭṭa, Pts. I, II, III, IV, Trivendrum Sanskrit Series, Nos. 106, 139, 153, and 174; Years 1931, 1938, 1948 and 1958.

Pratijñā-sūtra, ed. and tr. into German by Albrecht Weber, Abh. d. Kön. Ak. der. Wiss. zu Berlin, 1871.

PS Paribhāṣenduśekhara by Nāgeśabhaṭṭa, with the commentary Tattvādarśa by M. Vasudeva Shastri Abhyankar, ed. by K. V. Abhyankar, Revised edn. Bhandarkar Oriental Research Institute, Poona, 1962.

Puṣpa-sūtra, Das, mit Einleitung und Übersetzung, herausgegeben von Richard Simon, Abhandlungen der Philosophisch-Philologischen Klasse der Köngl. Bayerischen Akademie der Wissenschaften, 23, München, 1904-9.

Ṛk-tantra [A Prātiśākhya of the Sāmaveda], ed. by Surya Kanta, Lahore, 1939, reprinted by Meherchand Lachhmandas, Delhi, 1971.

RPr Ṛgveda-prātiśākhya, Pt. I, (Text only), ed. by Mangal Deva Shastri, Banaras, 1959.

Rūpāvatāra, by Dharmakīrti, ed. by M. Rangacharya, published by G. A. Natesan and Co., Madras, Pt. I., (no date given); Pt. II., Bangalore, 1927.

Śabdānuśāsana by Acārya Malayagiri, with his auto-commentary Vṛtti, ed. by Pt. Becharda J. Doshi, Lalbhai Dalpatbhai Series No. 13, Ahmedabad, 1967.

Śaiśirīya-śiksā, ed. by Tarapada Chowdhury, Journal of Vedic Studies, ed. by Raghu Vira, Vol. II., No. II., Lahore, 1935.

Śākaṭāyana-vyākaraṇa, with the auto-commentary Amogha-vṛtti, Murtidevi Jaina Granthamala, Sanskrit Series 39, Bhāratīya Jñānapīṭha, Banaras, 1971. [Page references are given to this edition.]

Sākaṭāyana-vyākaraṇa, with the commentary Prakriyā-saṁgraha by Abhayacandrasūri, edited by Gustav Oppert, Madras, 1893.

Sāma-tantra by Audavraji, [A Prātiśākhya of the Sāmaveda], with an anonymous Bhāṣya, ed. by Ramnath Dīksiṭa, Vedic Research Committee, Banaras Hindu University, Banaras, 1961.

Sārasvata-vyākaraṇam, vṛtti-trayātmakam, by Anubhūti-svarūpacārya, ed. by Narayana Rama Acharya, Nirnayasagara Press, 7th edn., Bombay, 1952.

Sarasvatī-kaṇṭhābharaṇa by Bhojadeva, with the commentary Hṛdayahāriṇī by Nārayaṇa Daṇḍanātha, Pt. I., Trivendrum Sanskrit Series CXVII, Trivendrum, 1935.

Śikṣā-saṁgraha, a collection of various śikṣās, Banaras Sanskrit Series, Banaras, 1893.

Śikṣā-sūtrāṇi, Āpiśali-Pāṇini-Candragomi-viracitāni, ed. by Yudhisthir Mimamsaka, Ajmer, 2024 Saṁvat.

SK Siddhānta-kaumudī by Bhaṭṭoji Dīkṣita, 11th edn., Nirnayasagara Press, Bombay, 1938.

SK(M) Siddhānta-kaumudī by Bhaṭṭoji Dīkṣita, with the commentaries Bālamanoramā by Vāsudeva Dīkṣita, and Tattvabodhinī by Jñānendra Sarasvatī, ed. by Giridhar Sarma and Parameshvaranand, publ. by Motilal Banarasidass, Delhi, 1960.

SKB Śabda-kaustubha by Bhaṭṭoji Dīkṣita, Chowkhamba Sanskrit Series 2, Vol. I, Fasc. I to IV, ed. by Nene and Puntamkar, Banaras, 1933.

TPr Taittitīya-prātiśākhya, with the commentary Tribhāṣyaratna, ed. and tr. with notes, by W. D. Whitney, New Haven, 1871.

TS Tarka-saṁgraha by Annambhaṭṭa, with the auto-commentary Dīpikā and the commentary Nyāya-bodhinī by Govardhana, ed. by Athalye and Bodas, second edn., second impression, Bombay Sanskrit Series LV, Poona, 1963.

VP Vākya-padīya, edited with appendices, by Abhyankar and Limaye, University of Poona Sanskrit and Prakrit Series, Poona, 1965.

VPr Vājasaneyi-prātiśākhya, ed. and tr. by Indu Rastogi, Kashi Sanskrit Series 179, Banaras, 1967. [Page nos. refer to this edn.]

VPr(W) Vājasaneyi-prātiśākhya, ed. and tr. into German, with notes, by Albrecht Weber, Indische Studien, Beiträge für die Kunde des Indischen Alterthums, bd. IV, Berlin, 1858.

VSSN Vyākaraṇa-siddhānta-sudhānidhi, by Viśveśvarasūri, ed. by Dhadhi Ram Sarma, Chowkhamba Sanskrit Series, Banaras, 1914.

Yājñavalkya-śikṣā (Yajurvedīyā), with a Hindi commentary by Brahmamuni, Arya Sahitya Mandal, Ajmer, 1967.

SECONDARY LITERATURE

Abhyankar, K. V. (1969)
Patañjali's Vyākaraṇa-mahābhāṣya, Āhnika I-II, ed. and tr. with notes, Sanskrit Vidyā Parisaṁsthā, Vasudeva Shastri Abhyankar Publication Series 15, Poona, 1969.

Aklujkar, A. N. (1970)
The Philosophy of Bhartṛhari's Trikāṇḍī, a doctoral dissertation, the Dept. of Sanskrit and Indian Studies, Harvard University, Feb. 1970.

Allen, W. S. (1953)
Phonetics in Ancient India, London Oriental Series 1, Oxford University Press, 1953.

Bare, James (1975)
Phonetics and Phonology in Pāṇini, a doctoral dissertation, Dept. of Linguistics, University of Michigan, Ann Arbor, 1975.

Belvalkar, S. K. (1915)
Systems of Sanskrit Grammar, Poona, 1915.

Biardeau, M. (1964)
Théorie de la Connaissance et Philosophie de la Parole dans le Brahmanisme classique, Mouton and Co., Paris, 1964.

Böhtlingk, Otto (1887)
Pāṇini's Grammatik, Leipzig, 1887.

Breloer, B. (1929)
"Studie zu Pāṇini," Zeitschrift für Indologie und Iranistik, Herausgegeben in Auftrage der Deutschen Morgenländischen Gessellschaft, Leipzig, Bd. 7, Heft 1, pp. 114-35, 1929.

----(1935)
"Die 14 Pratyāhāra-sūtras des Pāṇini," Zetischrift für Indologie und Iranistik, Bd. 10, Heft 2, Leipzig, pp. 134-91, 1935.

Brough, John (1951)
"Theories of General Linguistics in the Sanskrit Grammarians," Transactions of the Philological Society, Cambridge, 1951.

Burnell, A. C. (1875)
On the Aindra School of Sanskrit Grammarians, Mangalore, 1875.

Cardona, G. (1965a)
"On Pāṇini's Morphophonemic Principles," Language, Vol. 41. 1965.

----(1965b)
"On Translating and Formalizing Pāṇinian Rules," Journal of the Oriental Institute, Baroda, Vol. XIV, Nos. 3-4, 1965.

----(1968)
"Review of the Sphoṭa-nirṇaya by S. D. Joshi," Journal of the Oriental Institute, Baroda, Vo. XVII, 1968.

----(1969)
"Studies in Indian Grammarians I, the Method of Description Reflected in the Śiva-sūtras," Transactions of the American Philosophical Society, New Series,

Vol. 59, Pt. I, Philadelphia, 1969.

Chatterjee, Kshitis Chandra (1934)
"The Śiva-sūtras," Journal of the Dept. of Letters, Vol. XXIV, University of Calcutta, Calcutta, 1934.

----(1948)
Technical Terms and Technique of Sanskrit Grammar, University of Calcutta, Calcutta, 1948, revised edn. by Gaurinath Shastri, 1964.

Chattopadhyaya, K. C. (1974)
"Did Pāṇini Envisage 'A' as a Close (saṁvṛta) Vowel?" Charudeva Shastri Felicitation Volume, Delhi, 1974.

Chaturvedi, S. P. (1933)
"Homogeneity of Letters in the Pāṇinian System--A Critical Estimate of the Views Held by Different Commentators," Proceedings and Transactions of the Seventh All India Oriental Conference, Baroda, 1933.

Citrācārya, Jagadīśa (1969)
"Śikṣā-śāstram," (in Sanskrit), Bālārka-veda-mandirasya prathamam puṣpam, Bahrāich, U. P., India, 1969.

Deshpande, Madhav (1972)
"Pāṇinian Procedure of Taparakaraṇa: A Historical Investigation," Zeitschrift für vergleichende Sprachforschung, Band 86, Heft 2, Göttingen, 1972.

----(Forthcoming)
"New Material on the Kautsa-vyākaraṇa," appearing in the Journal of the Oriental Institute, Baroda (1975 ?).

----(Forthcoming)
"Phonetics of Short /a/ in Sanskrit," appearing in the Indo-Iranian Journal, 1975.

----(Forthcoming)
"Phonetics of /v/ in Pāṇini," appearing in the Annals of the Bhandarkar Oriental Research Institute, Poona (1975 ?).

----(Forthcoming)
"The Scope of Homogeneous-Representation in Pāṇini," appearing in the Silver Jubilee Volume of the Annals of Oriental Research, University of Madras, Madras.

Devasthali, G. V. (1969)
Sārasiddhāntakaumudī of Varadarāja Bhaṭṭa, ed. and tr. with notes, Publications of the Centre of Advanced Studies in Sanskrit, University of Poona, Poona, 1969.

Ghatage, A. M. (1972)
"A Sample Entry in a Historical Sanskrit Dictionary," Indian Linguistics, Vol. 33, No. 2, Poona, 1972.

Goldstücker, Theodor (1860)
Pāṇini: His Place in Sanskrit Literature etc., London, 1860, Indian edition, Chowkhamba Sanskrit Studies XLVIII, Banaras, 1965.

Joshi, S. D. (1967)
The Sphoṭa-nirṇaya of Kauṇḍabhaṭṭa, ed. and tr. with notes, Publications of the Centre of Advanced Studies in Sanskrit, Class C, No. 2, University of Poona, Poona, 1967.

----(1969) [In collaboration with J. A. F. Roodbergen]
Patañjali's Vyākaraṇa-mahābhāṣya, Avyayībhāva-tatpuruṣāhnika, ed. and tr. with notes, Publications of the Centre of Advanced Studies in Sanskrit, Class C, No. 5, University of Poona, Poona, 1969.

Katre, S. L. (1938)
"Kautsa-vyākaraṇa:A Detailed Notice; Recovery of Kautsa's Authorship," New Indian Antiquary, Vol. I, Bombay, 1938.

Kielhorn, Franz (1876a)
Kātyāyana and Patañjali, their Relation to each other and to Pāṇini, Bombay, 1876, 2nd edn., Banaras, 1963.

----(1876b)
"Remarks on the Śikṣās," The Indian Antiquary, Vol. 5, Bombay, 1876.

----(1887)
"Notes on the Mahābhāṣya, No. 7, Some Devices of

Indian Grammarians," The Indian Antiquary, Vol. 16, Bombay, 1887.

----(1891)
"Die Colebrooke'schen Pāṇini-Handschriften der Königlichen Bibliothek zu Göttingen," Nachrichten von der Königlichen Gesellschaft der Wissenschaften zu Göttingen, Nr. 3, 1891.

Konow, Sten (1943)
"The Authorship of the Śiva-sūtras," Acta Orientalia, Vol. XIX, 1943.

Liebich, Bruno (1891)
Pāṇini, Ein Beitrag zur Kenntnis der Indischen Literatur und Grammatick, Leipzig, 1891.

Limaye, V. P. (1974)
Critical Studies on the Mahābhāṣya, Vishveshvarananda Indological Series, No. 49, Hoshiarpur, 1974.

Lüders, Heinrich (1894)
Die Vyāsa-śikṣā, besonders in ihrem Verhaltnis zum Taittirīya-Prātiśākhya, Göttingen, 1894.

Mimamsaka, Yudhisthir (1961-2)
Saṃskṛta-vyākaraṇa-śāstra kā Itihāsa, Hindi, Vol. I, revised edn., Ajmer, 1962; Vol. II, 1961.

Misra, Vidya Niwas (1966)
The Descriptive Technique of Pāṇini, Mouton and Co., Paris-Hague, 1966.

Nooten, van, B. A. (1973)
"The Structure of a Sanskrit Phonetic Treatise (Āpiśaliśikṣā)," Acta et Commentationes Universitatis Tartuensis, Oriental Studies, Vo. II, No. 2, Tartu, U. S. S. R., 1973.

Palsule, G. B. (1953)
"A Glimpse into the Kāśakṛtsna School of Sanskrit Grammar," Proceedings and Transactions of the All India Oriental Conference, 17th Session, 1953.

----(1974)
"The Technical Terms in the Harināmāmṛta-vyākaraṇa

of Jīva Gosvāmin," CASS Studies, No. 2., Publications of the Centre of Advanced Study in Sanskrit, University of Poona, Poona, 1974.

Pandeya, Rāmājñā (1965)
Vyākaraṇa-darśana-pīṭhikā, in Sanskrit, Sarasvati Bhavana Studies, Vol. XII, Banaras, 1965.

Phatak, Madhukar (1972)
Pāṇinīya-śikṣāyāḥ Śikṣāntaraiḥ saha Samīkṣā, in Sanskrit, Banaras, 1972.

Raja, Kunhan (1957)
"The Śiva-sūtras of Pāṇini," Annals of Oriental Research, University of Madras, Vol. XIII, 1957.

Raja, Kunjunni (1963)
Indian Theories of Meaning, The Adyar Library Series, Vol. 91, Madras, 1963.

Renou, Louis (1966)
La Grammaire de Pāṇini, Vol. I-II, Texte Sanskrit, Traduction Française avec extraits des commentaires, École Française d'Extrême-Orient, Paris, 1966.

Sarma, K. Madhava Krishna (1968)
Pāṇini, Kātyāyana and Patañjali, Shri Lal Bahadur Shastri Sanskrit Vidyapith, Delhi, 1968.

Sarma, Venkatarama (1935)
Critical Studies on Kātyāyana's Śukla Yajurveda Prātiśākhya, University of Madras, Madras, 1935.

Scharfe, Hartmut (1961)
Die Logik im Mahābhāṣya, Deutsche Akademie der Wissenschaften zu Berlin, Institut für Orientforschung, Veröffentlichung Nr. 50, Berlin, 1961.

----(1971)
Pāṇini's Metalanguage, Memoirs of the American Philosophical Society, Vol. 81, Philadelphia, 1971.

Shastri, M. D. (1926)
A Comparison of the Contents of the Ṛgveda, Vājasaneyi, Taittirīya and Atharva-Prātiśākhyas, Princess of Wales Sarasvati Bhavana Studies, ed. by

Gopinatha Kaviraja, Vol. V, Banaras, 1926.

Shastri, Nemichandra (1963)
Ācārya Hemacandra aur unakā Śabdānuśāsana: Eka Adhyayana, Vidyabhavana Rashtrabhasa Granthamala, No. 62, Banaras, 1963.

Sköld, Hannes (1926)
"Papers on Pāṇini, and Indian Grammar in General," Lunds Universitets Årsskrift, N. F. Avd. 1, Bd. 21, Nr. 8, Lund, 1926.

Staal, J. F. (1972)
A Reader on the Sanskrit Grammarians, The M. I. T. Press, Cambridge, Mass., 1972.

Subramonia, Venkata S. (1972)
Nārāyaṇa Bhaṭṭa's Prakriyā-sarvasva, a Critical Study, Kerala University Sanskrit Department Publication, No. 7, Trivendrum, 1972.

Sukthankar, V. S. (1921)
Die Grammatik Śākaṭāyana's [Addhyāya 1, Pada 1, Nebst Yakṣavarman's Kommentar Cintāmaṇi], Leipzig, 1921.

Thieme, Paul (1935a)
Pāṇini and the Veda, Allahabad, 1935.

----(1935b)
"Bhāṣya zu Vārttika 5 zu Pāṇini 1.1.9 und seine einheimischen Erklärer," Nachrichten von der Gesellschaft der Wissenschaften zu Göttingen, Philologisch-Historische Klass, Fachgruppe III, Allgemeine Sprachwissenschaft, Östlische Kulturkreise, Neue Folge, Bd. I, Nr. 5, Göttingen, 1935.

----(1935c)
"Zur Datierung des Pāṇini," Zeitschrift für Deutschen Morgenländischen Gesellschaft, Neue Folge, Bd. XIV, (Bd. 89), 1935.

----(1937-8)
"On the Identity of the Vārttikakāra," Indian Culture, Vol. IV, No. 2, Calcutta, 1937-8.

----(1957a)
"Interpretation of the Learned," S. K. Belvalkar Felicitation Volume, Banaras, 1957.

----(1957b)
"Pāṇini and the Pronounciation of Sanskrit," Studies Presented to J. Whatmough on his sixtieth birthday, Gravenhage, 1957.

----(1957c)
"Review of W. S. Allen's Phonetics in Ancient India," Zeitschrift für Deutschen Morgenländischen Gesell-schaft, Bd. 107, 1957.

----(1958)
"Review of the second edition of Renou's Terminologie Grammaticale du Sanskrit," Göttingische Gelehrte Anzeigen, 1958.

Varma, Siddheshwar (1929)
The Phonetic Observations of Indian Grammarians, London, 1929, Indian Reprint Edition, Delhi, 1961.

Vasu, Satish Chandra (1891)
Aṣṭādhyāyī of Pāṇini, Vols., I-II, 1891, reprint edition by Motilal Banarsidass, Delhi, 1962.

Wackernagel, Jacob (1896)
Altindische Grammatik, I. Lautlehre, Vandenhoeck and Ruprecht, Göttingen, 1896.

Walleser, Max (1927)
"Zur Aussprache von skr. a," Zeitschrift für Indologie und Iranistik, Band 5, Leipzig, 1927.

Whitney, William Dwight (1884)
"On Lepsius's Standard Alphabet: a Letter of Explanation from Prof. Lepsius, with notes by W. D. Whitney," Journal of the American Oriental Society, Vol. 8, 1884-6.

Zgusta, L. (1969)
"Pāṇini--Descriptivist or Transformationalist?" Archiv Orientální, Vol. 37, No. 3, 1969.

THE UNIVERSITY OF MICHIGAN

CENTER FOR SOUTH AND SOUTHEAST ASIAN STUDIES

PUBLICATIONS

MP 3 Norman G. Owen, ed. Compadre Colonialism: Studies on the Philippines under American Rule. Illustration, tables, bibliography. 318 pp., paper.

MP 4 Frank Shulman. Doctoral Dissertations on South Asia, 1966-70. Appendices, indexes. xvii, 228 pp., paper.

MP 5 Harley Harris Bartlett. The Labors of the Datoe and Other Essays on the Bataks of Asahan (North Sumatra). Illustrations. xxiv, 387 pp., paper.

MP 6 John Stephen Lansing. Evil in the Morning of the World: Phenomenological Approaches to a Balinese Community. Illustration, bibliography. x, 104 pp., paper.

MP 7 Thomas R. Trautmann, ed. Kinship and History in South Asia. Diagrams. ix, 157 pp., paper.

MP 8 William P. Malm and Amin Sweeney. Studies in Malaysian Oral and Musical Traditions. Illustrations. x, 104 pp., paper.

MP 9 David M. Engel. Law and Kingship in Thailand during the Reign of King Chulalongkorn. Bibliography. 131 pp., paper.

MP 10 Thomas Poffenberger. Fertility and Family Life in an Indian Village. Tables. 108 pp., paper.

Sp 1 Thomas Powers. Balita Mula Maynila (News from Manila). Illustrations. 40 pp., paper.

LL 1 Peter Edwin Hook. The Compound Verb in Hindi. Index, bibliography. 318 pp., paper.

LL 2 Madhav Deshpande. Critical Studies in Indian Grammarians I: Theory of Homogeneity [Sāvarṇya]. Bibliography. xiii, 223 pp., paper.

CSSEAS Publications
130 Lane Hall
The University of Michigan
Ann Arbor, Mich. 48104

ERRATA

The reader is requested to make the following corrections

page:	line:	for:	read:
16	25	Mahākarūṇāvatara	Mahākarūṇāvatāra
28	6	Kāyavāṇ-	Kāyavāṅ-
30	8	bhaṣyamāne	bhāṣyamāṇe
”	12	smarami	smarāmi
”	18	katam asya	katamasya
”	22	adhyabhaṣata	adhyabhāṣata
”	23	bhūyasya	bhūyasyā
39	4	120 scrolls	10 scrolls
49	14	Fredrich	Friedrich
87	20	pragṛhnāti	pragṛhṇāti
234	22	Jam	’Jam

Printed and bound by CPI Group (UK) Ltd, Croydon, CR0 4YY
13/04/2025
14656538-0002